NAVIGATING ASEAN-NOVATION

The **Reservoir Principle** and Other Essays on **Startups** and **Innovation** in Southeast Asia

NAVIGATING ASEAN-NOVATION

The **Reservoir Principle** and Other Essays on **Startups** and **Innovation** in Southeast Asia

Editors

Yinglan Tan
Insignia Ventures Partners, Singapore

Paulo Joquiño
Insignia Business Review, Singapore

World Scientific

NEW JERSEY • LONDON • SINGAPORE • BEIJING • SHANGHAI • HONG KONG • TAIPEI • CHENNAI • TOKYO

Published by

World Scientific Publishing Co. Pte. Ltd.
5 Toh Tuck Link, Singapore 596224
USA office: 27 Warren Street, Suite 401-402, Hackensack, NJ 07601
UK office: 57 Shelton Street, Covent Garden, London WC2H 9HE

British Library Cataloguing-in-Publication Data
A catalogue record for this book is available from the British Library.

NAVIGATING ASEANNOVATION
The Reservoir Principle and Other Essays on Startups and Innovation in Southeast Asia

ISBN 978-981-122-774-5 (hardcover)
ISBN 978-981-4518-72-7 (paperback)
ISBN 978-981-4518-73-4 (ebook for institutions)
ISBN 978-981-4518-74-1 (ebook for individuals)

For any available supplementary material, please visit
https://www.worldscientific.com/worldscibooks/10.1142/8860#t=suppl

Desk Editor: Karimah Samsudin

Typeset by Stallion Press
Email: enquiries@stallionpress.com

Contents

Foreword 1: Unknown Unknowns

by Lim Siong Guan
Author of The Leader, The Teacher & You

I have a friend in Israel. We got to know each other when we were both attending the Advanced Management Program at the Harvard Business School some decades ago. Now, we are retired from our careers for many years, though we have discovered that retiring means to "go into the pit stop, get new tires, and run again."

When we last met, I asked him what he was now doing. He said he was going around schools setting up robotics clubs.

Robotics clubs, of course, are not a new idea. Many schools have them, and many wished they had them. So how would his venture be different, I wondered.

He explained. The first thing he did was to teach the students social responsibility. In other words, even as they built robots, they had to be able to answer the question of why is what they are doing socially responsible and good for society. The minimum has to be that what they are doing is not socially irresponsible or bad for society. This was interesting to me. That the first thing students who are interested in robots learn is that they need to be socially responsible.

Next, he taught them how to cope with failure. Students in the robotics clubs clamour to take part in international competitions. How many winners can there be? So, not winning in a competition will be a lot more common than winning. We hear a lot about how innovation and enterprise always require a measure of risk-taking and a positive perspective on failing. How many schools and how many robotics clubs make a conscious effort to teach their students how to cope with failure?

No one starts something new with the idea of failing. However, everyone needs to start conscious of the possibility of failing. Everyone needs to have a deliberate perspective on how to cope with failure.

It has been said that fatal failure — namely, failure which results in the demise of enterprises and programmes — is the result of failure to learn from the past, failure to adapt to the present, or failure to anticipate the future.

A failure to learn from the past is often so avoidable if only we were humble enough to acknowledge and learn from our past failure, or we were smart enough to learn from the slips and failures of others.

A failure to adapt to the present is often also avoidable if we were to recognise that all policies and practices are the best that could be with the resources and circumstances at the time they were introduced. However, situations change, the desires of people change, the possibilities of technology change, the demands of the market change. It is possible to adapt to the present if we were humble enough to accept that what we are doing is no longer the best that we can do.

A failure to anticipate the future is the most important reason for failing. This presumes, of course, that we can anticipate the future and position ourselves for it. To be in time for the future is a continuous challenge. A failure to do so is ultimately a failure of leadership. It is to fail to prepare for survival and sustainability.

How do we prepare for the future? How can we prepare for the future when the future is not only uncertain, but is also increasingly unknowable.

We all think we would be much more comfortable if we were living in a world which is continually understandable and predictable, a world comprising just the Known Knowns. It is where every cause has its predictable effect, where we know what we need to do to get a particular result, where success is guaranteed so long as we are not so lazy as to not do what is necessary to get that particular outcome. However, it is a world where everyone knows everything, business has no new opportunity, and competition has no meaning.

Consider next the world of Known Unknowns. This is where we recognise the unpredictabilities of life and enterprise. It is where we seek to understand the future in terms of the *predetermined elements* — those aspects of the future we can be reasonably certain of because they are the Known Knowns — and the *critical uncertainties*, like the different ways US–China relations could pan out over the coming years. The world of Known Unknowns is the world of scenario planning, where we learn from the past what we cannot control for the future but believe we can plan for the diversity of possible futures. We can develop, for example, a strategic plan that is not optimised to any particular scenario, but can work reasonably well irrespective of which scenario transpires.

However, in all humility, we now have to contend with the world of Unknown Unknowns. By definition, scenario planning cannot cater for Unknown Unknowns, because if an Unknown were known, it would have been recognised and thought about in scenario planning. Can an enterprise plan for a world of Unknown Unknowns and win against its competitor?

Winning in a world of Unknown Unknowns demands that we pay attention to a different set of attributes than we normally tend to do. Professor Rosabeth Moss Kanter, Professor of Business at Harvard Business School, has so aptly said, "Culture is a leading indicator. Culture predicts the future." She has further remarked that culture, in some ways, is more important than strategy.

Culture is that set of values and behaviors in an enterprise which the alert and observant worker can describe. It is what life and work is really like in the enterprise.

An enterprise on a journey to develop a winning culture will define the values and behaviours which it believes it needs to have in order to win. I find Insignia Ventures Partners' CRAFT — Collaborative,

Results-driven, Agile, Future-oriented, Trustworthy — to be an excellent statement. However, it will not work for every enterprise.

Each enterprise needs to define its own beliefs about what winning in a world of Unknown Unknowns demands. Once the target culture is defined, the enterprise will be much clearer about its priorities and will be much bolder in its decisions, because it has decided the direction it has to take over the long-term. Timing will be tactical, and will demand much in terms of wisdom and sensitivity. Direction will be strategic, and will demand "mid-course" corrections from time to time as tactical decisions along the way would have caused deviations from the desired direction.

This book, *Navigating ASEANnovation: Startups and Innovation in Southeast Asia with application of the Reservoir Principle* is well worth your time to read. Learning from the experience of others is smart. It adds to your reservoir of knowledge and pitfalls, and learning from a variety of enterprises in different stages of progress and development adds to your reservoir of beliefs and ideas.

Our interest is not only about Southeast Asia and about innovation and enterprise. It is about winning in work and life as we address our various situations in the worlds of Known Knowns, Known Unknowns, and Unknown Unknowns. We need humility, openness of mind, and goodness of heart to succeed.

Foreword 2

by Professor Josh Lerner
Harvard Business School

High-potential entrepreneurship has been with us for a long time. In the 18th century BC, the Code of Hammurabi laid out the sixth Babylonian king's rules for, among many other things, structuring and investing in promising new ventures. Over the millennia, entrepreneurship has been a driver of growth and wealth creation around the planet.

However, during the second half of the 20th century, a few dozen square miles in one nation appeared to have a virtual monopoly on one form of high-potential entrepreneurship — the Silicon Valley-based venture-funded start-up. The venture capital model proved to be enormously powerful in creating and nurturing new firms: the financiers engaged in careful screening of potential new ventures, provided tight governance and informal venturing, and gave young firms a stamp of approval and access to their bulging rolodexes.

The power of this model led to extensive wealth and subsequently transformed the world. For example, among publicly traded firms worldwide at the time that I am writing this foreword in August 2020, seven of the top eight firms by market capitalization have been backed by venture capital prior to their initial public offerings: Alphabet, Apple, Amazon, Facebook, and Microsoft in the United

States, and Alibaba and Tencent in China. More generally, although firms backed by venture capital comprise less than 0.5 percent of firms that are born each year in the U.S., they represent nearly half of entrepreneurial companies that graduate to the public marketplace. Indeed, Nobel Laureate in Economics Kenneth Arrow (1995) once opined, "venture capital has done much more, I think, to improve efficiency than anything."[1]

Nevertheless, as suggested above, during the 1900s, the venture model was very localized. Funds formed in locations such as Europe, Japan, and Australia by and large struggled, and generally did not achieve the financial success or spawn the types of world-changing enterprises that their Silicon Valley-based peers did. Even within the United States, the performance of venture capital funds was extremely uneven. Scholars and observers offered many explanations for these disparities, from differing appetites for risk to legal regimes.

All this began changing dramatically with the 21st century. The first manifestation of this was the growth of venture capital in China. The early successes of investors who transferred already-proven business models, particularly related to the Internet, in the Chinese market opened the eyes of many providers of capital to the potential of this market. This led to a "virtuous cycle". Entrepreneurial success attracted additional founders and investors, who then succeeded with ever more sophisticated business models, paving the way for yet other generations. In the decade after the Global Financial Crisis of 2008, the Chinese venture market generated some of the highest returns globally.

This experience inspired many other investors, entrepreneurs, and policymakers to take another look at their own markets, and seek to pursue entrepreneurial opportunities. To be sure, the money is still being allocated in a lumpy manner.[2] In the United

---

[1] Kenneth Arrow, (1995), "Interview with Kenneth Arrow, Federal Reserve Bank of Minneapolis," https://www.minneapolisfed.org/article/1995/interview-with-kenneth-arrow.

[2] Josh Lerner and Ramana Nanda, "Venture Capital's Role in Financing Innovation: How Far We Have Come and How Much We Still Need to Go," *Journal of Economic Perspectives*, 34 (Summer 2020), pp. 237–261.

States, National Venture Capital Association statistics suggest that three metropolitan areas — the San Francisco Bay Area, Greater New York, and Greater Boston — account for about two-thirds of the venture capital deployed by firms each year. The same phenomenon also seems to manifest itself globally, though good statistics are hard to find. For instance, a tabulation of PitchBook data between 2015 and 2017 concludes that the top 25 urban areas accounted for 75 percent of all disbursements globally.[3] Nevertheless, certainly, the diversity of where capital is being provided is far more diverse than was the case at the beginning of the century. In addition, as the world becomes less globalized —whether due to nationalist political pressures or to travel restrictions brought about by the COVID-19 crisis — the decentralization of the venture industry is likely to continue.

Today, one of the most exciting hubs of venture capital is in Southeast Asia. This region, as discussed in the essays in this volume, has many strengths: a diverse and youthful population, a strong emphasis on education, sophisticated consumers eager to adopt information technology, and an optimistic spirit. It is little surprise that venture capitalists, both local and from China, Europe, and the United States, are increasingly looking here for opportunity. This book explores this exciting territory, and the potential for entrepreneurs with great promise and those that seek to fund them.

Enjoy the essays, and may they inspire great entrepreneurial dreams!

---

[3]Richard Florida and Ian Hathaway (2018), *The Rise of the Startup City*, Washington, Center for American Entrepreneurship.

Foreword 3

by Wong Lin Hong
Venture capitalist and author of "Venture Capital Fund Management: A Comprehensive Approach to Investment Practices & the Entire Operations of a VC Firm"
(Thomson Reuters)

Appointed as a board member of the Insignia fund management company and as a member of the Investment Committee since Insignia's inception, I know very well the general partners, the investment team and the founders of the portfolio companies. I congratulate them for compiling their war stories into this book.

I have been in the venture capital industry since 1990 and have my share of stories. However, the personal accounts, interviews, views, and advice narrated in this book are most valuable since they are relevant and current, and of practical use to startup entrepreneurs in a world that is not only fast-changing, but also undergoing upheavals caused by the COVID pandemic.

Since 2017, the general partners and investment team have diligently combed through the ASEAN countries for the most promising early stage companies and in particular the most capable founders with the brightest ideas. As a consequence, the Insignia portfolio has a rich mix of industries, such as logistics, automotive, banking, insurance, health, education, food, gaming, and ecommerce, all exploded by the internet revolution. The companies operate in the ASEAN countries which encompass a variety of languages and cultures, different levels of economic development, infrastructure, and income. This vast diversity makes it almost impossible to replicate business success from one country to another without major modifications to models. Even within a country, such as Indonesia, new and novel business approaches are required when launching into the remote areas.

Therefore, the stories told in this book offer such an extensive scope and depth that any entrepreneur in the internet world of startups will find takeaways of relevance. Much of the learning points are also applicable in other industries, making them useful case studies. The recounting of many personal experiences undergoing the ups and downs of markets and pivoting of business strategies and product positioning provide vicarious thrill and immediacy to the reader.

As explorers of uncharted territories, the founders had to experiment and quickly learn from their trials and errors to best understand and serve the needs of the unfamiliar target markets. However, the strife of the marketplace is in turn entry barriers to newcomers and large players who lack understanding and agility.

Our explorers are not dreaming to change the world, now enveloped by chaos and calamity, but to find those market segments, be they rural or urban, that are left behind, unserved or underserved, and to innovate products and services to best meet their needs. Furthermore, the COVID-19 pandemic has rapidly and massively grown the trend towards online connectivity in a myriad of use cases, opening up attractive market opportunities for our explorers.

Besides bringing forth the stories of the frontline entrepreneurs seeking and tackling new market segments, this book has another layer of wisdom to share. This is captured in the articles written by the Insignia founding general partner and key investment team members. From their helicopter view of the portfolio companies as well as non-invested companies where they conducted extensive due diligence, the Insignia team has observed several common business themes that have enabled successful market traction and expansion, and also saw themes that did not or will not work. Some successes are new-found or newly minted business models and marketing strategies that have not been discovered or not so apparent in other world markets. Some are not new, but they serve to reinforce their relevance and applicability in Southeast Asian markets. These business themes are well articulated in this book, illustrated with examples from the Insignia portfolio. Enjoy the discovery of these themes as you explore through the book.

The Insignia team also highlights to entrepreneurs the importance of hiring the right crew (management team) and being well-fortified with resources (software) and sustenance (funds) when embarking on their explorations. They must also be able to "weather the storms" and "build the reservoirs".

While it appears that many Southeast Asian startups are adopting similar business models of Chinese companies, just as the Chinese companies have adopted those of American companies, there is one overriding factor which can ruin blind replication of the models in Southeast Asia. The USA and China are largely homogeneous markets. As previously stated, ASEAN countries are not homogeneous, and other than Indonesia as a whole, the size of the market of each country is not very attractive. Even within the large Indonesian archipelago, the disparity between urban and rural areas makes them totally different markets. ASEAN entrepreneurs have to treat their domestic markets as testbeds and launchpads, and modify their business strategies when expanding into other ASEAN countries. Thus, the need for creativity and innovation by our entrepreneurs when they attempt to penetrate the ASEAN markets.

Now other entrepreneurs can follow the footsteps and signposts of our explorers in this book. They can strike out further into virgin territories or deeper into the rich mother lode seeking more treasure, with less need for raw experimentation and reduced risk of failure.

The Insignia team presents their acquired wisdom in this book, backed up by adventures narrated by the founders of respective portfolio companies, generously contributing invaluable practical knowledge to all entrepreneurs in the fast-evolving and growing internet business world. The casual reader who may not be an entrepreneur or an investor will also find this book to be an interesting read.

Preface 1: Investing in Southeast Asia's Technology Market: Lessons from Indonesia's Biggest Floating Market

by Yinglan Tan and Paulo Joquino

Nestled in the Lok Baintan river on Banjarmasin island in the South Kalimantan province is Indonesia's biggest floating market. Every day just after dawn, traders on their traditional boats, or *klotok*, sell their goods until mid-morning.

Dating back to the 1600s, the Lok Baintan Floating Market is an enduring presence in South Kalimantan. It is not just a mecca of trade with a rich cultural heritage; it is also a dynamic ecosystem, influenced both by merchants and external factors.

In a way, the floating market is a microcosm of Southeast Asia's technology market. For investors looking at the region, there are some striking lessons to be learned from Lok Baintan and how it is changing — also potentially worth a trip once the opportunity arises!

(1) Invest in Companies that Foster Ecosystems

Chaos is a natural first impression of the floating market, with boats bumping into each other every so often. A closer look unveils order and collaboration. In this market, the "bumps" are necessary for them to communicate and trade with one another. There is also a culture of trust, with merchants bartering goods among each other.

This culture was formed over the years of existence and has allowed Lok Baintan to be more than just a floating market, but also a tourism hotspot. Most of the traders are women who fostered interdependence with local government and the greater community to market Lok Baintan beyond its traditional clientele, attracting buyers from the world over.

In Southeast Asia, working with complex ecosystems in local environments is part-and-parcel of the market entry of a technology venture. Communities have unique ways of communicating, and relationships that can be pivotal in introducing new technology. Startups collaborate with community fixtures like the *warungs* in Indonesia and the *sari-sari* stores in the Philippines to introduce online platforms for ecommerce and financial services.

Apart from collaboration with local communities for market entry, Lok Baintan also presents a model of entrepreneurial collaboration, where synergies and mutual respect among startups uplift the entire ecosystem as a whole. Investing in the region is about finding ecosystems that multiply the growth of entire markets.

(2) Invest in Simple Solutions that Solve Big Problems

Ten years ago, transactions at Lok Baintan were all in cash. Today, a large number of the merchants use the Payfazz application for transactions.

The shift from offline to online is inevitable, but what is interesting is how and why this transition is happening. In an area where most merchants have no bank accounts, companies like Payfazz built lightweight apps merchants could easily access on their first-generation smartphones.

Solutions like these are not the stuff of science fiction or even deep tech, but they are effective at closing the gaps in basic services in disconnected markets.

(3) Invest in Dis-Intermediating Technology

The merchants of Lok Baintan are mostly farmers who ply the river to sell their crops. Despite all the hard work that goes into those early mornings, these farmers do not make a lot of money. Other players along the value chain, from the one who leased their boats to resellers, take up most of the profits.

These intermediaries are a result of long-standing fragmentation in the market. Technology plays a large role in the dis-intermediation of these intermediaries. Farm-to-table startups have been using technology platforms to reduce costs and intermediaries. Producers make more, and buyers pay less.

Even in an ecosystem like Lok Baintan, there are inefficiencies that, if addressed, can unlock better livelihood for the people who have broken their backs to keep the market afloat.

(4) Invest in the Rare Fruits

The goods traded on Lok Baintan range from fruits like rambutans and guavas, to vegetables like cassava leaves and water spinach, to traditional snacks like *nasi bungkus*. Among these are fruits rarely seen or sold in big cities today, like the Kalimantan mango or Kasturi, and the rambai.

Just as many tourists come to Southeast Asia for its "exotic" appeal, the appeal of Southeast Asia's technology market for investors abroad is born out of the acclimatization of existing business models to local environments. It is especially more exciting to go beyond the big cities and see the startup activity in second and third-tier cities, where often, the most valuable technology companies created are the "new species".

(5) Invest early in the freshest produce

Tourists flock to the Lok Baintan for various reasons. There is the sunrise view with a backdrop of prayers sung from nearby mosques. There is a variety of cheap fresh produce, and the hot *'kopi'* is perfect for early mornings. There is the interactions with locals as they sell their goods. But, to enjoy all of these, you have to come in early.

The same goes for investing in Southeast Asia's technology market. Reaping the best returns means coming in early and committing to the endeavor. Sleeping in or hesitation can result in missing out on the fresher produce.

These are just five takeaways from a trip to the Lok Baintan Floating Market that illustrate where and how to invest in Southeast Asia's technology market. If you look back in history, the most significant creation in market capitalization are caused by two primary shifts: (1) the rise of technology and (2) the rise of the middle class. In the US, the former mostly drove the market. In China, it was a combination.

In Southeast Asia's internet economy, the rise of the middle-class income has been the main driver, but in the last five years, the rise of technology has enabled more entrepreneurs to speed up digitalization especially in untapped areas. As much as the startup investment landscape has matured in the last five years, the rise of technology in the region clashing with the internet-consuming middle class will continue to open new doors.

The sun has risen on the market, but just like Lok Baintan, the market continues to evolve day-to-day, and it is never too late to be early. This book is an attempt to show everyone, till now, only a handful people got to see — the dawn of the Southeast Asia technology marketplace.

Preface 2: Building Southeast Asia's Largest Automotive Marketplace: Carro

by Aaron Tan
CEO & Co-founder of Carro

"Being the best is not enough, you must better the best."
— Tan Yinglan

The year was 1996. I was 12 then, dialing in onto the internet for the first time. Yahoo!, Altavista, Excite, Lycos, and Geocities were all the rage then — though none of them exist today. These tech startups inspired me to learn programming early — starting my first company the following year when I was 13.

I subsequently sold my company and got conscripted for military service where I had the good fortune (while some may beg to differ) to meet Yinglan, whom had only just graduated from Stanford.

Soon, we were venture building and eventually launched a couple of company and products together. I later received a full government scholarship and was sent packing to Carnegie Mellon in the Pittsburgh.

Four years flashed passed, I came back to Singapore and served my scholarship bond as a venture capitalist in a newly formed corporate venture fund.

Being part of a venture fund was a dream come true, I learned everything from setting up the fund, renovating the office, down to investing in startups, negotiating valuations, dealing with legal documents, and sitting on the board of companies. I was subsequently transferred to the United States office which further sharpened my venture experience but more importantly, taught me how to run companies properly.

One of the best things about being in the Valley is that it is a hotspot of innovation — there is a demo day, pitch day, open house, and a new venture fund event almost every day. One of the most useful events that shaped my thinking till today was the corporate development discussion by the corporate development heads of Facebook and Google.

So what are you looking at acquiring at Facebook? I famously asked — the answer was simple yet profound: "We buy toothbrushes". The gentlemen went on to describe that in Facebook, they want companies that are super sticky ideally using the platform at least two to three times a day, like that of a toothbrush.

When my bond with the government was about to end in late-2015, I would have then returned to Singapore from my two-year stint in the United States. Yinglan, then already in Sequoia, appeared out of nowhere, telling me that I have overstayed and asked me out for a discussion.

We brainstormed on a few ideas and decided on anything that is in and around "衣(yī), 食 (shí), 住 (zhù), 行 (xing)" — which in Mandarin, loosely translates to clothing, food, property, or transport — the necessities in our daily life.

Having been a VC for the most of my professional career, I was mostly concerned on team (T), market size (M), comparable (C), good neighborhood (N), and weak competition (C). For me, a perfect investment should have most the following elements: $T + MC^2 + N$.

In any investment, the ***Team*** is the most important factor. As VCs, the pedigree, experience, and more importantly, the tenancy of the founders is what we invest in. One can have the best idea, but without a strong team, the idea will not work. Similarly, a strong team learns, adapts, and will make even a weak idea work.

Before I founded my company, I assembled a few classmates from the same scholarship program as myself — this formed the core team and baseline of the company. During this team forming process, I purposefully got in my classmates who were not Singaporeans — instead, they were mostly Indonesians and Thais. This gave the company a natural advantage over all competitors early on — we had local co-founders everywhere we went.

After the core team was sorted, the next most important thing was product-market-fit and how big the **market size** is. What is the Total Addressable Market (TAM)? What is the Serviceable Available Market (SAM)? Something that worked in Indonesia does not mean that it will work in the Philippines or Singapore, so it is important to understand what works and what does not early on and how big is the opportunity across different geographies in Southeast Asia. Be strategic and purposeful on the order of market entry.

Sometimes, we do see entirely unique business models being created, but more often than not — an idea is merely an adaptation of existing business models executed better across various markets. If you have an idea, it is very likely that it has been implemented somewhere around the world in some shape, way, or manner.

From **comparable** companies, we can determine many variables and more importantly, we can shortcut the learnings. The ideal situation is if there are many large (more than $5 billion market cap) comparables overseas and none in your home/target market.

Assuming the comparable is sometimes in the local market (and thereby a **competitor**), then we need to ask ourselves if we want to compete head on with them? How can we win? Are there many of them?

In certain winner-takes-all businesses such as the classifieds space, it takes a lot of time and often hundreds of millions in investment dollars to take on a competitor. Sometimes, rather than go after a red ocean, it may be smarter to avoid competition (in the interest of time) to go after a blue ocean entirely.

Lastly, assuming once we decided on an idea, what are the adjacencies we see? What is the hyper loop? How do we capture and retain the customers across the entire spectrum of the business thereby increasing the **neighborhood** and network effect of the business?

Based on the four necessities of life and the principle of $T + MC^2 + N$. We quickly (as a team) agreed that building Southeast Asia's largest transactional marketplace is the way forward and we launched Carro in 2016.

Four years in, we raised over \$100 million from top-tier venture funds to strategics including Softbank Ventures Asia, Insignia Ventures, Singtel Innov8, MS&AD, B Capital, and more.

Carro is present across Indonesia, Malaysia, Vietnam, Thailand, as well as in Singapore. We transacted over half a billion worth of vehicles last year netting over \$100 million in revenues and the company has close on to 500 people now across Southeast Asia.

We are no longer just a marketplace for trading vehicles we are also a financier, an insurer, and an aftersales provider all in one roof. The best thing about the automotive/ transport space is that the adjacent spaces. Financing, workshop, and insurance are super lucrative.

We have only just started going after the trillion-dollar automotive industry, barely hitting 1% of the overall Southeast Asian market. Competition, while present, has also been largely mute.

This book touches upon various topics with real war stories and experiences that would be super useful for anyone exploring to start a company, build a sustainable reservoir, or weather the storms of crisis.

In summary, I always remember the quote in my scholarship application, "Being the best is not enough, you must better the best". Similarly, in running a company, we cannot rest on our laurels, we must be aware and be on the constant move to excel and be a cut better than the best.

Preface 3: The Talent Behind Southeast Asia's Software Revolution

by Ridy Lie
Partner and Head of Tech at Insignia Ventures Partners

When I decided to return to Southeast Asia around five years ago, I came with the conviction that engineering innovation would help leapfrog various traditional businesses into the future. At that time, I had spent nearly a decade working for arguably one of the most innovative and successful startups in the United States. I had seen how technology could produce the best customer experience and at the same time reduce costs, and technology's capacity to do so has only progressed further.

Software innovation has progressed to a point that just a handful of engineers could produce a meaningful impact. In 2015, Whatsapp was illustriously able to serve half a billion users with only a few dozen engineers. Hackathons have consistently demonstrated that a small group of engineers armed with pizza and sodas could build useful products over a weekend. With the proliferation of tools and services available through the cloud, scaling to millions of users no longer takes months of gargantuan effort, but mere days.

Returning to Southeast Asia, I found that the rapid and collaborative nature of software development has attracted some of the best minds in the region as it had back in the United States.

Throughout the last five years, I have had the pleasure of working with some outstanding talent. In my judgment, the top talents in the region are every bit as outstanding as their counterparts in Silicon Valley. They are as bright, as hardworking, and as hungry for learning. Unfortunately, there are broader factors that often prevent these top talents from building the best products. These are often embedded deeply into the region's cultures, institutions, and management practices. At the same time, they offer clues as to how things can evolve in future for the region's tech talents.

(1) *Southeast Asia's strong culture of hierarchy.* In the workplace, employees felt a sense of duty to please their superior. Their sense of community and collectiveness leads to camaraderie and teamwork that few Sillicon Valley teams can achieve. However, this strength also leads to one crucial weakness: the team's vision is only as good as the vision of the leader. As the company grows, the leader is further removed from customer interactions, and so too will his vision be further removed from what is happening on the ground. Startups in the region will benefit from emphasizing that every employee should place pleasing the customer as a higher mandate than pleasing their superior.

(2) *Work arrangements not suited to better performance.* Managing tech talents is vastly different from managing employees with clear and measurable objectives. Incentivizing software engineers to meet a managerial deadline will lead to a completed system that works well, but needs to be rewritten in a year. Incentivizing for individual accomplishments will lead to a brittle system, like a chain is only as strong as it weakest link. Worst of all, forcing them to work longer will only backfire against long term productivity as quality is compromised.

A tech talent needs autonomy to excel at his job. He needs to be given a clear objective, and then given autonomy to execute the objective in his own way, without the need to constantly ask for approvals or produce progress. To illustrate, tech talents are like scouts rather than a foot soldiers, exploring unknown terrains and exercising their best judgment on which path to take. And if they find dead ends, they should still be lauded for providing valuable information for the army. Many companies in Southeast Asia fail to develop the environment of trust that is needed for this autonomy, and thus remains pinned with tech mediocrity.

(3) *Low labor costs incentivizing manual practices over automation.* Labor cost in many regions of Southeast Asia is still relatively low. This leads to a greater inertia to move a tech platform that requires significant investment of resources; why move to an automated solution when an army of admins could do the job at an acceptable cost? Take for example the financial ecosystem in Indonesia. Top payment channels still include manual bank transfer (through ATM or manned kiosks) and cash payment on delivery to customer. Furthermore, many major banks do not have a programmatic interface, so fintech companies are forced to use a complicated and brittle solution of website scraping and even makeshift hand robots to operate physical security tokens.

(4) *Fragmented education systems and hiring market.* Lastly, hiring remains as a perennial struggle in the region. The relatively few demonstrably strong talents are fiercely sought after by established companies and even global tech companies. For the rest, uneven education quality makes it difficult to find the diamonds in the rough. In general, tech talents are hard to come by, but I can see this changing. The success stories of multiple unicorns in the region are piquing the interest of many young minds. I am seeing more and more people, from Vietnam to Indonesia to Myanmar, choosing tech as their career choice.

Looking back, I have no regrets returning to the region. I am optimistic that the era of information is unfolding in Southeast Asia, and bringing the much-needed efficiency upgrade to business and the ways of life of its 650 million residents. This book is a testament to this unfolding narrative, with the stories it contains about those leading software innovation in the region.

And my belief in this revolution has only strengthened because of, and not in spite of, the challenges that face the region's tech talent. After all, software engineers like myself love a tough challenge.

Introduction: Explorers, Ecosystems, and Endurance

by Paulo Joquiňo

"Sometimes reality is too complex. Stories give it form."
Jean Luc Godard
film director, screenwriter, film critic

When I was invited by Yinglan to co-author a Southeast Asia version of *Chinnovation,* his previous opus featuring "star" entrepreneurs innovating China's industries, it was difficult to figure out from what angle to write this narrative of a rapidly evolving startup ecosystem like Southeast Asia's.

We decided not to overthink or look too far. While ideas for angles on the book were baking in the oven, we had also been sharing insights from the Insignia Ventures team and portfolio founders on a blog, *Insignia Business Review,* since the start of 2019. This blog was one way the firm was widening its mindshare in the ecosystem.

So instead of creating something entirely from scratch, we decided to use what we already had at our disposal — essays written throughout the year from January 2019 all the way to June 2020. The book became an anthology of essays and interviews from *Insignia*

Business Review, as well as other channels of content ranging from webinars and panels, to podcast conversations. *Essentially the book became an imprint or insignia, if you will, of the ecosystem of mindshare Insignia Ventures has been building on Southeast Asia.*

An Explanation on Form

Navigating ASEANnovation is like a multi-artist exhibition in an art gallery, or an anniversary album featuring star-studded collaborations. It is not meant to be a definitive guide to the region. Southeast Asia is too complex (and in some ways, abstract) that make any one perspective insufficient to encapsulate. Instead, like an exhibition or album, it is a curation of interpretations that adds more meaning to the collective understanding of a subject.

Of course, the curation reflects the venture capitalist lens. We are all too familiar with questions like, "What do you look for in founders?" or "What do you consider when investing?" Our answers to these questions were used in framing the essays together, but ultimately, it is a single narrative that holds this anthology together: the narrative of the explorer.

The book is divided into three parts according to this narrative. The first part covers the setting (Southeast Asia) and the characters (founders and their team) in exploration. The next is about the venture itself and the core approach we believe makes the most impact as a business. The final part is about the uncertainties and externalities startups have to deal with along the way, and how these outside forces can be sources of strength and endurance.

Even with this narrative however, the book is made up of various essays written in different times over the past 18 months — 18 months which have been momentous and historic in many ways. And all these essays are preserved in their original state as they were published, save for the ones formatted as interviews, which were curated and edited for narrative purposes. Each essay is collected into a chapter that explores a specific aspect of building and growing a tech startup, and a list of takeaways for the explorer at the end of each chapter.

This diversity inherent to the anthology means that there is more than one way to piece this book apart, not just the narrative of the explorer. There are several essays on logistics, fintech, and e-commerce, many discussions on the rural economy, and an entire chapter and an essay devoted to the COVID19 crisis. Founders' views are juxtaposed with that of venture capitalists.

This anthology can be different things to different people. It can be a guide for the reader who wants to dip his/her feet in the sea of Southeast Asia's tech startup ecosystem. It can be a source of inspiration for the aspiring entrepreneurs. It can be a framework for the founders to look at building their company. It can be a perspective for the investors with which to compare their own. It can simply be a collection of stories and wisdom.

Part 1: Explorers

The parallels between explorers and startup founders have always fascinated me. Even in management classes, the feats (and failures) of expeditions are pieced apart for what wisdom they might hold for the business leader.

Startup founders in particular face more extreme environments and seemingly impossible odds, akin to scaling the heights of Mount Everest, traversing the Antarctic tundra to reach the South Pole, or landing a lunar module on the Sea of Tranquility. This makes the comparison with explorers all the more poignant and relevant.

However, instead of mountains, seas, and outer space, these startup founders traverse the landscape of the internet. Throughout the book, we refer to the startup founder as an innovator. What they innovate is not confined to the technical limits of the internet; it encompasses the human experience online. Since the internet emerged out of clandestine military laboratories, it has evolved to become an inseparable part of the human experience. Today, the lines even blur between the internet and physical objects, with applications like Siri and IoT devices.

In Southeast Asia, the internet as a landscape of human experience remains largely uncharted. Leading the charge to explore the myriad of ways the internet can impact the human experience are these innovators. The first three chapters set this motivation, and lay out the conditions facing the innovators in their quest.

Chapter One, "Mapping Southeast Asia," covers Southeast Asia as a startup ecosystem, how it evolved, the various factors involved in its development, and possible trajectories it can take in the future.

Chapter Two, "Setting sail with the captains of innovation," looks at the ways explorers are molded by their environment, experiences, and ventures, and the steps the best founders take when setting sail as an early stage company.

Chapter Three, "Getting a crew," talks about talent — how teams are formed, developed, and grown. There are solo explorers who sail oceans and fly over continents, but ventures like these need a strong team from ideation all the way through market expansion.

For these innovators, it is not just about finding new applications and addressing longstanding inefficiencies with digitalization. There has to be sustainable ways to ensure that the venture creates significant and meaningful impact.

Part 2: Ecosystems

Explorers are often catalysts for changing worldview. The crew of Apollo 11 and the astronauts that followed on the moon gave the world a new way of looking at the Earth. Explorers laid the foundation for even more explorers to follow their path. Generations that follow even gain value from their ventures well beyond what the explorers initially expected. Eventually, the voyages taken by astronauts helped bring together the ISS, which now enables studies of many kinds. It is no longer simply about stepping on the moon or getting into space.

Such are the first-order and second-order effects of exploration. For tech startups, the creation of impact is not just an effect, it is the core motivation of the venture. In Southeast Asia, the impact is generally directed towards enabling access towards the part of the internet experience the startup has explored and materialized into a product or service — for example, developing an app for the unbanked to do banking on their phones. To sustain this access, an ecosystem that enables those using the product or service to maximize its value needs to be built.

Just as the idea of an ecosystem influenced this anthology, so does it take center stage in this narrative. In particular, the book focuses on the growth trajectory of platform companies, from acquisition to retention and eventually creating sustainable ecosystems. Chapters Four to Six trace this path from aggregating supply and demand to leveraging on data to cross-pollinate use cases.

Chapter Four, "Boarding the technology platforms," sets the stage for platform companies as a compelling business model in Southeast Asia, introduces the Reservoir Principle as a framework for growing platform companies, and goes over different acquisition strategies to get users on board.

Chapter Five, "Dropping the anchor on the market," surveys the different aspects that come into play when driving retention and stickiness on a platform business.

Chapter Six, "Settling in the Reservoir," wraps up the Reservoir Principle by tackling monetization and sustainable ecosystem building.

This focus on platform companies is the basis for the Reservoir Principle, the title essay of this book. The most impactful and enduring startups grew to become ecosystems of value, and platform companies are best suited to achieve this. In a way, these companies are all descendants of the original ecosystem — the internet itself.

Part 3: Endurance

These explorers, as much as they can prepare for their goal, are often subject to the whims of the environment. They are often a few degrees, a few centimeters, or a few seconds away from life-or-death scenarios.

In the same way, no matter how effective the ecosystem or motivated the founder and team, these platforms are not siloed in their own universes, nor do they exist solely as applications for the online human experience. There is the fundraising environment that supercharges the growth of startups. There are crises that come by threatening to topple the growth of the company, but also offer an opportunity to lead the way into the future. Then there are the options to exit that come along the path of growth. It is impossible to fully anticipate, much less prepare, for all these possibilities. *To endure means to build for uncertainty and optionality.*

The final three chapters cover these scenarios and frameworks to approach these eventualities.

Chapter Seven, "Unlocking the treasure chests," covers different takes on fundraising in Southeast Asia and ways to make the most out of fundraising.

Chapter Eight, "Weathering the storms," traces the impact of COVID19 on startups to the opportunities they present for the future, as a look into crisis management for startups.

Chapter Nine, "Exit Ahoy!" wraps up the book with insights on what it takes to exit a venture, and why exits are not the end of the exploration.

***

In stringing these aspects of growing and building a tech startup into the narrative of exploration or adventure, the intent is not to romanticize the everyday struggle founders face to turn their ideas into reality. Instead, the book offers an approach to this struggle inspired by these feats of human ingenuity and perseverance. It is an approach that also comes from insights developed over years of investing in tech companies and the experience of the founders and investors with whom we have had the privilege of conversation. It is not one-size-fits-all; there is no such thing. Like a good story passed on from generation to generation, it finds meaning in the context of the receiver. I hope that in this collection of essays, you can find meaning in it too.

1 June 2020
Manila, Philippines

Chapter One

Mapping Southeast Asia

Innovators stay ahead of the game.

"The winds and waves are always on the side of the ablest navigators."

— Edward Gibbon Historian, *"The History of the Decline and
Fall of the Roman Empire" Vol. 1, Chap. 68*

Every great adventure begins with a map — or the realization that
none has hitherto existed. For the innovator, a map is not a hand
drawn illustration with a clearly marked "X" for the treasure.

The innovator's map does not exist, for two reasons. First,
innovators are uniquely disposed to their exploration. Due to an
array of factors, each journey is different. While lessons can be
drawn from others, every innovator's "X" is unique. There is no
copy-paste template to achieve "X" because that "X" will never be
truly the same. Second, the landscape before them is always
changing, defeating the purpose of a map — unless that map itself
can change. And so, innovators look to nature as a guide, following
the stars (the ventures that came and went before them) and paying
attention to the direction of the wind (the markets).

And even though the innovator's journey leads to no singular
"X," there are destinations that capture the interest of many. Over
the last decade, one such destination has been Southeast Asia. As

economies in this region showed great promise to hit the technology market stride and the infrastructure to introduce digital technology became more widely accessible, tech companies, venture capitalists, and startup founders followed.

Composed of several countries connected by relatively recent historical and political circumstance, Southeast Asia from a startup ecosystem's point of view is less a singular region and more a conceptual framework with which startups and investors have approached this part of the world. Those expanding into the region are often cautioned about mistaking the forest for the diversity of trees.

The region's positioning globally has brought in the fuel to accelerate relatively similar growth trajectories among countries, closing gaps even further as capital and talent flows within the region thicken.

With more activity, the region has evolved into hotspots for tech startups. The successes of regional unicorns set the tone for local founders and the investment landscape. While the region has certainly become more crowded, there remains a lot of uncharted, nonobvious territory — arguably the more valuable areas for innovation.

This first section of essays revolves around this theme of change in Southeast Asia's startup ecosystem, and how startup founders can stay ahead of the pack as the competition thickens in the region.

Essays in this Chapter

(1) **Moving the needle.** It takes more than startups to build a startup ecosystem. With the Philippines as an example, the essay delves into the ingredients necessary for a startup ecosystem to grow. *Based on "Startup Ecosystem in the Philippines" by Paulo Joquiño and Yinglan Tan. Published 15 April 2019.*

(2) **Chinnovation in Southeast Asia.** The expansion of tech companies and movement of capital from China to Southeast Asia is a relatively recent development in the two regions' long history. The essay outlines the motivations for these development

and opportunities for local founders. *Based on "Big Tech's Chinatowns in Southeast Asia" by Paulo Joquiňo. Published 28 February 2020.*

(3) **Giants shape the landscape; outliers break the mold.** The essay illustrates the dynamic landscape of Southeast Asia's tech players, from the marketplaces that have amassed enough capital and resources to draw in other players, to the startups in sunrise sectors in the region. *Based on "The world is flat, but Southeast Asia is a bowl" by Paulo Joquiňo. Published 18 July 2019.*

(4) **Beyond the third wave.** Insights collected from interviews for publications illustrate the possible future waves of innovation in Southeast Asia, specifically for e-commerce. *By Paulo Joquiňo, based on interviews of Yinglan Tan with 7.5 degrees and simmondsstewart.sg (written by Liz Fox, published 20 September 2019).*

(5) **A model for sustainable growth.** Amidst the shattered illusions of unicorns and Silicon Valley narratives, Japan's shock-absorbent skyscrapers present a model for more resilient and enduring companies. *Based on "Dancing skyscrapers" by Paulo Joquiňo. Published 14 February 2020.*

(1) Moving the Needle

Based on "Startup Ecosystem in the Philippines" by Paulo Joquiňo and Yinglan Tan. Published 15 April 2019.

Every story begins with a setting on which it unfolds, and every journey a landscape on which it takes place. For startups, its ecosystems of resources and support that make it possible for many emerge and scale. From this essay zooming in on the Philippines' startup ecosystem in the first half of 2019, it is clear that there are local elements, from talent to regulatory support, that are needed along the different stages of a startup's growth. These elements have to be present at a critical mass to be needle-moving for technology companies in a country to rapidly scale regionally and attract foreign investment.

***

Factors Underlying the Deal-making Lag

With 6.55% real GDP growth in 2018 and a population of 107 million, the country holds great potential to be the next rising ecosystem. To put it into context within the region, Indonesia is like the King, Vietnam the Queen, and the Philippines is the Jack. The level of deal-making and capital-raising activities in the Philippines are a direct effect of the overall health of the country's startup ecosystem. There are certain changes in the ecosystem which need to happen before the Philippines can reach the heights of Indonesia and other countries.

Institutional support

A 2017 PWC study on the Philippine's startup ecosystem reported that there are more than 300 startups in the country and over 200 of them are actively operating. There are notable incubators, accelerators, and early stage VCs, such as Ideaspace and Kickstart. However, there is a gap in institutional support for post-Series A startups where significant capital is needed to help the startup grow and cross the chasm. Startups at this stage reach a significant scale where many internal changes take place within its team, culture and processes.

Regulatory support

Up until recently, there has not been a coordinated effort to lay the foundation to a vibrant startup ecosystem in the country. The collaboration between the Department of Science and Technology (DOST), Department of Information and Communications Technology (DICT), and the Department of Trade and Industry (DTI) should produce a roadmap to coordinate support efforts from different pockets of the ecosystem. Initiatives such as targeted regulatory sandboxes would help open up resources from the government and corporations while protecting startups from unfair competition.

A key factor among this would be political stability. This would help ensure long-term foresight in policy planning and continuity in the initiatives implemented for the community.

Talent and human capital

Education is still geared towards the service industry rather than entrepreneurship or the creative economy. Many graduates aspire towards corporate jobs or Business Process Outsourcing (BPO) companies with attractive and stable pay checks. Aside from this, brain-drain is still a significant trend and the Philippines has yet to experience the same influx of highly-educated returnees or 海龟 (hǎiguī) witnessed in other countries.

There is a limited set of rock stars that aspiring entrepreneurs can look up to, and success stories are limited to first movers in fintech or HR solutions. There has not been a success story which has reached the level of Gojek in Indonesia, and this impacts how far local startup founders in the Philippines dare to aim beyond their local market. Founders are generally conservative when it comes to how they look at growth.

Industry support

There is a general lack of widespread industry support which has, until recently, been largely dominated by the telcos. This has affected the nature of startups which succeed in the country. Infrastructure support and resource access have to open up to ensure that development can progress beyond major cities and into second and third tier cities.

Investment Stimuli

Critical mass of entrepreneurship and startup activity

The base level of entrepreneurship and startup activity (i.e., the propensity for talents to create new businesses or work in young companies) have not reached the same heights as what is currently witnessed in other parts of the region.

This is directly linked to the talent pool in the country, be it technical talents or talents with business backgrounds or industry expertise. A deep pool is needed to fuel the growth of startups. In addition, it can produce a generation of founders/entrepreneurs with the grit and smarts to innovate new business models, create new products, and solve complex problems in the market. In contrast to the current brain-drain phenomenon, the country should also start witnessing a trend of highly-educated returnees returning to start new businesses.

Openness of the Startup Ecosystem and Capital Markets

There are already pockets of activity in different parts of the local startup ecosystem. It is critical that efforts are made to coordinate and link up the ecosystem. In addition, an active startup ecosystem needs to be open in order for new local players and other foreign stakeholders to easily participate and connect resources. This is especially critical if the goal is for local startups to ultimately expand into other markets in the region.

The government's stance and regulatory attitude are important factors in sending a message to foreign investors that the country is ready to open up. This includes policy changes to make it easier for foreign capital to flow into local companies by easing foreign ownership limits in specific industries. Other important areas include creating clearer regulations and simplifying regulatory approval and other legal corporate processes.

Possibility of Profitable Exits and Corporate-startup Partnerships

Ultimately, foreign investors also need market evidence that the ecosystem is mature enough to support the growth of mid-market companies and attractive investment returns can be made. The best evidence would come from the emergence of the first generation of successful thriving startups valued US$100 million and above.

Corporate-startup partnerships are key to helping the country to reach that stage. There are already large conglomerates specifically in real estate, retail, telcos, banking, energy and insurance. These industries have potential for partnerships including acquisitions, buy-outs, and strategic investments which can boost tech companies and further spur the local economy.

Opening for a Regional Presence

With its population and growing middle class, the Philippines definitely has a large enough market to produce a unicorn — either a horizontal platform or a player focused on a sufficiently large vertical. The local market also has its own unique set of intricacies to support a local champion, i.e., "mutants" that adapt successful business models in the region for local differences.

Take the fintech space, for example. The regulation, underwriting environment, attitude towards credit, and trust towards tech startups as business partners differ from market to market. Thus, market-specific customer on-boarding processes, proprietary underwriting models, and highly localized datasets are key to winning each market. This creates the opportunity for local champions like First Circle to create a superior product over foreign entrants entering the local trade financing space.

The active participation by regional and global tech giants in the country is clear evidence supporting this. This includes Gojek's "substantial investment" into Coins.ph, Tencent, and KKR's investment into Paymaya and Ant Financial's investment into Mynt. What the Philippines needs is a generation of startups (US$100 million valuation and above) that have been around for three to five years, crossed the chasm with its initial product, and are rapidly expanding into adjacent services or markets.

In recent years, the Philippines has been working on its ecosystem fundamentals, highlighted by the formation of support systems like the DICT, QBO (a PPP initiative for startups), and VCAP (Venture Capital and Private Equity Association of the Philippines), the active involvement of legislation through the Philippine Startup Bill and the One-Person Corporation, and the launching of "sandboxes" for entrepreneurs like in PhilDev,

Ideaspace, Founders' Institute, Globe Future Makers, among others. However, these efforts are still concentrated in the early stage and do not address the missing growth stage where startups are scaling up towards mid-market and becoming a unicorn.

The above foundational initiatives can lead the way for support from more diverse sources. This includes attracting regional VCs to place a bigger focus and allocate more capital to invest in the country, encouraging corporate participation from a wider set of local conglomerates (beyond telcos and banks) either through CVCs or by funding local VCs, and getting HNWIs and family offices (e.g., old Chinese families in the Philippines) to start looking at startup investments. Participation from foreign conglomerates (i.e., Japan and Korea) can play an important role as a source of Foreign Direct Investments.

Beyond funding capital, support also needs to come in the form of technological infrastructure (5G and stable mobile networks beyond the major cities) and education to create a deep talent pool. Also, the government has to create incentives and actively make efforts to woo the Philippine diaspora overseas to return to the country.

(2) Chinnovation in Southeast Asia

"Being a distribution expert in Singapore brings little insight into distributing packages throughout Indonesia's 17,500 islands. For that sort of thing, it is difficult to have a one-size-fits-all approach for different countries. Such intricacies, in other words, might be better delivered by local entrepreneurs who can be bought out once they have cracked them."

— *Tan Yinglan,* in *The Economist,* Jul 7, 2018

Based on "Big Tech's Chinatowns in Southeast Asia" by Paulo Joquiño. Published 28 February 2020.

While many of the factors discussed in the previous essay can apply to startup ecosystems around the world, one factor unique to Southeast Asia is the constant, yet ever-changing role of China.

This "Chinnovation" impacts Southeast Asia in two ways: direct and indirect influence. Chinese innovators who have seen success in China and are looking to grow even further find Southeast Asia as an attractive destination for expansion. Alibaba and Tencent are leaders in this regard, but more Chinese tech companies in various verticals are placing their stake in the region.

Apart from the direct expansion of Chinese companies into the region, local founders and investors are also looking to successful models in China (or China's internet economy growth trajectory in general) for inspiration on what might be next for Southeast Asia. This mirroring effect between the two regions is not entirely abstraction; there are shared behaviors and perceptions that have enabled the translation of Chinese business models into the region.

Even with these similarities, there are many more differences that also make it difficult for Chinese innovation to simply uproot and find traction here. Born-and-bred founders in the region are using this local understanding to their advantage, especially those that have found success in the rural economy.

This essay is a telescope into the direct influence of Chinnovation, panning across China's tech activity in Southeast Asia, then zooming in financial services and zooming out to what the future looks like for Chinese tech companies that have entered the region.

***

Chinese influence in the region traces centuries back to sampans and Chinese junks making their way across rivers and seas to trade with locals, and later on the rest of the world that made Southeast Asia their trading outpost with the Middle Kingdom. The world's oldest Chinatown can be found in Manila, a historical signpost for just how entrenched China has been in the region and how valuable the region has been for spreading Chinese influence globally.

Digital Merchants

This past decade has simply been an evolution of this dynamic in the digital age. When China became a tech powerhouse, it made sense for the winners to take their technology and talent where their forebears took their spices and sails several centuries ago.

Apart from the geographical and even cultural proximity, China tech's huge splash in the region can largely be owed to their overall investment approach, which did not just involve watering companies with cash, but cultivating their growth with talent (i.e., training), technology (e.g., 5G), and expertise.

Alibaba and Tencent set the precedent in this regard for the companies that followed, albeit to varying degrees. While Alibaba is known to have deployed talent and infrastructure, Tencent's involvement remains largely in the boardroom and on the cap tables of their investments.

They also seem to have different approaches in terms of verticals, with Alibaba sticking to e-commerce with Lazada and Tokopedia. Meanwhile, Tencent is inclined more towards the content and gaming ecosystem with investments into Sea, Ookbee, and Gojek, given its dependence on the messaging super app WeChat for scale. Another model for expansion into the region is JD's where they did a joint venture with Gojek and Traveloka to setup JD.ID, which is now reported to have joined Indonesia's unicorn club.

Hands-on Approach to the Market

This hands-on ability stems from investors seeing the region's digital transformation as almost mirroring that of China's nearly a decade ago, only this time going at a faster pace with better technology and more sources of capital. Indonesia, for example, is currently viewed as being at the inflection point where China was when Alibaba's Taobao took off. The business models that succeeded in China, with their strength in generating user stickiness at low cost, are also proving to be crucial to expansion in Southeast Asia's fragmented landscape.

The recent slew of startups hitting the brakes on the public markets has certainly pushed tech investors globally to re-evaluate their positions and become more scrutinous when it comes to profitability and quality overall, and Chinese tech investors are no different.

Even then, their moves in the region have not abated and are becoming more focused on securing stronger positions in the region and supporting the path to profitability for local investments. Instead of the pure investments and joint ventures which have characterized most of China tech's activity in the region in latter half of the decade, Chinese tech companies will strengthen their ground up initiatives in the region, with Ant Financial, Xiaomi, and even Tencent (through Sea) joining the digital banking race, Ping An launching telehealth consulting services in Indonesia with Grab, and JD launching a mobile wallet in Thailand with Central Group.

Fintech Point-of-entry

Chinese tech unicorns are leveraging on the ubiquity of financial services to compete in the region, taking advantage of their massive user base and gain penetration across different markets. Finance is a foundational vertical for tech companies in Southeast Asia, where most of the region's population is unbanked or has difficulty with financing. Enabling access to financial services opens up opportunities to tap into other verticals, like e-commerce and logistics.

Many of these tech giants also have a high number of active users and traffic — personal finance allows them to monetize these users effectively, and also in the process, collect transaction data that underwrites many financial services. Tencent and Alibaba have already shown how tapping into a financial services platform play, whether by acquiring local players or setting up subsidiaries, has enabled them to extend their reach into regions like Southeast Asia and Africa.

The stiff competition in China's fintech sector is pushing tech companies to tap into the growing opportunity in Southeast Asia for financial services, where the majority of the online population transact heavily on e-commerce and ride-hailing. It also helps that financial services in the region serve both as a strong moat from which to expand into other offerings and an expansion strategy for platforms with already deep market share.

Apart from Singapore where the digital banking race is afoot, markets like Malaysia, Thailand, and the Philippines are becoming more open and structured in terms of financial services regulation and bank partnerships with tech companies.

Another key motivation is expansion. The best offense begins with setting up good defense. Covering financial services entrenches their position in the market, creating stickiness with existing customers. This lays the foundation to expand into new markets and across more services. Integrating financial services would not necessarily ensure profitability, but when done right, it can result in better unit economics and create more breathing space for these giants to grow.

Coming into the region, the tech platforms have traffic, data, often superior artificial intelligence or machine learning capacity, and cloud computing capabilities. They often also have a more acute sense of the user when it comes to engineering retention on their platforms. However, what they lack is often the regulatory license, low funding cost, risk management capabilities, product offerings, and in certain cases like private banking, personalized services.

When it comes to regions like Southeast Asia, regulations vary with each country, and this can be a hurdle for platforms seeking to tap into finance. Some markets can be proactive with their regulations (like Hong Kong and Singapore, which are issuing virtual banking licenses), while others tend to wait for players to make more considerable moves before stepping in.

With the variability across markets, the key for tech platforms venturing into finance is to form the right partnerships with local banks and financing institutions. These partnerships would not only get a foot in the door, but also set a defensible moat for these platforms should competitors follow.

Long-term Opportunities for Local Founders

A combination of local competition, pushback from other markets, and the raw market potential will continue to attract Chinese investment into Southeast Asia. With the market uncertainties and tension across the Pacific heightened, the relatively China-friendly regulation in Southeast Asia stands more favorably versus the pushback companies like Huawei and Bytedance have received in the West. The trade war has also resulted in supply chain diversification driving manufacturing growth in insular countries like Vietnam, which will only serve to make the region an even more attractive destination for Chinese investment.

What differentiates the impact of Chinese investment from the rest of the world's in the region is that it has gone well beyond capital and the play for these big tech companies is long-term. For local founders, opportunities abound to leverage on China tech not just for investments but long-term infrastructure plays as well. The question is who to partner with and which platforms will benefit your business model. This degree of influence has played a huge role in accelerating the region's digital transformation thus far and will continue to do so in the next decade.

(3) Giants Shape the Landscape, and Outliers Break the Mold

Based on "The world is flat, but Southeast Asia is a bowl" by Paulo Joquiño. Published 18 July 2019.

In part due to Chinnovation in the region, Southeast Asia's landscape has been shaped by the fast growth of marketplace leaders like Grab, Gojek, and Tokopedia in the latter half of the 2010s. In turn, these companies have opened the doors for other startups, many of whom have ended up following the money into the arms of (or getting knocked out of the ring by) these regional heavyweights. At the same time, there are others invested in creating impact specifically within their own verticals, away from the pull of these large marketplaces.

***

In 2005, Thomas Friedman's book, *The World is Flat*, described a democratized and accessible innovation landscape shaped by globalization. That same year, University of Toronto Professor Richard Florida responded with a spikier view of the world, where the benefits of innovation and economic progress concentrate in a few metropolitan centers around the world. Southeast Asia is somewhere in between — a bowl.

Innovation "Gravity Well"

Investments have been flowing in this bowl, with the region drawing in international players amidst the global economic slowdown and tensions. While the M&A and investment activity opens opportunities in the region, the competitive landscape is not flat. Tech giants, regional unicorns, and key markets have been pulling these investments and innovation towards them, creating an innovation "gravity well."

This innovation "gravity well," akin to how Albert Einstein described heavier bodies in space bending the fabric of spacetime, bends trends towards the heavyweights like Grab, Gojek, and Traveloka, who are themselves riding on the shoulders of Alibaba and Tencent.

The mass of these companies, measurable by their user base, draws smaller startups towards them, especially those whose solutions are in nearby verticals. Founders looking for an easy exit will likely then position themselves as prospective acquisitions, which is not as easy.

Not all startups in verticals critical to a unicorn's operations are prospects. There are some services that unicorns can easily deploy on their own, like loans in the case of Tokopedia. In the case of critical services beyond their existing capabilities, then unicorns will use their momentum to pull in the right acquisition.

The "gravity well" extends to markets, with Singapore and Indonesia keeping up a significant lead in VC investments against their neighbors and drawing in more startups to launch there.

When a Bowl with Cracks is not Broken, but Valuable

The bowl can only hold so much, as cracks emerge on the frontiers of innovation. Some startups are pulling away from larger players, establishing themselves in underserved verticals or venturing into cross-border operations. They develop unique capabilities and their own networks, reducing dependencies from unicorns. Serving unicorns is not their main motivation or driver of growth.

These companies have set themselves up as their own gateways into the region for foreign stakeholders and are looking for more than just an exit. Founders on these cracks are pioneering solutions in sectors like agriculture, where Sayurbox is digitizing farm-to-table in Indonesia.

Markets apart from Singapore and Indonesia are also building their capacity to raise more unicorns. The recent partnership between Thailand's Kasikornbank and Vietnam's Business Startup Support Center signifies capacity-building beyond individual economies. Local conglomerates in the Philippines are extending more capital to local startups through new CVC funds. As other markets in Southeast Asia attract interest towards them, certain verticals will also benefit and be able to support the growth of unicorns in these spaces.

What do you do when there are cracks on a bowl? There is the Japanese tradition of Kintsugi, where pottery cracks are filled in with gold, silver, or platinum. In the same way, investors and governments can fill in these cracks made by pioneer startups and emerging markets, raising the bowl's value over time. Ultimately, the goal is for these startups not to stay long in this bowl, but to grow out of it into the flat (or spiky) world.

(4) Beyond the Third Wave

By Paulo Joquiño, based on interviews of Yinglan Tan with 7.5 degrees and simmondsstewart.sg (written by Liz Fox, published 20 September 2019).

Staying ahead of the waves of innovation is critical to avoiding the "gravity well" of larger players and being a pioneer in the region. The previous essays in this chapter identified and characterized a few of these waves that came, but what might the future waves of innovation hold for Southeast Asia? This compilation of insights from interviews is no crystal ball, but there are emerging sectors and trends within more established sectors like e-commerce that hold clues to the future of Southeast Asia's tech landscape.

***

Enabling the Second Wave

Third-wave tech innovation in Southeast Asia is all about enablers. E-commerce and ride-hailing are horizontal marketplaces that amassed users by targeting compelling needs, and now they need the support of payment gateways and logistics providers to create a more efficient and engaging user experience. So, these enablers come in to support these functions and address with technology some of the issues that these marketplaces have.

One great example of this third-wave innovation is Janio, a 4PL cross-border logistics solutions platform. Their proprietary software layer provides end-to-end logistics solutions for e-commerce marketplaces, including COD and customs clearance. This platform enables e-commerce players in Southeast Asia to ship more efficiently cross-border and even expand their reach beyond the region. Janio's platform finds optimal routes for these e-commerce businesses to receive goods from suppliers and deliver to their customers, which is especially important these days when global supply chains are being disrupted and diversified.

Incoming FADs

With marketplaces enablers leading the third wave, the next wave of innovation in the region will likely see a departure from the horizontal marketplaces as Southeast Asia's startups tackle more problems and pain points in the region.

(1) *Funding at the frontier*: Specialized investment will open up for emerging verticals in the region like healthtech, entertainment, logistics, and smart cities

(2) *Away from the center*: Second- to fourth-tier cities will become the focus of more startups as the regional unicorns and bigger players take up online segments and more developed localities

(3) *Data sources and use cases*: New sources and use cases for data will emerge as platforms engage more consumers, enabling verticals like robotics process automation (RPA), healthtech, and insurtech to tackle industry inefficiencies.

Hyper-vertical Unicorns

What does this FAD mean for what unicorns might emerge from the region? Southeast Asia's past unicorns have come mostly from e-commerce, ride-hailing, and entertainment/gaming. As tech startups become more industry-focused, the region's next generation of unicorns may well be hyper-vertical platforms that are able to create an ecosystem of products or services within their specific industry or vertical.

Instead of the generalist consumer-facing super app model that can spread itself thin, the next unicorns would emerge from the verticals, working within low-hanging adjacencies. With the crisis and shifting expectations of investors on startups, the key here for these platforms will be to go beyond acquisition and nail down monetization.

The New Waves of E-commerce

Although e-commerce has long been in the region, it is rapidly evolving to meet the unique needs of new markets. This is happening in rural communities where social commerce is preferred. Through group-buying and agent-driven models, social commerce platforms like Super in Indonesia are able to cater to users who do not only prefer to transact with people they trust but also benefit from the lower costs of these transactions.

As consumers in Southeast Asia becomes more digitally literate, the success of social media-based e-commerce features will depend on the seamlessness and convenience of the experience. The platforms that can flywheel into or from e-commerce the most effectively will win over the consumer.

E-commerce still has a large part to play in the future of Southeast Asia's internet. In the beginning, it was all about aggregating buyers and sellers. Then logistics and fintech came in to make the purchase experience more seamless. More recently, marketplaces have popped up, targeting more specific segments and needs. Last year, we invested in Eezee targeting the Maintence, Repair, and Operating (MRO) needs in the B2B space, while platforms like Super are tackling FMCG needs of second-tier and third-tier cities through social commerce. We expect that these marketplaces will continue to evolve to cater to more specific goods like cosmetics.

Moving forward, as Southeast Asia's population increases its screen time and e-commerce activity, it will be about diversifying the user experience on these platforms. Social media, entertainment, and e-commerce will come together in various ways. E-commerce players like Lazada and Shopee have already added live streaming shows onto their platforms, while social media platforms like TikTok are enabling purchases links through their short-form videos.

(5) A model for Sustainable Growth

Based on "Dancing skyscrapers" by Paulo Joquiño. Published 14 February 2020.

Towards the end of the decade, the growth-at-all-costs paradigm with which the likes of Facebook, Uber, and their venture-backed contemporaries skyrocketed showed its cracks. A slew of lackluster IPOs and IPO attempts, capped off by the WeWork/Softbank debacle, has had investor sentiment shifting significantly. Tech startups are being sought for paths to profitability and more sustainable business models.

It is becoming less a matter of choice than a matter of necessity as the pandemic-induced economic slowdown weighs heavily on startup activity. Even then, the innovation of business models continues unabated in the face of new challenges and new norms.

With the help of Japanese architecture, this essay illustrates how it is possible to balance scaling skyward and maintaining flexible foundations.

***

Accounting for 20% of global earthquakes with magnitude 6.0 and above, Japan's history has been shaped by seismic events. The Ansei Edo earthquakes in the late 1800s weakened the bakufu military of the shogunate, leading to the rise of Imperial Japan at the turn of the century. More recently, the Fukushima nuclear power plant collapse in 2011 shifted public perception globally when it came to nuclear energy.

Even Japan's most famous startup war chest — Softbank — was not spared from its own earthquake, and the aftershocks rippled investor sentiments globally. Much has been said about the WeWork/Softbank fallout, from its singularity as an event (i.e., it does not change anything) to its role in the larger narrative of a "reckoning" befalling companies at the cusp of an IPO. Regardless, it is clear that this seismic event has been building up pressure for a long time, and the IPO pull-out was the one with the magnitude to pull the rug from underneath the big players and private investors.

Unicorns Grounded

Primarily WeWork's downfall brought other Softbank investments like Oyo and Grab under more intense scrutiny. The pressure mounts for unicorns to prove profitability in their models as they expand further into later stage rounds.

In the property sector, major players have been taking cover from the fallout. Property Guru coincidentally missed what would have been an arguably pivotal $256 million exit for the region, and Oyo diversified its board in a bid to step out of Softbank's mushroom cloud.

The once palpable excitement among technology companies to take-off in the public markets in three to five years is now overrun by the sobering reality that internal stability and sustainable profitability are key to a successful IPO. Technology companies that have grown accustomed to scale and expansion at all costs cannot make this transition overnight.

Companies that have raised several mega rounds in anticipation of a public exit are staying private longer, presumably in an effort to reconfigure their growth trajectory. This is a trend that has been observed long before WeWork with companies exceeding $10 billion on private fundraising, and it is one that the past year's IPO flops have only intensified.

The crowding at the IPO gates is thinning out, especially with capital flows shifting due to trade wars and economic uncertainties. Even then, fast growth remains the rule for venture-backed companies, only this time, it cannot be done the same way, given what WeWork and Softbank have brought to light.

Seismic Isolation

Even though Japan is inextricably tied to earthquakes, this does not stop them from building skyscrapers. The country boasts the second tallest building in the world, the Tokyo Skytree. As the high-rises of Tokyo, Osaka, and Yokohama are built, a process called seismic isolation allows these skyscrapers to dance with the earthquakes. Shock absorbers and motion dampers are built in throughout their entire height.

In the same way, fast-growing technology companies need to undergo their own "seismic isolation" that encompasses the entire company. This approach extends from installing organizational checks and balances to tapping into multiple high-margin revenue streams.

With the biases uncovered by the WeWork case and overall uncertainty in the global markets, investors are flocking to safety in dancing skyscrapers — companies that are still able to grow fast while withstanding market uncertainties and adapting to the limits of their own business models.

Industry-sensitive Architects

Architects of these dancing skyscrapers have an industry-sensitive perspective. It is difficult to build on land you have not studied well.

That the co-sharing model has an immensely high cash burn due to capital procurement should be clear from day one. This means a venture-backed, sustainable growth trajectory for co-sharing cannot be the same as that for an asset-light, volume-driven e-commerce or entertainment platform. The co-sharing model has to establish value-add to their clients beyond leasing space and generate cash flow through these adjacencies, from tenant support services to community engagements.

Having an industry-sensitive perspective also means being nimble enough to adjust strategy and tap into opportunities amidst changing market conditions. Given the unsustainable economics of the WeWork model shaking up investor sentiment, an IPO may not be the best exit, and instead an M&A with a more established property developer may be a better alternative.

Investor appetite can be expected to focus on this founder-market fit, as it will define how the investor-founder relationship will work out. How involved should the investor be? And on the other hand, what value add does the founder really need from each stakeholder on the cap table?

The "ownership" aspect of the deal was vastly underestimated in the case of WeWork and Softbank. While it is easy to diagnose the issue as a lack of true investor-founder collaboration, the challenge will still remain for founders to choose the best deals, which does not always mean the most cash or highest valuation. The challenge for investors is to find founders who can live up to the heights of their story or at the very least have clarity on how to get there.

Dancing Skyscrapers of the Future

The earthquakes will continue to happen, and skyscrapers will still be built. Sentiments may have shifted but appetites remain strong as increasing amounts of capital search for smarter investments. In East Asia, capital from the north continues to flow south as bulked up investors from China, Korea, and Japan seek dancing skyscrapers in Southeast Asia for high return liquidity opportunities.

To that end, it i not just about following the money, but the evolution of models as the waves of innovation take on new forms beyond Silicon Valley, Hangzhou, and Bangalore. Seismic isolation is not limited to rubber shock absorbers, and engineers are becoming creative working with what they have, designing polyhedral meshes to support age-old temples.

In Southeast Asia, the geography and diversity of the region have given rise to vertical-focused ecosystems and growth in terms of depth instead of breadth. The dancing skyscrapers of the future will no longer be monolithic structures thriving solely on the vanity of their height. Instead, the immense heights they attain will be precisely because of their ability to balance aggressive speed and measured expansion.

Perhaps it is these emerging buildings of the future that will exceed any post-WeWork expectations, and this time it would not be the result of a flop in the public markets.

Innovators Stay Ahead of the Game

Takeaways on being competitive in a fast-growing market:

(1) *Staying ahead of the "waves of innovation" leads to creating more long-term value.* Better equipped with lessons from experience and other players, more local founders are exploring uncharted territory in secular industries or markets where foreign players previously missed.

(2) Big tech and regional heavyweights present both threat and opportunity. *While positioning the business towards the latter seems to*

be the more favorable option, there is a third option: steer clear early on and create one's own "gravity well" to attract users, talent, and capital independently. With this in tow, it becomes easier to leverage for partnerships with bigger players.

(3) Structuring a business for both growth and profitability requires *nuanced understanding of the market and the ability to translate this understanding into "seismic isolation"* (e.g., strong retention strategies, internal protocols) to survive market shocks.

Chapter Two

Setting Sail with the Captains of Innovation

Behind the innovator is the market, a story, and a singular focus.

"We all have dreams. But in order to make dreams come into reality, it takes an awful lot of determination, dedication, self-discipline, and effort."
— Jesse Owens *Four-time Olympic gold medalist*

As explorers pave the way to the future, they are also heavily defined by their past and the present. Throughout history, we have seen how circumstances of politics and society enabled explorers to go on expeditions that would outlive them.

Marco Polo's historic journey would have been significantly more short-lived without the Mongol Empire's trade routes linking up Europe to China. When Marco Polo did return, his writings unveiled a world hitherto unknown to most of the Western world.

The competition between European powers opened the coffers for to seafarers to traverse the Pacific. When his expedition returned, they were living testimony to the roundness of the earth — a revelation that ran against the beliefs of the strongest institutions of their time.

The space race brought the pilots of Apollo 11 to the moon, and many more astronauts thereafter.

In the same way, founders — these captains of innovation — are shaped by the landscape they are in and the journeys they have taken to get where they are. This section covers essays that paint broad strokes of the founder in the context of Southeast Asia and how they go from idea to execution in the early stages of growth.

Essays in this Chapter

(6) **Understanding founders in Southeast Asia.** The development of Southeast Asia's startup ecosystem, as covered in the previous chapter, shapes how founders look at growth and innovation. *"Rising above the noise: What makes great founders in Southeast Asia" by Paulo Joquiño. Published 25 November 2019.*

(7) **The making of a startup founder.** Indonesian edtech founder Rousyan Fikri shares his journey from a 19-year-old PhD candidate to top Youtuber to tech startup founder. *Based on "An education on entrepreneurship" by Rousyan Fikri. Published 23 March 2020.*

(8) **Seven S's for early stage startups.** We look at seven characteristics an early stage startup needs to position itself for growth. *Based on "Leading Asia's Digital Disruption" originally written by Yinglan Tan for Stars Insights in conjunction with the Stars Singapore Symposium 2019. Published 15 March 2019.*

(9) **The case of an early stage startup.** We take a look at Indonesian fintech AwanTunai's early days, how the founders came together, and landed a unique approach to MSME financing. *Based on "Tapping into traditional markets" by Paulo Joquiño Published 24 June 2019.*

(6) Understanding Founders in Southeast Asia

Based on "Rising above the noise: What makes great founders in Southeast Asia" by Paulo Joquiño. Published 25 November 2019.

In the first essay of the previous section, we saw how Vietnamese founders had to rewrite their approach to tackling the local logistics industry at that time. This was a function of the market that these founders responded to.

From a wider perspective, the region's characteristics affect how founders build companies. This essay tackles how Southeast Asia's growth and geography have molded the mindsets and attitudes of founders, essentially disrupting the way startups form and grow.

***

Against the backdrop of a global ecosystem of equal parts uncertainty and maturity, the rapidly changing conditions of Southeast Asia's tech landscape have given rise to a unique outlook on growth among founders in the region that, if leveraged well, provides key advantages to:

(1) overcoming the uncertainty of tackling a nascent or new market, which is largely the case in Southeast Asia
(2) starting up and growing in a region with vastly different laws, cultures, and politics, especially within industries
(3) strategically managing options for growth in a region where there are many roads but only a few that will ultimately lead to winning in the market

Such founders are more often than not:

(1) students of the "startup playbook",
(2) have the ability to localize from the get-go, and
(3) are tactical when it comes to growth.

Students of the "Startup Playbook"

Successful founders are more often than not students of the "startup playbook" who have been exposed to the know-how and wisdom needed to make their own rules in home court. Whether they received education in the US or China, and were ex-Rocket Internet, Alibaba, or Amazon, these founders were behind-the-scenes of the growth and failures of companies in more mature markets and sectors.

Having that depth of experience from US, China, India, or even bigger regional players provides an edge in innovating underserved sectors or localising existing innovation. Introducing new business models to more traditional markets poses high barriers to entry. The cost of market education and customer acquisition will inevitably weigh down as the business starts.

On the other hand, localization also poses the risk of larger players coming in, taking advantage of the fact that the initial, often smaller wave of startups had already warmed up the market for them, and pouring in all their war chests into converting existing users and unlocking new ones at a faster rate than a local startup would. While this strategy for larger players does not always work, there is still that risk.

Nevertheless, the experience of being a founder in markets that have gone through several crests and troughs or the experience of leading pioneering companies to dominating the market can be needle-moving for a new venture. This familiarity with the "playbook" presents an opportunity to create a strong moat for the business, as well as a strong pull for valuable investors.

The trend of returnee entrepreneurs is evolving to include not just seasoned founders from China or Stanford MBA graduates, but also experienced operators from regional unicorns like Gojek and Traveloka, who leave their leadership roles to get back to the grind of solving problems on-the-ground. Hence, there is this so-called "Gojek Mafia" of founders who have successfully set out on their own. The trend itself is localizing as more companies in the region grow.

When Dino Setiawan finished his Stanford Sloan program after several years in the finance industry, he wanted to bring P2P lending to Indonesia, but realized the market was not ready. It took another five years before he finally found an opportunity working with ex-Gojek Product Head Rama Notowidigdo and Vice President of Growth Windy Natriavi to build an MSME financing platform. By then, he had experience building a fintech startup in Palo Alto and was already a well-versed fintech consultant at home. These experiences played well into providing him an edge when it came to building a product for Indonesia's MSMEs.

Founder Localization

Having roots in the region puts Southeast Asian founders in a unique position to tap into elements of the economy that multinationals will find more costly to do. In order to develop and distribute products that work and are valued in local environments, while remaining competitive against global players, founders themselves have to be "localized."

This means developing an affinity or familiarity with the local industry, often entrenched in idiosyncratic tradition and politics, and the willingness to work with these nuances to ship product and deliver on the promise of their business models. Such founders are willing to get their boots-on-the-ground regardless of the upfront costs because they understand the value of building strong relationships with customers and key industry stakeholders as the business scales across the region.

The region's many unique and disparate markets, even within a single country, provide a lot of opportunities to mutate models from other markets like Europe or China. At the same time, the implementation of such mutant business models across these different markets requires careful consideration.

For example, in the rural economy, many startup founders looking to bring in financial inclusion and more efficient supply chains are faced with practices and infrastructure (or lack there of) that slow down the adoption of digital technology. It often helps to have had first-hand experience of the inefficiencies in the local industry and the connections to introduce a new approach to doing business.

When Linh Pham returned home from the UK after her degree in Cambridge and some time at Goldman Sachs as a technology analyst, she spent time working at her family's fertiliser business. There, she witnessed first-hand the inefficiencies in Vietnam's vast trucking sector and found an opportunity in the high productivity that could come from improving the efficiency of loading and assigning trucks. She leveraged the network she had built and the experience she had gained to grow a platform that now matches all kinds of trucks to tens of thousands of shipments.

Tactical Short-term Growth for Better Long-term Odds

With all the hype around the region, variability across local markets, and global market uncertainties, Southeast Asia's founders cannot afford to be reckless with growth. A sense of clarity is needed when it comes to profitability and it reflects in decisions even pre-revenue. They focus on building loyalty with consumers while staying asset-light and efficient. As they are tactical with growth, the impact they can deliver through their businesses has better chances of being more sustainable and long-lasting.

For example, car marketplace Carro's growth into four markets is not purely a result of the amount of resources they pooled with every fundraise but clarity when it came to allocating those resources, from the key partnerships made in each market to their expansion into financial services for the automobile industry.

Not many startups can afford or sustain betting on long-term market share growth by burning heavy amounts of cash. It is far more prudent (and profitable) to be the turtle that conserves its energy and uses it at the right time than the hare that becomes complacent at the most crucial moments.

(7) The Making of a Startup Founder

Based on "An education on entrepreneurship" by Rousyan Fikri. Published 23 March 2020.

Even with the unique outlook founders have on growth as a function of the region's diversity and development, founders are also greatly affected by their own personal backgrounds and journeys. This is part of the reason why the founders themselves are a large part of the due diligence of investors. It is also why the founder's own story often plays into the company's communications.

Rousyan Fikri, an education technology startup founder in Indonesia, reflects on his university education, which he began at the age of 15, his PhD work at Singapore's Nanyang Technological University (NTU), and his Youtuber experiences. All of these contributes to the kind of entrepreneur he is today. What is striking from his narrative is how in spite of how random or roundabout his journey may seem, everything he picked up along the way contributes to what he aims to do for the long-term — improve Indonesia's education system.

***

There is the famous quote of Steve Jobs from his 2005 Stanford commencement address, "You have to trust that the dots will somehow connect in your future. You have to trust in something — your gut, destiny, life, karma, whatever. This approach has never let me down, and it has made all the difference in my life."

Being an entrepreneur, I have realized that these dots are all the more ambiguous and roundabout than other journeys, but at the same time, they all fall into place. We have recently graduated from Y Combinator's Winter 2020 batch with $150,000 in funding, following the launch of our app for senior high school students last year.

This milestone coincides with education systems around the world being forced to make sudden adjustments with the coronavirus, and where the value of edtech platforms are being put to the test. As we gear up for growth in the face of the changing education landscape ahead, it is important to take stock of these dots and the lessons I have picked up along the way.

An Education in Indonesia's Education System

I did not go through my education determined to be an entrepreneur. I entered the top engineering institute in Indonesia, Institut Teknologi

Bandung (ITB), when I was 15 years old without the slightest entrepreneurial vision in mind. During my time in ITB, I was a student representative on the board of trustees, which gave me deeper insight into Indonesia's education system. The experience inspired me to find ways to improve the way things were being done in my country, even as I took my postgraduate studies in Singapore.

From my research and observation, there are three major gaps in Indonesian education, and these are not necessarily infrastructural, but problems embedded within the kind of mindset and culture our education system has promoted.

First is the gap between the one-size-fits-all approach and the reality that everyone learns differently, at different paces.

Second is the misalignment between career and education. There is a lack of institutionalized guidance when it comes to linking studies and career plans. Students do not feel that what they are learning will be important to them later on, especially before they enter university.

Finally, students learn a lot, but do not necessarily learn how to learn. According to the Programme for International Student Assessment (PISA) test, Indonesian students are highly motivated, but it does not reflect in their performance. This means that there is a gap between what they want and how to achieve these aspirations.

In spite of these gaps, the momentum in Indonesia's education system has been towards improvement. There has been changes in the system everywhere, especially for the college entrance examination. This is the wave my co-founders and I rode on more than two years ago, and we are committed to accelerating this improvement in the long-term.

An Education in Learning

For my postgraduate studies, I went to NTU when I was 20 years old. As I was being trained as a researcher, I also became hungry for innovation that could be applied in real life situations. Seeing the struggle of my professors getting grants made me think twice about becoming a professor myself if I wanted to make real and effective change in Indonesia.

At the same time, my studies in NTU helped me discover my passion for teaching. On the side, I began a YouTube channel, inspired by the concept of flipped based learning. As the channel took off, I decided to focus my efforts on teaching through YouTube, and so I decided not to complete my PhD. There was joy in communicating things in a simpler way for others. The concepts I talked about in my videos were things I had been taking for granted, but were amazing to my viewers.

Over the course of making YouTube videos, I learned about startups and realized that bringing together technology, education, and content is what I want to do and what I believe could really bring change to Indonesia. That is how Pahamify came to be.

My experience as a Youtuber was the starting point for Pahamify. With the curriculum as our mold, our team collaborates on the content, produces videos following the mold, tests it with students to get feedback and iterate. With this process, we quickly put together content early on, and continually update this library of content.

At the core of our content creation is the constructivist learning theory. It simply means that in order to make learning effective, one needs to be able to relate it to a personal experience or another idea one is already familiar with. That is actually how our brain works, and that is how we produce our content. We tell stories that reinforce what students already learn in the classroom by allowing them to relate concepts to things they are familiar with.

As we built an app to distribute our library of content, we have also leveraged gamification to add another layer of constructivist learning and make the learning experience more engaging. We turn lessons into levels where students can answer questions after viewing videos and gain points as users on the platform. These levels fall into categories according to subjects and skillsets, organized in a way that students can easily start where they left off or sync up with what they are learning in the classroom. Another way we have leveraged on gamification is through avatars. Students with enough points can purchase avatars that can reflect their future aspirations, say pilot or rocket engineer.

When it comes to careers, we have also gone a step further and included information on colleges they can go to and in-app consultation with career advisers. This way, we have geared our app to make the experience more personal to each student, and in doing so, address the second gap I mentioned earlier.

With this app supplementing what students learn in the classroom, we want these engagements to also shape what happens in the classroom of the future. With information from the app, we want to be able to equip teachers with the information they need to be good mentors to their students and teach more effectively. That way students can talk about the videos and interactions they have on the app with their teachers.

When it comes to product development, we devised the "PAHAMI Framework" to translate key research findings in neuroscience into effective, student-centered features that improve learning retention. That way the constructivist learning, flipped classroom, and all these theories goes into creating a user experience designed for students. This experience begins with the lessons they learn in the classroom, then their interactions on the app, and finally back to the classroom through their teacher.

An Education in Entrepreneurship

It has been more than two years since I co-founded Pahamify. Throughout the process of building Pahamify, I am very fortunate to have had what I call "lucky networks." These "lucky networks" are people with whom I have had an authentic relationship and then they turned out to be in a position where they provided me with advice and help later on. When I became one of the YouTube Top Creators, I found out the country manager and I took the same class in college, and he was very helpful in guiding me as a startup founder. I also gained many insights for management and strategy from college friends who hold management positions in Indonesian unicorns.

As I sought to reimagine education in Indonesia, I have also received my own education in entrepreneurship. From making tough hiring decisions, to learning the ropes of finances, and building a culture and structure for the company, it was many miles apart from the PhD program I was once taking. However, I have never been alone in figuring these things out, having been able to seek advice from my college friends who have been through it all. I was also lucky enough to learn the "science of start-ups" in Y Combinator as Pahamify was accepted in the Winter 2020 batch of the Silicon Valley incubator.

After hearing the stories of top startup founders, I learned that there is no one road leading to Rome. There are many ways the startup journey can go wrong, but a good startup treads on the right path where it matters. And that is what I am focusing on. As we continue to grow Pahamify, the learning continues, hopefully not just for me, but for the millions of students in Indonesia.

(8) Seven 'S's for Early Stage Startups

Based on "Leading Asia's Digital Disruption," originally written by Yinglan Tan for Stars Insights in conjunction with the Stars Singapore Symposium 2019. Published 15 March 2019.

The outlook of Southeast Asian founders on innovation and growth in the region (as outlined in the previous essay) stems from the nature of the region and its relatively recent emergence as fertile ground for tech startups. However, this is limited to the founders themselves. How it reflects in an early stage startup as it aims for digital disruption is another story altogether. This essay lists seven concrete characteristics early stage startups need to successfully position themselves to disrupt industry and grow their impact.

***

Leading digital disruption requires a change to the status quo. Having strong industry credentials does not have any strong causality with the eventual success of the startup. Out of 195 unicorn startups founded from 2005 to 2018 in the US, over 50% were founded by CEOs with no directly relevant experience. We have learnt that digital disruption requires an outsider less bogged down by traditional industry norms coming in with a fresh pair of eyes.

Most importantly, it requires a new breed of startup with the following seven key attributes:

(1) *Speed*: Size of organization is inversely proportional to agility
(2) *Stealth*: Stay under the radar as long as possible
(3) *Smarts*: It is not the "how" or "what" but the "why"
(4) *Simplicity*: The simplest answer is usually the best answer
(5) *Singularity*: Focus and aim your resources
(6) *Svelteness*: Stay lean and lose the fat
(7) *Symbiosis*: Build symbiotic platform companies

Speed: Size of Organization is Inversely Proportional to Agility

Unstoppable founders act with speed. Decisions made at nine are executed at noon. Time is their enemy and speed is their friend. This is in stark contrast to what happens in a corporate setting, where a product launch goes through multiple approval layers from the manager to business line heads and top executive committees.

The process involves a lot of human herding, from cross-functional coordination like the clearance of marketing collaterals by marketing departments to press release approvals from public relations teams. Say you are a product manager who has an idea, you will surface it to the division director, who surfaces it to the director, who will surface it to the vice-president, who will surface it to the assistant CEO, who will surface it to the CEO, and this whole process takes six months. At this point, your original idea does not look like the end product anymore.

So, the size of the organization is inversely proportional to agility, and unstoppable founders have the ability to make things happen with great agility and speed. At a startup, decision-making is kept within small product teams, and minimum viable products are built and shipped out within the week.

Interbank transfers in Indonesia cost around US$0.50 per transaction, which can be a hefty amount for remittances and those dependent on bank transfers for a living. This pain points pushed the founders of Indonesian fintech Flip to create a product that could facilitate fund transfers at scale across multiple banks. They wasted no time and started out with a Google Form and accounts in multiple banks. They quickly found out people were willing to take the risk to save on transaction costs. They transitioned to a website in late 2015 when the traffic was too much for a Google Form to handle. By mid-2016, their platform had facilitated roughly US$920,000 worth of transfers. The speed with which they proved product-market fit also helped them secure a license with Bank Indonesia in just 10 weeks versus the usual one to two years.

Stealth: Stay Under the Radar as Long as Possible

When standing against industry behemoths with capital and resources to burn, stealth is key. A lot of people think that every time a startup has a new product or new launch of a service, they need to do a big press release and get covered on publications like TechCrunch. Counterintuitively, it can do more harm than good, especially early on in the life of the company.

Staying under the radar as long as possible and being strategic with publicity pays off in the long run. Doing a press release at the wrong time could potentially put a startup up against competitors who can easily copy your product and move a lot faster. Venture funds who do not invest in one end up investing in competitors. Investment bankers arrange meetings and learn all about the company with not much clear benefit for the company itself.

The only time there is a benefit for a startup to run a campaign is if it is for hiring or user acquisition. Ideally, startups should become too large to be crushed or ignored before industry incumbents and big tech players can get a whiff of the potential disruption. It is more cost effective to go down the path that avoids glitzy marketing campaigns and attention-grabbing headlines if there are more effective ways to hire and acquire users for the business.

AwanTunai is a supply chain services platform providing distributors, wholesalers, and micro retailers in Indonesia with a range of digital solutions. Their flagship product allows access to affordable supplier financing that alleviates the chronic pain point of insufficient working capital among micro retailers. This product was the result of rapid experimentation, where the team executed more than 10 different products. Staying in stealth mode allowed them to focus on finding out which one worked while staying ahead of the market and introducing a compelling flagship product when they finally launched in the market.

Smarts: It is not the "How" or "What" but the "Why"

Smarts is the ability to ask not the how or the what but the *why*. The why reflects the bigger calling of the organization — why the company does what it does.

Smarts also stands for the ability to learn, because in the world of tech, things move so fast, that what is common knowledge a year ago will be obsolete in 12 to 18 months in certain things.

Smarts also means having a strong technical core team. This human capital determines whether a startup is able to bring lasting digital disruption, especially when the company reaches scale (think Grab level of scale) and the tech infrastructure needs to support the product.

Growing an agile and lasting tech infrastructure starts by planting the right seeds and working with the right "smarts."

Most people attribute the success of Apple to Steve Jobs, but in the early days, Steve Wozniak was just as critical as Steve Jobs. Notwithstanding the marketing genius of Steve Jobs, Apple's early success was built upon Steve Wozniak's engineering chops and his ability to engineer a world-class product.

The "smarts" of your first few engineers spell how the rest of the tech team will grow. 'A' engineers hire 'B' engineers and 'B' engineers hire 'C' engineers, and 'C' engineers cannot hire anybody.

Carro's founding team all had strong engineering backgrounds from Carnegie Mellon and this gives it a technology advantage as the leading used car marketplace platform in Southeast Asia. Carro analyses real-time data of car purchases in each country and inputs that data into a proprietary pricing algorithm. In this way, customers receive information on the best deals in the market and improve their decision-making process.

Simplicity: The Simplest Answer is Usually the Best Answer

A lot of times people try to explain their business and it is more complicated than it needs to be, but the best companies are able to articulate what they do with clarity and simplicity. A simple mission allows startups to focus on solving the core user problem and ensure that this focus is pervasive throughout the company. A mission statement should be less than 10 words long with a clear purpose. It runs in the company's DNA and acts like a compass which guides its paths, every product can be traced to that single purpose. The best products are usually uncluttered; you look at Dropbox, Google, and WhatsApp; these focus precisely on what the customer needs.

Since its founding, Indonesian fintech Payfazz has been focused on a singular mission to enable the unbanked to access financial services. Banking the unbanked in Indonesia has long been a problem of many institutions and organizations, but Payfazz approached it simply by enabling *warungs* and restaurants to facilitate digital transactions through their mobile app. This simple solution of putting the bank in the "hands" of people has allowed them to build a network of financial services from bill payments to bank transfers and loans.

Singularity: Focus and Aim Your Resources

In the West, you have the case of the serial entrepreneur, one who does one startup after another often in rapid succession. In the East, there is the phenomenon of the parallel entrepreneur, who has a lot of ventures going on simultaneously. The process of digital disruption always involves facing many false positives — varying advice and distractions which pulls the business in competing directions.

However, the key is to nurture a core group of 'early adopter' customers by having a singular focus on one thing and doing it well. At startup pitching competitions, you often see entrepreneurs presenting wordy slides flushed with product features. However, the winning startups with the best pitch decks often only have one slide with one key feature.

Even the most valuable companies like Apple have no more than 10 core products, because each product requires engineering and marketing. The key is to focus and aim your resources so your chances of success are much higher.

A startup needs a laser-like focus to test multiple hypotheses, scope a compelling value proposition and find the right product-market fit for this set of customers. Vietnamese trucking startup LOGIVAN identified that in order to improve a trucker's life, the company needs to build a product with an Uber-like experience. This involves running on-the-ground operations at highway tolls to explain the product, encourage adoption from truckers and drive network effects on the platform.

Svelteness: Stay Lean and Lose the Fat

Svelteness is all about staying lean. If you picture the image of a heavyweight sumo wrestler and the Karate Kid, we would always bet on the underdog who can run circles around the sumo wrestler.

Corporates tend to be like these sumo wrestlers that have grown to a large size and have gained the benefit of scale resources. While they cannot be underestimated and can deal decisive blows when placing their full weight, startups have the agility to quickly change the game and lead the charge.

Startups embrace the "fail fast, learn fast" mentality and rapid iterations of hypothesis testing, small experiments, and learning from data insights. At corporates, bigger teams mean an increase in scale across every aspect — more human coordination, more delays, and more resources committed. The resulting fallouts and costs of any failure increases.

This svelteness is particularly important in introducing new business models while competing with longstanding practices and the capabilities of larger players. While leading the adoption of social commerce in second- and third-tier cities in Indonesia, social commerce startup Super has also been agile with its operations, understanding the communities they operate in and leveraging on this on-the-ground knowledge to find the right agents for distribution (mom-and-pops and individuals at the end of the value chain). This allows them to stay ahead of more traditional e-commerce platforms and coexist with wholesalers and big retailers, while still making FMCG goods accessible and affordable.

Symbiosis: Build Symbiotic Platform Companies

Symbiosis happens when two organisms are able to thrive off each other. In the same way, the most successful companies are able to create a self-sustaining ecosystem that enables symbiosis between demand and supply.

This model is best executed by platform companies as they are built on the aggregation, retention, and matching of supply and demand for a certain (set of) transactions. By building a platform that facilitates and incentivizes the symbiosis between supply and demand, the business is able to devote more resources to monetization and value extraction on top of these interactions.

For example, Airbnb is able to generate a continuous stream of revenue from both hosts and guests because they've essentially engineered a way for hosts and guests to exchange value — space for cash — and for this exchange to happen at scale.

Not only does a symbiotic platform enable long-term value extraction from the core interaction, it also opens up exploration into high margin revenue streams. As platforms like Uber and Grab were able to retain users through ridesharing, they could then introduce other services like food delivery, which have proven to be more lucrative in terms of margins.

This symbiosis goes beyond two-sided interactions. 4PL cross-border logistics platform Janio facilitates symbiosis across an entire ecosystem of logistics players from e-commerce marketplaces to freight forwarders and cargo companies. Their propriety software layer links up different service providers to optimize shipping routes in and out of Southeast Asia.

(9) The Case of an Early Stage Startup

Based on "Tapping into traditional markets" by Paulo Joquiño Published 24 June 2019.

The seven S's outlined in the previous essay are best implemented in the early stages of growth when the business is still a startup and is getting the product and business model in place to scale. These attributes are important specifically to early stage startups because it is during this time that (1) the organization and scope of the business is well-suited to exhibit these traits, (2) the nature of these startups as disruptors within their industries demands the level of focus common to all these traits, and (3) these traits, if embodied well, reflect throughout the journey of the company as it grows.

This essay follows the story of Indonesian SME financing startup AwanTunai in three parts: (1) how the co-founders came together, (2) how they found an innovative way to underwrite loans for unbanked MSMEs, and (3) how they executed this approach. Their story brings together several of the S's discussed in the previous essay, as well as reflecting the unique features of founders in Southeast Asia touched upon in this section's first piece.

***

Entering into traditional markets waving the technology flag bears huge potential of reaching vast underserved customers, but it can be challenging for startups. These markets exact a high cost of customer acquisition given the effort needed to change consumer behavior. The intuitive reaction would be to slow down or turn back.

For AwanTunai's co-founders Dino Setiawan, Rama Notowidigdo, and Windy Natriavi, neither of those was an option. It would take forming a team around a vision, finding out where data is accessible, and focusing on fast growth.

Form a Founding Team of Complementary Specialists Under a "Holy Grail" Vision

After more than two years as Chief Product Officer at Gojek, Rama sold his shares and travelled the countryside. There, he found farmers borrowing at 20% interest to buy seeds and fertilizer, then selling to the same lenders at harvest. Rama wanted to break this wheel and replace it with more inclusive financing for the self-employed, who comprise 80% of the Indonesian workforce.

Using offline loan cycles, Rama proved lending at bank interest rates to the unbanked SMEs significantly grew their business. Now, it was a question of scale. He brought up his idea with his friend Dino, a Silicon Valley veteran and finance specialist. Rama's vision was the holy grail for Indonesian financial inclusion, and despite knowing how difficult it is to start from scratch, Dino was onboard. "It kind of just came together [over lunch]. This [was] an opportunity I couldn't pass up."

One of Rama's former colleagues at Gojek, Windy, often met with him to catch up. During one such occasion, she brought up the lack of access to financing problems she was following as VP for Growth. Finding out her mentor had a plan to solve that was all Windy needed to hear. She left Gojek the same way she went in two and a half years ago — following problems to solve and waiting for no one.

And so, a product specialist, finance specialist, and growth specialist came together under one mission — the holy grail of Indonesian financial inclusion.

Address Limitations to Key Resources through Unconventional Channels

Having a founding team of experts with complementary skills makes it easier to navigate traditional markets, but it was only the first step. For fintechs, what data is accessible determines what can be done.

Many of their fintech peers went into online consumer loans, with more accessible data and easier adoption. However, their mission was to focus on the larger offline market. Building a distribution network there would open up possibilities beyond loans.

"The question is, 'How do we get the offline folks online?' It all boils down to data," shares Dino. However, it was not enough to know where to go. Knowing limitations down the road is just as important. Tight regulations on Indonesian fintech early on made accessing data more complicated.

Enter supply chain financing. It meant leaving the conventional route of fintechs behind, but it also made a lot of sense to them. Suppliers have merchant transaction data (i.e., inventory purchases) that is highly predictive for fraud and credit risk.

Focus on Fast Growth to Secure Partners, not the other Way Around

More than access to data, the supply chain entry point made it easier to set up a distribution network into the offline market. However, instead of dragging through lengthy negotiations with big principal suppliers, they initially went to work on their own. Not relying on these big partnerships for growth enabled them to move fast.

"We love to execute at speed... We wanted to work with [principal] suppliers at first, but instead of waiting for [business development], we started rolling out [the product]," shares Windy.

From there, the numbers built a compelling case for productive loans, attracting financing and supply chain partners to their side. Merchants could purchase twice as much inventory than before. Repayment on loans went up more than 97% versus status quo 30% to 50% default rates.

Tapping into a traditional market is laden with challenges, but AwanTunai played their cards well to grow fast and reduce risk.

Behind the Innovator is the Market, a Story, and a Singular Focus

Takeaways on what drives founders:

(1) We often talk about founders disrupting markets, but *markets also affect how founders build companies*. In Southeast Asia, we have seen how this creates an outlook on innovation and growth specific to the region.

(2) The best founders are able to envision the future, but *their past plays a significant role in their approach to living in the future*.

(3) *Focus best summarizes the seven S's of early stage companies (speed, stealth, smarts, simplicity, singularity, svelteness, symbiosis).* It is essential for early stage startups to lock in with clarity what they want to achieve. This not only saves on cash and resources in the short-term but results in more stability in the long-term.

Chapter Three

Getting a Crew

Innovators do not fish for talent; they cast nets for teams.

"Talent wins games, but teamwork and intelligence win championships. "
— Michael Jordan *Six-time NBA champion*

Every captain needs a crew. Finding those first few hands to go on deck is a challenge that fleshes out the reality of running a business, and the challenge never really ends with the first few hires — although as mentioned in one of the previous chapter's essays, having the right "smarts" onboard early on is critical. Employees come and go, the organization becomes more complex, and the needs of the business change. All of these will test the capabilities of the company to acquire and retain talent over time.

This challenge is not limited to tech startups, but with the kind of scale and backing these companies have *vis-à-vis* their size and stage of growth, the pressure is paramount. This is compounded by the often-overlooked realities that (1) first hires have an indelible impact on the company's outlook and culture, and (2) the startup eventually has to install internal controls and strengthen cultural practices over time to keep up with the complexity of the organization as it grows.

This chapter contains essays that explore the different strategies startups in Southeast Asia are taking to build teams fit to disrupt specific industries, handle international expansion, and hire industry veterans.

Essays in this Chapter

(10) **Hiring to disrupt.** Before casting a net for talent, it is important to know how deep the market is. Approaches to finding, attracting, and managing talent across different industries are compared. *Based on "Markets maketh talent" by Paulo Joquiño. Published 23 March 2020.*

(11) **Going international.** This is a case study into how a cross-border startup handles communication across multiple markets. *Based on "Developing effective local teams for cross-border companies" by Paulo Joquiño. Published 23 August 2019.*

(12) **Bringing in the giants.** Hiring industry veterans is crossing a two-way street. The essay shows how this should reflect in the job interview. *Based on "How Davids Hire Goliaths" by Paulo Joquiño. Published 5 October 2019.*

(13) **Finding strength in the middle.** High calibre middle management for fast-growing startups is in short supply in Southeast Asia. Fortunately, middle managers are not hired but developed. *Based on "Unlocking agility in middle management" by Paulo Joquiño. Published 14 May 2020.*

(10) Hiring to Disrupt

Based on "Markets maketh talent" by Paulo Joquiño. Published 23 March 2020.

As startup founders are often faced with the challenge of changing the way things are done within industries, the teams they build need to have both the tech/innovation skillset and industry expertise. Depending on how many players there are already in the market and how resistant the industry is to change or digitalization in particular, it can be very challenging for founders to find this mix. This essay covers various approaches to bringing together tech and industry in a team, all of which begin with a deep understanding of the available talent in that specific market.

***

Hiring the right people is a challenge for any business. When it comes to early stage startups, this challenge is heightened by the limitations on capital and brand, as well as the drive to grow the business immensely. To compensate for this, founders have had to draw in the best talent they could with a clear vision, all the charisma they can muster, and what skills and experience they have on hand — three things, if wielded properly, that can bring together a loyal team.

This worked to great effect with the likes of Ele.me's Mark (Xuhao) Zhang and Alibaba's Jack Ma. Mark was able to rally seven of his classmates at Jiao Tong University to help him build a delivery app for free, while Jack Ma had his founding team of 18 people all working in a difficult office of around 300 square meters.

It makes for a great narrative, but there is another underplayed factor that affects how startup teams form and grow — the market. What we have learned is the depth of talent in a sector often influences how founders are able to form and structure their companies.

In the case of Jack Ma, 1999 was a critical time to introduce e-commerce, as internet platforms became more widely adopted in China. Alibaba was not his first internet company, so it helped that he could invite his former employees to join him on his next venture. For Mark Zhang, his classmates shared the same pain point as he did, and in his university, there were already many startup teams working on similar projects.

In both cases, there was a clear presence of talent within the sector that had exposure to the kind of innovation these founders wanted to introduce. Even though these sectors were arguably young at the time, these founders also had access to the available talent, with Jack Ma being a serial entrepreneur and Mark Zhang studying in a university that supported these kinds of ventures.

Fishing in Shallow Depths

On the other hand, it becomes more difficult if you were a founder looking for solid ground in a heavily entrenched industry with low exposure to digital technology, and where the existing pool of product and business talent are not in the headspace for innovation. This can be the case for founders in Southeast Asia who are trying to introduce technology to traditional and secular sectors.

The ideal situation would be to attract talent that can tick both the experience box and innovation mindset box. However, especially for very fresh sectors, it will be difficult to find this fit, so founders may tend to take things slowly and be meticulous in finding the gems. This approach conserves cash for hiring, but entails that each hire brings strategic value to the team. It also requires that the founders are well-versed in the space to be the best possible judge for these hires.

"Because [agritech] is a new space, I think the experience in agriculture is a lot of help but it is difficult to find people who have a deep understanding of the space and also the hunger, speed, and ambition to make things happen, as a lot of the players in this industry are traditional players," shares Amanda, co-founder and CEO of Indonesian agritech Sayurbox. "So we do hire slowly to find people who can adapt to a fast-paced culture, but have experience and connections in the [agriculture] side."

Focusing on Capabilities

Most of the time, a founder will have to find talent from other industries. What is key is that coming into the company they have high aptitude, a passion for the industry they are entering, and have the capacity to keep up with the company. As they settle in their role, the founder and earlier hires contribute to grooming them on what the business needs. Then, as these hires become more familiar with the business, it becomes easier for the founder to pass on responsibility.

Hiring outside of the industry and easing them into the business seems reactionary to the depth of talent, but it is also necessary to get the job done, as logistics industry veteran and startup founder Iman Kusnadi realized. Instead of focusing on experience, he looked at the capabilities his company would need to operate and be effective.

"For example, for an operation manager or COO, I used to think that I would simply need someone with 15 years of experience running a logistics business. Now I realize that operations in Ritase run like a factory," Iman shares. "I don't necessarily need a logistics veteran. I need someone with factory experience, with a Kaizen, Six Sigma black belt to run operations, someone who can manage all the moving parts in a process."

Hiring with a Net of Diverse Talent

Taking off from this capability perspective, another approach to hiring is to build the team around the capabilities of the ideal candidate, instead of looking for one. This is what cross-border logistics company Janio did to work with the shallow depths of relevant talent in Singapore and Indonesia. Instead of fishing for the ideal hire, Janio brought together their ideal team. They cast a net with their existing team's mix of technology talent, business acumen, and industry expertise.

"Functionally, we see this mix through our team. My teammates have twenty years in the logistics space. We complement each other. The majority of our company does not come from the logistics industry," shares Junkai Ng, co-founder and CEO of Janio. "The ones who do come from the logistics industry serve as advisors or mentors while the rest, mostly product guys and developers, have the freedom to build something they believe is valuable based on everyone's input and feedback. They go back and forth with each other to figure out how to innovate within boundaries."

Simply hiring is not enough. The company has to have an environment that supports the different kinds of hires, especially when you have industry expertise used to a certain way of doing things and technologists who want to change the way things are done.

"We are building a technology trucking company [in Vietnam]. The people who often work in the trucking industry are usually very different from the tech people. Bringing these two types of people together in company is a challenge, because one is more used to the traditional way of trucking and doing logistics and the other wants to change it," explains Linh Pham, founder and CEO of LOGIVAN. "It is always an interesting challenge for us to create the best environment and the right combination of policies and resources to support both types of talent."

Leveraging on Competition in Deeper Waters

As more startups race to disrupt traditional markets, they will be faced with this constant challenge of finding and balancing experience and innovation talent. For businesses in hotter markets with more depth in talent, like e-commerce for example, it is less a quest than it is competition for talent.

It is possible to use the presence of many competitors to one's advantage by following talents who have performed well working with other players and are looking for a new opportunity. Of course, it is non-sequitur that any particular talent will perform the same miracles twice, but the chances are high especially if they are hungry for new challenges. Listening in to what is happening to talent in the market, especially if there are massive events like layoffs or conversely a surge in hiring notices, will be crucial in determining a specific strategy for hiring.

At the same time, hiring in hot markets also means that players need to have clearly defined vision and direction. No one will want to board the ship of a lost captain. This goes back to what Ele.me and Alibaba's founders were able to do with their vision and determination.

(11) Going International

Based on "Developing effective local teams for cross-border companies" by Paulo Joquiño. Published 23 August 2019.

Not all tech startups go international at an early stage. This is the case if the market is highly localized, meaning there are no network effects to support international expansion and it is not cost-effective to replicate operations in another country. That or the market is already sizable within one country (e.g., Indonesia).

Those that do expand internationally, however, not only have to deal with the tech-industry conundrum but also the HQ-locality question. How local should a team be? How far should HQ be involved when it comes to local operations? This essay takes a look at the approach of Singapore-based logistics technology company Janio, and how they manage a team that spans several countries all over the world.

***

While startups in Southeast Asia often figure out product-market fit and develop their defensibility in an origin market — usually the country where the founders are based — it is inevitable that these companies grow regionally in order to thrive. That not only comes with building an adaptive product but also an adaptive organization, one made up of teams in different localities catering to different market needs.

Janio Asia co-founder and CEO Junkai Ng shares how they set up their local teams, find talent for a fast-growing startup in a traditional industry, and manage product implementation across different markets.

Set up the Local Team by Building Top-Down AND Bottom-Up

There are generally two ways to go about setting up a team in a new market. Either HQ can hire a local as head of country first or send people to do the initial setup.

It is too much to expect that a fresh local team would be able to lead country operations with 100% cultural and direction alignment. They may be able to move faster, but they would operate with their own agendas and SOPs. If not handled carefully, this can have severe consequences down the line. On the other hand, sending over a team to a new market trades off speed for alignment. The team's acclimatization can weigh heavily on the company's runway.

Janio got rid of the trade-off problem and did both approaches.

"What we do now is station folks we trust in Singapore overseas for three to six months and give them a fixed set of agenda to achieve within that period. Once they hit those milestones, we build a secondary local team below them who can inherit those roles. By then the culture has set in and is closely aligned to what Janio represents in Singapore. Imagine in Southeast Asia you have six or seven offices across the region. If every country office has a different culture, you're screwed. That's something that we are very cautious about."

This approach does not apply for all countries they operate in, however. Given Janio's adaptive approach to cross-border logistics, full-service hubs, or countries with strategic value in terms of import and export, receive more attention in terms of human resource development.

Pure origin markets have less functional requirements and tend to be more commercial heavy than operational. The culture is still there, but it doesn't have to be as strongly ingrained as a full-service team with many moving parts.

Weave in "People Managers" for Seamless Product Implementation Across Diverse Markets

Going through the process of building a local team with a top-down, bottom-up approach and pulling in talent that works is all for nothing if the product cannot be rolled out effectively across markets. For Janio, it is all about placing the right conduits — channels for HQ to validate and communicate product development issues.

"When the country team reaches critical mass — for example recently in Indonesia we hit 20 people — we'll get a people manager, someone who is very international but at the same time understands the locality they are assigned to. Oftentimes, the local teams are not very vocal about problems with implementation. With strong interpersonal skills and local language ability, these people managers are able to extract the essence of the problems, and translate that to the HQ so we can target those issues."

(12) Bringing in the Giants

Based on "How Davids Hire Goliaths" by Paulo Joquiño. Published 5 October 2019.

There are many incentives to hiring industry veterans, especially as a startup goes from achieving product-market fit to scale. These hires do not only bring in years of experience and expertise, but also their own individual network effects that can be needle-moving for the business.

It is not as easy as filling an entry-level or junior position however. These senior hires should not only be the right fit for the company at this particular stage in their growth, but the company should also be structured so that their talent will be productive within the company. This essay focuses on pointers for the interview proper, and the crucial mindset shift that founders should embrace even before interviewing candidates.

***

Hiring industry giants can be a huge asset for growth, but it is less about hiring and more about being the right fit for the senior person.

For technology companies in Southeast Asia, true growth is all about digitally transforming entire industries and capturing several markets in the region. This means having a top-notch executive team who can follow through on company vision and strategy with on-the-ground experience. To form these A-teams, founders need to be able to source candidates and find the ones with the right fit for the company's needs.

Filling in these leadership roles with top-notch talent often means approaching giants in the industry, long-time executives and veterans who have seen the playbook, waged their fair share of battles, and established a name and career for themselves. As a David on the field, relatively inexperienced and much less established, founders need to take a different course from the usual hiring approach when winning over these Goliaths to their side.

Battle-readiness Goes both Ways

It all starts with embracing a mindset shift from "Please come work for me" to "I believe we are the best fit for each other." Once these senior candidates apply, you can expect them to be battle-ready for the role they will play in the company, so the company needs to be at least as ready as they are.

This means clarity. Value exchange and culture alignment, while applicable regardless of experience or position, is more pronounced when dealing with senior candidates, who already know what they want in their career and what they can bring to the table. Given your growth trajectory and company culture, it should also be clear who exactly you are looking to bring into the company.

Interviewing Industry Goliaths

From our experience linking our portfolio companies with seasoned candidates to key executive roles, here are the things to take note of when interviewing senior people:

1. Have a compelling origin story.
    Keep it short, but set the tone of your conversation with some good old inspiration. Give them the most aspirational statement on why you are running the company. For example, "I was doing

XX, but saw the problem YY. I decided to spend the rest of my career doing this."

2. Put your best foot forward, only.
   It is an interview, not an intervention or reflection period. There is no point in volunteering or addressing any company issues or problems.

3. Show clarity in explaining the role.
   Level with them on why you are having the conversation. Tell them you already know how to do X. Now you are looking for the person who bring X to scale, and you personally wanted to interview him/her because you want the best fit.

4. Listen to their origin story.
   Figure out if you are on the same page in terms of #1. Get them to talk about their experiences, and also what their aspirations are — this is a huge clue to winning them over!

5. Speak in their "language".
   Professional language is a safer option unless getting more colloquial (e.g. Singlish) builds rapport. This is one unique case where it is neither easier said nor done. Instead, it is best to listen.

6. Frame metrics positively, if needed.
   Senior candidates have seen the playbook and worked with big companies and numbers. Do not volunteer your company's numbers; and if asked, try to couch it in a good light, e.g., "Revenue grew XX% M/M."

On the Shoulders of Giants

As much as you would want to find the best fit through the hiring process, the true test will come when the company is on the shoulders of these giants and they are brought to the front lines of growth. The company should be an environment where they can fully embrace their responsibilities, take point on the teams they are in charge of, and be trusted to call their own shots. Here, it comes down to company culture — a great company nurtures great talent as much as it attracts them.

(13) Finding Strength in the Middle

Based on "Unlocking agility in middle management" by Paulo Joquiňo. Published 14 May 2020.

As a startup grows in size, organizational complexity is unavoidable. At the same time, the hierarchical barriers to rapid innovation characteristic of multinational corporations given their size are not as inevitable. Core to growing as an organization while remaining agile as a business is the middle management.

In order to be effective, these layers of leaders need to have the tools and voice to communicate to higher ups the reality of the situation on the ground and implement company direction in various environments. This is especially important in times of crisis, when radical decisions need to be made urgently. Through the lens of various founders, this essay proposes different ways to develop an agile middle management.

***

In Southeast Asia, startup founders face difficulties finding capable middle management, especially as they expand into new markets or lines of business. It is a struggle that is part-and-parcel of a startup's growing pains.

Apart from competing with corporates, unicorns, and larger companies for talent and others starting their own companies, there's the prevailing top-down management culture in the talent pool clashing with the need for managers capable of running an agile operation in the region.

Middle managers are not just there to fill in the leadership gaps of a startup overcoming its growing pains. Cross-border operations and cross-cultural teams require leaders who can keep the organization agile and flexible. The ground rules vary for each market and industry and are all the more uncertain in this crisis.

The role can often turn into a "stuck between a rock and a hard place" situation. Middle managers need to make tough calls, and founders are hard-pressed to find the talent willing and capable. Even then, developing agile middle management is a necessity for any business to grow in the region.

Business expansion means that senior management will naturally tend to know less than people on the ground when it comes to specifics. Add a highly uncertain landscape into the mix, and top brass will need multiple perspectives to get a better sense of what needs to be done.

Effective middle managers cannot be hired, given the nature of their job as critical links in the organization. Middle managers are trained and molded into their roles, which are unique to the needs of the company. For fast-growing tech companies, there is not always enough time or resources to spend on training and development, which is why development also needs to come from the organization's structure, processes, and culture itself.

At the core of this approach is developing the ability of middle management to communicate their perspective from the ground. It is a perspective built from acclimatization with the local or specific teams and expertise from their career. There are ways founders can develop their organization to unlock agility in middle management:

(1) Developing Effective Middle Managers begins with Hiring the Right Culture-fit.

Middle managers develop into their roles, but it is crucial to have filters early-on when they first join the company that ensures they are comfortable with the culture of working at a startup.

Coming up with criteria for hiring can be difficult, but culture-fit should be at the foundation, and for fast-growing startups, that often involves finding talent with hunger.

"We [at AwanTunai] don't prioritize your technical skill above all else. We hire and promote based on how fast you grow and your leadership," shares Windy Natriavi, COO and co-founder of AwanTunai, in an interview with her last year. "In reality, it's hard... I want to find a good technical middle manager, but without the same hunger, they could jump around, so the investment and training you put into them [becomes] useless."

(2) Overcommunication Enables Ownership.

Ownership begins with middle managers understanding the bigger picture, which means overcommunication from top leadership. This involves regular updates and calls. Counterintuitively, it is a healthy level of over-communication that puts middle managers in a better position to call the shots.

For Windy, this is important to retaining talent. "How [you] retain [talent] is overcommunication...creating that environment in which they can perform. It doesn't mean you always have to be at the forefront. Create an environment where they can call the shots so that they can understand the full context."

(3) Integrating Openness into Standard Operating Procedures (SOPs) Overcomes Cultural Defaults.

Traditional East Asian business cultures will encourage a default of staying quiet and not voicing out opinions to authority to avoid putting discussions in an awkward position. One way to circumvent this default is to force middle managers to speak up and bring their ideas to the table. Placing this as SOP ingrains it into the company's operation, so the default becomes speaking up rather than staying quiet.

This SOP is especially essential to maintain agility in a crisis as it allows top leadership to have optionality. Various perspectives can be noisy, but it is better than placing all bets in one basket that doesn't have the full picture.

One way startups can integrate this into SOPs is to actually place people whose job is dedicated to ensuring open communication across teams. This was brought up in a previous essay in this chapter where 4PL cross-border logistics platform Janio embeds what they call "people managers" to "extract the essence of the problems [in local teams], and translate that to HQ so we can target those issues."

(4) Useful Feedback Loops begin with Measuring the Right Things.

It is vital to keep middle managers in check, but doing that correctly means knowing what to look out for.

In a crisis, these checks-and-balances are all the more critical. As co-founder and CEO of Carro Aaron Tan shared in our first webinar, conducting surveys with employees across the various countries they operate in is essential to get a sense of how each team is handling the crisis. Gaining this nuanced understanding is critical because the situation (and response) varies from country to country.

"...we have done this survey and [are following] up. So we are implementing it across various countries, understanding what is happening, [asking questions like], "Do you have enough direction from the various CEOs?... Are you coping well?... Do you have good instructions from your bosses?"

In getting a sense of the situation on the ground, it is essential to know what metrics to check. "For me, it is about understanding which metrics are important. For instance, I'm watching my NPLs like a hawk nowadays. So it means like, even if it is 10 days late or one day late I need to know. So it's very important to measure each of your countries accordingly, each of the business lines according to what matters and how it will matter," Aaron adds.

(5) Technology can Reduce Informational Asymmetry.

Informational asymmetry can quickly happen in a company as a grows, and the more decentralized it becomes. It is vital to have infrastructures for information to be easily presented and accessed.

Technology automates information flows and makes communication more real-time. There are workplace collaboration platforms that companies can use, while others have the talent and resources to build their infrastructure better suited to their needs.

Innovators do not Fish for Talent; they Cast Nets for Teams

Takeaways on hiring and building teams:

(1) *Understanding the market and the depth of talent available* is a key first step to coming up with the right strategy for hiring and structuring the organization. Shallow waters call for creativity in attracting talent and focus in prioritizing hires, deeper waters attentiveness to competition and clarity in differentiation.

(2) *Effectively managing cross border teams is all about thinking in terms of the team as a whole* — growing top-down from HQ and bottom-up from local country/regional teams, as well as establishing transparent communication across teams.

(3) *Hiring senior talent is a two-way street.* It is not about finding someone to fit into the role, but ensuring that the hire can both bring value and benefit from the position.

(4) *With growth comes complexity, but that does not have to eliminate agility.* Developing an agile middle management is key to retaining speed while growing in size and across borders.

Chapter Four

Boarding the Technology Platforms

Innovators build reservoirs market-first.

"If you want to go fast, go the old road."
— Ancient Burmese proverb

Explorers gathering a crew, setting out in the wild, mapping their discoveries and returning to tell the tale is always just the beginning. The impact of an expedition can be gauged by how many more expeditions that follow it.

Pioneering expeditions often inspired others to follow with the prospect of seeing the exotic and invaluable. That was the case for early navigators who first mapped out the routes that trade ships eventually followed, and it is still the case today for travelers like mountaineers, deep sea divers, and astronauts whose narratives of the uncharted inspire succeeding generations of explorers.

More long-term impact can be gauged by how much these expeditions changed world views and behavior. Magellan's journey cast doubt on the age-old belief of a flat earth; men on the moon centuries later took photos of the round earth. For the innovator, these signs of impact translate into a large user base, competitors (followers), and disruption (changed world view).

However, achieving any of those begins with driving adoption — getting an initial following and scaling that. In the landscape of Southeast Asia's internet economy, growth has been driven by customers and businesses demanding more frictionless and faster access to products and services across various aspects of work and living.

Such driving forces from both industry and consumers have led to the rise of technology platform companies designed specifically to speed up flows and processes that would otherwise have continued to be absurdly bureaucratic and inefficient. These technology platform companies are uniquely geared to cater to this demand for speed, convenience, and visibility. They are able to utilize existing infrastructure (e.g., cloud) and techniques (e.g., AI, modelling) in bringing together suppliers and consumers on an interface that facilitates any number of transactions and interactions.

This is what makes technology platform companies so prevalent in our world today. The model is not focused on any particular market or vertical. It simply accelerates and makes more efficient what we know markets do from our economics 101 classes — bring together supply and demand.

Many successful technology platforms have attracted many companies to follow suit and improve on the user experience or business model. They have also changed world views and societal behavior.

However, these tech platforms do not just pop out of anywhere and transform industries in one decisive stroke. Certain elements have to come together for tech platforms to be relevant, game-changing, and enduring.

The next three chapters of this book will tackle these elements using a framework called "The Reservoir Principle." The Reservoir Principle describes the development of a technology platform as analogous to how a reservoir collects and stores rainwater for long-term use, and eventually evolves to support other applications beyond storage like irrigation and electricity.

The model is tackled in this book across three stages: adoption, retention, and ecosystem-building. Each of the next three chapters covers one stage in the development of a technology platform, citing tactics employed by businesses across various industries to clear these stages.

This chapter in particular tackles how user acquisition is unlocked in different industries in Southeast Asia, and the market conditions that tech startups leverage to drive adoption of their products or services.

Essays in this Chapter

(14) **The Reservoir Principle.** This will provide an overview of the framework that will guide our exploration of technology platforms in the next three chapters.

(15) **E-commerce: Driving logistics digitalization.** The growing usage of e-commerce platforms in Southeast Asia is driving logistics for an upgrade. *Based on "Southeast Asia's retail boom fuels the rise of logistics" by Yinglan Tan. Published 23 January 2019.*

(16) **Insurtech: Rethinking distribution.** Increasing demand for the convenience of online transactions combined with more accessible technology infrastructure opens the door for insurtechs to introduce new ways of distribution. *Based on "Distribution insurtechs' boarding call for industry" by Paulo Joquiño. Published 22 July 2019.*

(17) **Healthtech: Balancing technology and user needs.** With all the high-tech solutions out there in healthcare, Southeast Asian countries do not necessarily need such "fancy" remedies. Instead, what works best is a mix of technology and in-person care suited to the market's available resources. *Based on "Finding Healthtech's Golden Ratio" by Linh Nguyen. Published 17 January 2020.*

(18) **Fintech: Winning consumers in the offline market.** For fintechs in Southeast Asia, the next frontier is the unbanked and offline market. Fintech founders share their approach to driving adoption. *Based on "How digital disruptors serve the unbanked in Southeast Asia" by Yinglan Tan. Published 23 January 2019.*

(19) **Rural economy: Going distribution-first.** The rural economy poses great opportunity for digitalization, but the conventional

approaches to finding PMF need to be overturned. *Based on "Exploring Southeast Asia's Uncharted Rural Economy" by Paulo Joquiño. Published 9 January 2020.*

(14) The Reservoir Principle

By Paulo Joquiño

We have seen how the enduring tech companies of our day are built on self-sustaining platforms that on its own is able to monetize and extract value from customers with a lifetime value that far exceeds the cost to acquire and retain them. Such a self-sustaining platform can be illustrated as a reservoir or a manmade lake, where the water it holds represents the user base it was not only able to acquire but manages to retain.

***

The reservoir principle is founded on the reality that fighting for market share against competitors or incumbents will wear a business down, and a startup all the more quickly. In the technology market, it is becoming easier to deploy products, and more importantly, link these products together on a platform. With enough resources, a single company can be the platform for anything a consumer or business needs.

That is how the likes of Google and Alibaba have managed to thrive — by going beyond search and e-commerce into nearly every aspect of our lives, from IoT devices (Google Voice) and financial services (Ant Financial). The ease of movement from one product to the next has greatly sped up the growth of many companies and has even resulted in the "super app" ubiquity becoming the Holy Grail for these platforms.

At the same time, the low barriers to entry for the technology market means the cost to acquire every new customer is rapidly rising, as the competition thickens faster than ever before. Even non-technology companies have joined the digitalization rush, making it harder for startups to find space to fit in. This is especially the case of well-developed verticals like e-commerce, where traditional brick-and-mortar companies are creating their own digital storefronts and designing online customer journeys.

Along with the mechanisms for venture capital and private investing powering tech companies, the possible speed of growth for a company has accelerated further. Even then, companies that do succeed in dominating the market will find it challenging and costly to constantly maintain that lead and eventually match up scale with unit economics, especially if that growth was built on purely low-margin, high acquisition cost business.

What the reservoir principle offers is an approach to scale where acquisition is only one piece of the puzzle, and the heavy costs to scale can be reduced with a focus on the depth of customer (experience) instead of capturing more and more of the market.

***

Simply depending on rainwater or the natural flow of rivers for survival would not suffice. This is something the pioneers of agriculture realized. Enter the reservoir.

Reservoirs are an age-old innovation, with the oldest known dam in the world called the Jawa Dam built in Jordan's Black Desert around 3,000 BC to store water for irrigation. The capabilities of these artificial lakes have since expanded, from flood control to electricity, but core to achieving any of these capabilities is the reservoir's ability to hold water.

In the same way, companies that spend a lot of money acquiring customers at the expense of proper unit economics without any mechanism to retain them will either trip up their own scale or face the pressure later on to generate profits — both of which are more difficult to mitigate as the organization becomes more complex.

Hence, while a reservoir still depends on the natural flow of water, it stores water and maximizes the value it can derive from storing the water, acting as an ecosystem for flora and fauna, source of electricity, and so on and so forth.

Acquisition

There is no removing acquisition from the equation, but at the same time, tech platforms need to do more than just accumulate a huge user base (B2C) or build up a portfolio of big-ticket accounts (B2B). The reservoir has to store the water it collects. For the business, this means crafting a user experience that tremendously improves the status quo, converting a significant portion of customers into loyal followers or fans. Leveraging on distribution and network effects can speed up this process and increase chances of success.

Discounts, incentives, and subsidies will work initially, but there has to be deeper engagement for these users on the platform, otherwise the platform will end burning tons of cash just to keep users onboard. Referrals specifically tend to be more powerful, but there is still cash lost on the incentives for these referrals.

Adjacencies

Once you have a sizeable reservoir, you can start breeding fish and prawns. In other words, the users came in through rainfall, but you have to create other use cases to get them to stay engaged and increase engagement, and as more rainwater falls and your user base grows bigger. Scaling up your platform increases your moat by including customer service and allowing users to cross-pollinate the various use cases more conveniently. Platforms can achieve rapid growth by extending into high margin extraction channels with least amount of resources.

Ecosystem

And as reliance on rainwater for survival comes to a minimum, you can charge people to fish in the reservoir as well. So, once the platform is self-sustaining, you can start monetizing and extracting value much like a fisherman can do in a reservoir. Over time, the resources that is built up allows for sustaining value creation. You do not need to fish for prawns, you can build a hydro dam, to allow for limitless creation.

One can think of this as a setting up a greenhouse, where external resources are hardly needed to run the ecosystem of flora and fauna enclosed within. From a technology platform's perspective, the demand side drives engagement and interactions to the extent that it keeps the supply side running and able to continue providing what the demand side, well, demands.

***

These stages of acquisition, adjacencies, and ecosystem do not have to be entirely separate and chronological. It is better to already have clarity on what the stages mean for the business, even if they are not necessarily deployed yet.

Of course, this is easier said than done. However, the most enduring companies are able to build that reservoir and get users to stay engaged. This means creating a breadth of services that build on top of the core vertical, enabling flexibility and responsiveness to changing market needs.

(15) E-commerce: Driving Logistics Digitalization

Based on "Southeast Asia's retail boom fuels the rise of logistics" by Yinglan Tan. Published 23 January 2019.

One way to drive acquisition is through the necessity of digitalization. With the emergence of cross-border e-commerce marketplaces in Southeast Asia like Lazada and Shopee, the need for keeping logistics up to speed and affordable with discount-fueled consumer demand has opened up the arena for logistics enablers.

There is a wide range to cover in logistics, but in general, these startups offer e-commerce platforms and sellers flexibility in managing their logistics networks. This is critical in a region like Southeast Asia where standards for import and export can vary across countries and crises events can shake up supply chain routes in and out of the region.

By leveraging on Fourth Industrial Revolution technologies, they create optionality for stakeholders in the supply chain, and this optionality reduces logistics costs. As a result of these benefits and the necessity of it all, the barriers to acquisition will tend to be lower, and it becomes a matter of performance.

When it comes to reservoir building, these enablers are tied to the health of the platforms they enable. The customers are usually e-commerce players, SMEs, and more traditional brands and manufacturers but it is ultimately consumer demand for more e-commerce that opened up the space for these logistics startups. As these enabler startups are an embedded necessity within the customer journey on two levels (the businesses they support and the customers those businesses serve), the reservoir they build is stronger.

***

Southeast Asia's robust economic growth is supported by an increasing number of consumers from across the region gaining access to the web. In 2018, the internet penetration in the region reached 58%. With another 3.5 million users coming online each month, consumer behavior is rapidly shifting, which is fueling a boom in the e-commerce industry.

Developing 3PL Capabilities for E-commerce

China's logistics market became the largest in the world back in 2012 after the country's retail sales posted an annual growth rate of more than 15% for several years. Southeast Asia is in the midst of a similar boom in consumer spending. According to a study by Google and Temasek, the region's retail sales are forecast to almost double to $1.38 trillion in 2025 from the $720 billion it recorded in 2019. Although the 11 countries of Southeast Asia share the mutual goals of development and expansion, they also share similar logistical problems.

The region's logistics sector is still currently dominated by third-party logistics service providers, better known as 3PLs, which have traditionally been characterized as asset heavy and labor intensive.

Seeing where the current trends are headed, 3PLs will need to further develop their digital capabilities in order to meet the needs of the region's rapidly growing retail sector, which presents an opportunity for tech-enabled startups to offer their expertise.

Millennials are the biggest adopters of e-commerce. These young consumers are accustomed to receiving the instant gratification offered by today's apps and services and have similar expectations with online retailers. Thus, e-commerce players in Southeast Asia are continuously focused on catering to this generation. They are racing to provide fast and engaging experiences to win over and retain customers, while capturing a higher average revenue per user (ARPU) and extending lifetime value (LTV).

Despite this, long tail merchants in Southeast Asia are still consolidating bulk orders before sending them to 3PL storefronts in order to save on delivery costs. This delays shipping and poses a major problem in maintaining customer satisfaction, let alone loyalty. Things get even trickier in countries with inadequate infrastructure and higher geographical barriers, like Indonesia.

High E-commerce Demand vs High Logistics Costs

From 2017 to 2020, the Indonesian government has been spending a great deal of time and effort to accelerate the country's infrastructure development and solve logistical problems. There have been significant improvements in the sector, as seen in the Logistics Performance Index, a biannual report published by the World Bank. Indonesia jumped 17 positions to 46th place out of 168 countries covered in the report.

Despite the remarkable achievement, Indonesia accounts for most of the region's e-commerce market, but unfortunately still has some of the highest logistics costs across the region, accounting for 24% of the country's GDP. While the ratio in neighboring countries, like Thailand and Malaysia reached 13.2% and 13%, respectively.

Quite a few industry players, including those from the digital sector, have tried to come forward and offer their solutions. While e-commerce giant Lazada has built up its own delivery operations in Indonesia to ensure timely delivery, tech startup Shipper intends to help cut the inefficiency in local logistics business by creating a first-mile logistics aggregator platform that offers pick-up and delivery services in the hopes of complementing its 3PLs services, while providing merchants the option to have their products delivered to customers on the next day — if not the same day.

Introducing the Fourth Industrial Revolution to Logistics

The age-old logistics industry is primed for technology disruption. Southeast Asian businesses are often run on relationships, with multiple agents facilitating each deal, eating away at the supplier's profits and driving up prices for consumers as a result. Thus, some form of disintermediation has become essential to reinvent the current processes, especially now that the Fourth Industrial Revolution technologies are enabling, while at the same time, demanding logistics providers to embrace tech and take their services to another level.

One of the proofs of this inefficiency can be seen in the trucking sector, which has been used by large fast-moving consumer goods (FMCG) companies to carry inventory in bulk. This is a result of the lack of a single data point connecting all FMCG companies, trucking companies, and drivers together, resulting in several problems, such as under-utilized fleets, empty backhaul, and insufficient drivers to arise in certain regions.

In Vietnam, another startup called LOGIVAN has been exploring the possibility of utilizing data to better manage resources. By collecting data on truckers' routes and company fulfilment needs, managers can function like control towers, directing demand to truckers to prevent empty backhauls. Adding to the potential benefits, pricing transparency may also be improved by utilizing a two-sided marketplace that can obtain the fairest price for both truckers and FMCG companies. Seeing the success of models like BlackBuck in India and ManBang in China serves to illustrate the untapped potential of these startups.

With advancements in technology, warehouses will no longer just be locations for storing a wide array of items, but instead can be transformed into fulfilment centres that are able to analyse consumer purchasing patterns and anticipate demand for certain products. By shipping and storing selected items in advance, 3PLs can respond to orders faster and utilize bulk shipments at a lower cost.

3PLs continue to seek ways to expand their service coverage. Aside from offering lower prices and faster delivery services, 3PLs compete with each other by working with agents to open storefronts nationwide that can better serve consumers. Although spreading physical collection points has been the go-to expansion model for ages, it is ultimately expensive to set up and maintain. Meanwhile, 3PLs have the opportunity to shorten the distance between the hubs and consumers by considering several options, such as utilizing spaces like mom-and-pop stores as sorting hubs. This way, it is easier for consumers to drop their packages at the hubs and more efficient for the 3PLs to distribute.

(16) Insurtech: Rethinking Distribution

Based on "Distribution insurtechs' boarding call for industry" by Paulo Joquiño. Published 22 July 2019.

Apart from leveraging on necessity (and affordability) to drive acquisition, there is also the value proposition of distribution. While logistics enablers support the back-end efficiency of e-commerce marketplaces and sellers of all sizes, some insurance technology (insurtech) startups offer greater distribution for incumbents. They set up platforms and APIs for providers to reach more customers and rebundle products for specific needs.

Rethinking distribution goes hand-in-hand with a greater ability to capture and process data, the lifeblood of the insurance industry. This ability has been upgraded significantly by the digital technology we have today.

Building a platform that offers pathways and tools for distribution online makes for a more diverse reservoir. Insurtechs with this general value proposition can experiment with the technology capability they have to open up new use cases, allowing providers and customers to connect in more ways than one.

***

Back in the 1800s, housed in Lloyd's coffee shop in the UK, were the world's first underwriters. They peered out from the shop's windows, watching ships come in and out of the port and painstakingly noting which ones returned, damages to ships, among other details.

These days, big data is seen as one of the next big disruptors of industry. For insurance, data has been its staple since birth 200 years ago. So, as data for insurance has evolved far from its pen-and-notebook beginnings in the coffee shops of London, so has its potential uses.

"The insurance industry is ripe for [using data] — the industry is trying to grapple now how to make the most out of different data sets, structured and unstructured," shares Laurens Koppelaar, CEO of Symbo Singapore, the Southeast Asia HQ of an India-based insurtech company.

Distribution Models Amplifying Data Use in Insurance Ecosystem

As with most industries being disrupted today, many insurtechs are using technology to make specific insurance processes, like claims analysis and fraud detection, more efficient. For example, claims analysis insurtechs would use non-conventional sources of data like social media or weather stations. Others are taking the distribution route, focusing more on the linkages in the industry. Their concern revolves around the asynchronization of information and inefficiencies across the value chain.

When it comes to using data in the 21st century insurance industry, distribution insurtechs push the role of data in insurance beyond filling in gaps in processes. Instead, they use data to amplify the capabilities of insurers and brokers across all lines of insurance. For example, a distribution insurtech could advise insurers in their network on what insurance products have seen more success in sales, and how specific agents could be of stronger service to their customer bases.

The benefits also extend to affinity partners. Affinity partners can be a risk champion by heralding protection awareness to its customers, now empowered on far more accurate data points. In turn, affinity partners further strengthen their offering while also unlocking additional revenue streams.

Double Impetus to Take Action

While the industry has not yet fully embraced the distribution technology platform yet, industry shifts create a double impetus for incumbents. Expectations of both retail and commercial consumers are moving towards faster feedback loops as digital communication speeds up.

The second shift is happening on the other end with technological integration becoming more accessible for business. Some players are taking a step forward in the right direction even though there was still a long way to go with cultural norms and legacy systems that have to be changed. For example, while a handful of insurance companies are releasing API-enabled insurance products, most only cater to retail customers.

Nevertheless, with this double impetus to take action, the opportunity is there to strengthen linkages between customers and industry players. That is what distribution insurtechs are working towards, by building digital storefronts for insurance players and forming partnerships with non-insurance platforms like travel service aggregators. The biggest hurdle of companies and incumbents is culture and that kind of cultural fabric and DNA in a company to allow for that to happen.

Equipping the Ecosystem with Data

Accelerating this trend goes back to how distribution insurtechs are uniquely structured to use data. As distribution insurtechs expand their network, data shortens feedback loops between stakeholders — claims for a flight delay can be made immediately as opposed to going through tedious paperwork, and travel insurance can be "turned on and off" as customers need it. The benefits ripple across an ecosystem of industries, not just insurance.

Ecosystem building, especially in Southeast Asia, requires navigating the regulation, distribution models, and technology adoption. Having worked insurance roles in the region for close to a decade already, Laurens believes in finding the right fit of insurance products for the opportunities present in each market. In spite of differences, Symbo Singapore capitalizes on learning from their "bigger brother" in India, which has been operating for the last two and a half years.

Data has always been the lifeblood of insurance, but it is not going to be of much use if the industry remains docked at harbor. Distribution insurtechs like Symbo are setting sail into the future. "If you believe the ecosystem is helping to groom and grow startups, a big part of that is sharing data, and information, and knowledge, and experiences, the good and the bad, so collectively you move the needle," says Laurens.

(17) Healthtech: Balancing Technology and User Needs

Based on "Finding Healthtech's Golden Ratio" by Linh Nguyen. Published 17 January 2020.

In both logistics and insurance, the answer to acquisition seems to lie in digital technology offering a new, radically improved way of doing things. In healthcare, however, it is not as clear-cut as plugging in the industry online. Industries where needs are highly personalized and nuanced also require what we will call human "care."

For example, telemedicine is not just about connecting patients and doctors. A platform that wants to retain users needs to ensure these online consultations actually translate into "care" offline. Biotech software used to accelerate the development of antiviral drugs, ultimately proves itself in the efficacy of these drugs in the real world. The translation from online tech to offline "care" varies not just on a market-to-market level but a person-to-person level.

In Southeast Asia's healthcare industry, driving acquisition is less a question of how to bring in the technology but more a question of what technology will complement the existing elements in the market to create significant value for users.

With this amount of nuance, building a reservoir as a healthtech startup will be limited to the specific area or segment the startup is targeting. For a 4PL logistics platform or SaaS logistics startup, the technology could be refined for various applications across the supply chain, from customs clearance to managing airfreight. In healthcare, it is not practical (at least for an early stage startup) to move from consultation (telemedicine) to diagnostics and treatment (biotech), especially for an outsider company entering the industry.

A simpler trajectory for expansion is to build a specific function for different customers (small clinics, large hospitals) in different countries. Barriers will still be there, and to that end, it requires a deeper understanding of the ratio of "care" to technology needed in each market.

***

The Changing Landscape of Healthcare

In ancient times, holy men dominated the practice of healing. Powerful leaders like the Pharaohs of Egypt were flocked by priests, the only ones who could read the books of medicine, proclaimed to be the work of the gods. Healthcare at this time was widely considered a religious affair, left to magicians whose care was bought with prayer and power.

Nowadays, it is not uncommon to find people monitoring vitals on smart watches as they do their morning jog. It is also not a foreign concept to use DNA ancestry to predict the likelihood of disease. The power of data for healthcare is being harnessed at manifold levels by tech companies, and healthcare can be reached within the tap of a screen. It seems almost magical, and yet, technology solutions are powering many healthcare services in developed markets and highly urbanized areas.

At the same time, many communities, especially those outside of urban areas, remain without basic health centres or access to treat diseases like polio. Data, even from basic medical records, are unavailable. This disparity results in an expanse of healthcare solutions equally vast, ranging from new age hospitals to deep tech. These solutions vary in dosage of technology — is it a pure technology solution, or does it involve delivering resources for "care" as well (e.g., doctors, physical establishments, medicines, etc.)?

Finding the golden ratio of technology and care in Southeast Asia

In Southeast Asia, healthcare startups are generally more focused on improving the delivery of healthcare services, from insurance to doctor's appointments and antibiotics. Even then, there are stark differences in focus for each market in the region.

Tech solutions best suited for each market depend on how the public healthcare system evolved in the country and the ratio of doctors to patients. Inefficient public healthcare systems with low doctor-to-patient ratio have a stronger focus on equipping and supplying resources across the market, as with new age hospitals and smart clinics.

For example, Vietnam's overloaded public healthcare system, exclusive private hospitals, and rising out-of-pocket expenses are pushing health techs to focus on delivering healthcare services at an affordable cost to more of the population.

Meanwhile, those with more developed healthcare systems and higher doctor-to-patient ratio tend to prioritize affordability and convenience with standalone technology platforms like mobile health apps and AI diagnostic solutions.

In Singapore and Thailand, well established, centralized healthcare systems have led to consumer preferences evolving from need to convenience. Telemedicine, teleconsulting, and online insurance platforms dominate the landscape as consumers prefer services on-demand, online, and highly personalized.

Technology startups need to deliver value where it is truly needed in the market. Such value can address either shortage (balancing the doctor to patient ratio), affordability, or quality. The onus for founders is to find the golden ratio of "care" (healthcare resources) and technology that applies for the problem they are addressing.

Adjusting the Golden Ratio for the Long-term

It is not just about figuring out this "golden ratio" of care and technology, however. Successful models in healthcare globally are focused on providing solutions that decrease or prevent risk of disease rather than curing or medicating. This can be seen in companies in the US which focuses on diagnostics, like HeartFlow, and detection, like Grail, important tools that can increase prevention. In China, iCarbonX is digitalizing a holistic view of healthcare, combining genomics with a host of other health factors including lifestyle to create health profiles for users.

This proactive approach to healthtech adjusts the golden ratio for more long-term value for the patient. It is no longer just about tackling inefficiencies and problems in hospitals and clinics but across the patient's entire lifestyle, from physiological concerns to day-to-day living.

(18) Fintech: Winning Consumers in the Offline Market

Based on "How digital disruptors serve the unbanked in Southeast Asia" by Yinglan Tan. Published 23 January 2019.

The offline, unbanked market has long been one of the frontiers of financial institutions in Southeast Asia. E-commerce has initially solved their entry into the offline market with COD, but COD is not a long-term option to dominate the payment mix.

In these markets, speed can make a world of difference, where traditional channels can take days or weeks to complete transactions. Selling on speed alone can be enough to cross-pollinate usage from one use case (e.g., cash transfer) to another (e.g., bill payments) within the same platform. However, growing the platform's user base takes more than speed. It requires a strong offline network. For certain financial transactions like financing, data sources for credit scoring and underwriting are core to enabling adoption.

***

Just last week, DHL launched a new service to allow the unbanked in Southeast Asia to buy online through its Cross Border Cash-on-Delivery (COD) service. This follows other new-age players like Grab/Gojek aggressively launching initiatives of their own to provide financial services to people who do not have banking accounts.

Banking services are synonymous with convenience. In modern society, making transfers, paying bills, and making loans have all been enabled by banks and they have continued to innovate as we increasingly embraced technology. Many regional banks in Southeast Asia have created mobile applications, a solution seemingly tailor-made to the young population who access the mobile internet more than anybody else in the world.

However, banking penetration remains low in the region, with only 47% of the population in Southeast Asia having a bank account despite these new initiatives. This gap is highlighted particularly in the Philippines, where a staggering 77% of the population is unbanked, according to a recent survey by the Bangko Sentral ng Pilipinas. A similar magnitude of people are afflicted with the same problem in Vietnam and Indonesia at rates of 65% and 52% respectively. With this in mind, how can the unbanked be better served in the region?

Online Platforms have to be Augmented with Offline Network

"The supply of the banks can't accommodate the burgeoning number of users. It's the equivalent of being in Union Square in downtown San Francisco. The people in Mountain View and Oakland would find it difficult to get there," said Hendra Kwik, CEO of Payfazz, an Indonesia-based mobile platform for financial services, in reference to the banking ecosystem in Indonesia. As most Indonesians store their money as cash, a tech-only approach to banking the population does not suffice. A physical presence is required to digitize the cash for consumers, and Payfazz hopes to provide a solution with its army of offline agents.

While technology makes life much easier for the masses, sometimes the masses are required to make technology work, and companies have to tailor their products to each individual market. For lesser developed areas of Southeast Asia, establishing a strong offline network is key.

Unconventional Data is the New-age Credit Scoring

Consumers are not the only ones suffering from a lack of financial services, with only 33% of SMEs in Southeast Asia having access to loans and a line of credit. This prevents them from executing their growth plans effectively and limits their ability to scale quickly when demand surges. "There are 78 million small businesses in Southeast Asia, that's three times more than the US," said Andrea Baronchelli, CEO of Aspire, a Singapore-based company offering direct loans to SMEs.

SMEs often fail to get loans from banks due to their lack of credit history and assets for use as collateral. To counter the lack of credit history or collateral these SMEs face, Aspire's proprietary risk assessment engine taps onto non-conventional data, such as business transactions, data from online accounting software, online ratings, and social activities to create a new-age credit scoring for SMEs.

In this era of social media, there are huge amounts of data freely available online. Customer feedback, ratings, and the traction of a company's social media account can be used to determine the health of a business. Companies that have perfected the method of tapping this data will have a key competitive edge moving forward.

The Need for Speed to Win Over Consumers

For the few companies who are fortunate to have their loans approved by banks, the approval often comes after extensive research and credit verification, which typically takes many weeks. SMEs often lack sufficient cashflow to deal with surges in demand and thus need capital quickly. New methods of credit verification and increased processing speed are therefore key in revolutionizing the traditional SME financing method and to help these businesses reach their full potential.

Patrick Lynch, the CEO of First Circle, a Philippines-based startup providing PO financing and invoice financing to SMEs, said, "A typical bank loan takes multiple in-person visits and months to process. First Circle uses a combination of trading history and network data to understand what each SME does and how they interact with their trading partners, cutting down the entire loan process to just three days."

Embracing data analytics through their own proprietary software has allowed First Circle to safely underwrite tens of thousands of invoices for large SMEs as well as those with no credit history in a short amount of time.

Companies must innovate to stay agile, such as automation via data analytics. Additionally, the usage of collaborative cloud platforms and the flattening of decision-making processes will be key to maintaining a competitive edge.

Innovation and Adaptability is Key

Southeast Asia internet economy is expected to grow exponentially over the next few years, with both customers and businesses starting to demand new frictionless and faster access to financial services. Adapting quickly to the ever-changing needs of consumers is a competitive advantage for startups. As Charles Darwin said, "It is not the strongest or the most intelligent who will survive but those who can best manage change".

(19) Rural Economy: Going Distribution-first

Based on "Exploring Southeast Asia's Uncharted Rural Economy" by Paulo Joquiňo. Published 9 January 2020.

In the previous essay, building a strong offline network was key for a fintech to drive adoption in the offline market. This takeaway of building distribution first applies not just to fintechs but other startups venturing into the rural economy.

Southeast Asia's rural economy has attracted many startups across verticals, from fintech to logistics and e-commerce. As digitalization rushes in, it will be a race among startups not just to deliver the most compelling products, but to first build the strongest distribution to support their operation. Even if the customer journey happens entirely on the app, driving adoption in the rural economy requires tapping into local behaviors, offline infrastructure, and relationships to gain trust and retention.

While the norm is to build a product and run iterations with customers to find product-market fit, this essay emphasizes the value of going distribution-first in the offline market.

***

Going Back to Basics

Heavyweight marketplaces in the region have broken ground in transforming the consumer experience online. This ushered e-commerce into the region at an unparalleled pace, projected to hit $300 billion gross merchandise value (GMV) in 2025 from $5 billion in 2015.

However, these transactions are concentrated in urban areas, with around 52% of Southeast Asia's internet economy limited to major metropolitan areas in the region. Much of Southeast Asia still lacks reliable access to basic services and infrastructure like banks, hospitals, and schools, and this has created barriers to the adoption of internet services and digital tools.

At the same time, and precisely because of this lack of access, these market segments present huge opportunity for growth, with online consumption in areas beyond metros projected to grow twice as fast as urban centers moving into 2025.

This is because more technology companies are venturing into the rural economy, akin to expeditions sailing across uncharted oceans or traversing unmapped lands. Whether they make it out alive or thrive in such environments is another matter entirely, but what is clear is tapping into the rural economy means going back to basics.

It is less about competing for eyeballs, bandwidth, or wallets, and more setting up channels first for them to access basic services more efficiently and at lower costs than makeshift alternatives. Small businesses, for example, would resort to loan sharks without the presence of dependable platforms for financing. Enabling access to these immediate needs and addressing these glaring pain points can pave the way for more services to be introduced down the road.

Leveraging on What is Already there

When travelling, maps always help to plan out itineraries. However, what if there is no map or prior records that exist in the area? When in unfamiliar territory and with nothing else to depend on, explorers make use of what is within reach and try to acclimatize as fast as possible to their environment.

To succeed in the rural economy, technology companies are also taking this approach. Conventional wisdom dictates building the product first, then supporting it with a strong distribution plan. However, in the rural economy, where the population is largely offline or not as tech-savvy, the reverse is proving to be more effective for digital products and services. Unlocking a deeper understanding of the resources available not only enables product development and delivery at a lower cost, but also sets up a competitive advantage against potential market entries and even bigger players.

Hendra Kwik, co-founder and CEO of Payfazz, a fintech company leading in Indonesia's rural economy, shares how they started out.

"In order to become the best distribution channel for the offline rural population, we needed to have a very strong distribution network in the offline space — in the same way that apps go on Google Play. That Google Play for us is the warung (neighbourhood retail stores), followed by small town restaurants. We brought these retail stores and restaurants inside of our own distribution network by building a platform with features catering to each of their needs. Essentially we're creating for financial services in the offline market what Google Play and App Store are for the online market — financial apps distributed through warungs."

These features, primarily financial services, filled in the lack of banks in many rural communities across the archipelago, but did not require the same infrastructure and human resource costs that come with setting up a physical bank.

Figuring out distribution first is also economical because it avoids the unnecessary costs that come with introducing a pure digital product or even the physical alternative, say a bank or warehouse.

Going distribution-first leverages on what is already there in these rural communities — what infrastructure or information is under-utilized and what capabilities are untapped. It catalyzes the adoption of these products and strengthens customer stickiness, as user engagement already involves elements, they are familiar with. People and data native to these areas become valuable resources for innovation to take root.

In the case of Shipper, an Indonesian logistics platform for e-commerce, they leveraged on the presence of people looking for flexible, part-time work from the comfort of their homes, like stay-at-home parents, to scale their courier services, essentially turning these homes into micro-fulfilment hubs. Also, this not only applies to infrastructure but data as well. AwanTunai digitizes transaction data in Indonesia's traditional supply chain to underwrite micro-merchants at very low cost.

Explorers Survive, Pioneers Thrive

As technology startups race to capture more of the region's rural economy before bigger players come in, it is also a competition to build on top of these basic services to maximize distribution and stretch out the breadth of available services for users. While innovating in the rural economy begins by uncovering foundational needs and addressing these with digital technologies, it is ultimately about pioneering new ways of living, with which communities become more productive, financially secure, and healthy.

Innovators Build Reservoirs Market-first

Takeaways on building sustainable platforms and driving acquisition:

(1) Platforms are able to do more than just connect demand and supply. *They can also grow to become reservoirs that capture an ecosystem of products and services for the users onboard the platform.* This trajectory offers tech startups a sustainable way to grow and endure.

(2) Industry enablers *tap into key (digital) pain points* of incumbents, be it the speed and affordability demanded by end-consumers (logistics for e-commerce, fintech), or the ability to reach these end-consumers online (distribution insurtechs, healthtech). Proof-of-performance not only helps acquire users, but can retain them as well.

(3) *Bringing online platforms to offline environments can be done cost-effectively by going distribution-first.* This requires an understanding of the consumer behavior and existing infrastructure and network effects in the market.

(4) *Both (2) and (3) are best done with deep market understanding.*

Chapter Five

Dropping the Anchor on the Market

Innovators do not grow platforms; they engineer platforms for growth.

"Planting a flower in the desert takes greater skill than growing a garden in a rain forest."

— Matshona Dhliwayo *Philosopher and author*

Frontiers are eventually settled upon and explorations standardized over time. As more astronauts went into space, agencies created training programs, astronauts themselves built the International Space Station, and tours were set for astronauts to take shifts on these stations. European traders set up outposts on coasts and islands along routes outlined by earlier seafarers. Mount Everest hikers and locals set up base camps and planned routes to reach the summit. The goal of this standardization is to ensure these trips can be taken repeatedly over time with relative safety and set expectations. In the process, what was once uncharted eventually becomes more accessible with lower barriers to entry.

In the same way, as a technology platform is introduced to the market, driving adoption is not just about acquiring users. It is about retaining supply and demand as it acquired and aggregated, enabling the platform to keep them on board for the long-term. Once product-market fit is found, platforms need to be quick to drop the anchor on their market and secure a foothold from which growth can continue.

From a business perspective, this ensures the company is not entirely dependent on acquiring new customers and even opens up the possibility to focus more resources on lengthening the value of any single customer on the platform. One can even venture to say that structuring the business around retention can also act as a draw for new users to come in, as they see how much value existing users get from the platform.

From a user perspective, the services and features on the platform become part of their routine (consumer) or their operations (business) as the opportunity cost of using the platform increases.

This aligns directly with the adjacency and ecosystem aspects of the reservoir principle. Effective retention strengthens a reservoir. It reduces the reservoir's dependency for survival on rainfall (acquisition), and opens up multiple areas for monetization based on the information it acquires from customers retained over time.

In Southeast Asia, the race to scoop up as much rainfall as possible is a costly pursuit. In the arenas of e-commerce and ride-hailing, players are locked in battles for market share where subsidies and discounts have become hard-fast rules in a business with already thin margins. As a result, these players become dependent on raising capital from external sources.

The costly race to grab market share is complicated by the reality that Southeast Asia is not a single market. Some investors would say the true market of a Southeast Asian startup is Southeast Asia, but this true market is many markets with different consumer behaviors, regulations, and politics that can affect a company's strategy.

This makes retention all the more important for startups in Southeast Asia, because the company needs to come to a point where it can create enough margins to support further expansion. The business model itself has to incorporate elements that boost cashflow, and a strong retention strategy can achieve this. Regardless of the approach, there are three elements common to any retention strategy:

(1) The core of the strategy is achieving matching efficiency between demand and supply. That means the product or service is supplied to the user in a way that meets their needs (e.g., real-time information, instantaneous feedback, personalized content).

(2) There is rule setting on the platform to ensure quality as efficiency is being achieved. This in itself contributes to retaining users on the platform — creating a level of assurance for users to continue their activity in spite of the risk of certain scenarios. This rule-setting often includes certain standards for supplier and user behavior, incentives for going above and beyond these standards, penalties for breaking them, and feedback mechanism for quality assurance (e.g., driver rating, NPS surveys, quality compliance checks).

(3) Retention creates a self-evolving loop that allows the data generated by user activity to be collected and enriched over time. This self-evolving loop enables the platform to eventually branch out beyond the initial type of engagement or transactions users had on the platform. The platform becomes an engine for a kind of "blue ocean strategy" on steroids, opening new areas of growth that traditionally would have taken longer to do.

Technology platform companies have been observed to generally create more tech market cap and more enduring companies, and it is primarily because of the ability to create this data-driven, self-sustaining mechanism. This chapter covers various retention strategies tech startups use to drop the anchor in their market with the three elements above — achieving matching efficiency, ensuring rule setting, and creating a self-evolving loop for data enrichment.

Essays in this Chapter

(20) **Tech-driven personalization.** Matching efficiency can be achieved within the platform by creating feedback loops to curate the user experience to their specific needs. *Based on "Growing an edtech startup by going micro" by Linh Nguyen. Published 9 September 2020.*

(21) **Irreplaceability Factor.** The goal is to be irreplaceable for the customer, where even the customers themselves become agents for acquisition and retention. *Based on "To change the tide, go with the flows" by Paulo Joquiño. Published 21 February 2020.*

(22) **Platform-driven growth.** As a startup finds product-market fit and gears up for scale, there needs to be a shift from market-driven growth to platform-driven growth, especially in a market where the costs to acquire new customers and expand into new services are high. *Based on "Revisiting the rural economy" by Paulo Joquiño. Published 16 March 2020.*

   a. **Exhibit A: Trucking in Vietnam.** *Based on "Why you don't want the APPLE to fall far from the platform" by Linh Pham. Published on 19 March 2020.*

   b. **Exhibit B: Agriculture in Indonesia.** *Based on "Planting seeds of digitalisation in Indonesia's agriculture" by Paulo Joquiño. Published on 1 April 2020.*

   c. **Exhibit C: Southeast Asia's automobile marketplace.** *Based on "How to be the Alibaba for cars in Southeast Asia" by Joolin Chuah. Published 19 September 2019.*

(20) Tech-Driven Personalization

Based on "Growing an edtech startup by going micro" by Linh Nguyen. Published 9 September 2020.

Personalizing user engagement drives retention by improving matching efficiency and creating a data-driven feedback loop with users. This is particularly useful for tech startups in industries where customer experiences are by nature highly personal or have personal impact (e.g., education, healthcare, and entertainment).

By enabling the platform itself to curate its features depending on user behavior, users are able to benefit or derive value more effectively from the platform. This reduces the need for sales and marketing at scale and has the potential to extend the life of a customer on the platform. Indirectly, users are also contributing to the quality of the platform with their activity. In order to achieve personalization, deep technical skill and a more complex back-end infrastructure to support the platform are often needed.

In the edtech space, this personalization is achieved by creating a content feedback loop with the students. Student engagement with the supply of educational content creates data points that can be used to curate the supply of content to the student's capabilities and even career goals.

***

It is 5 pm in a high school in Hanoi. Parents crowd around the school gate, waiting for their children to come out. They are not going home though. For many Vietnamese kids, 5 pm means after-hour classes. There is no time to grab dinner — their parents already brought snacks to power them through another three or four hours of study. When their day ends, they will finally get some sleep, wake up, and repeat. All in the hopes of landing a spot in a prestigious university in Vietnam or even abroad.

These classes that parents go to extra lengths to for their kids have become part and parcel of a culture that takes pride in education and espouses the onus to spend the extra dong for it. This culture plays hand-in-hand with an education system catching up with workforce globalization. Accessibility has become a luxury when it comes to the intense and often slanted competition for career opportunities.

Edtech Unicorns Creating an Edge

The asymmetry between career opportunities and formal education, and the lengths parents go to close this gap is not a phenomenon limited to Vietnam. Eighty percent of Asian parents are willing to pay extra to send their children for private tuition.

Gaps across the global education landscape combined with increasing access to digital solutions have created the space for technology startups to step in and reach a massive number of students and parents looking to gain an edge in education, amounting to a $260 billion opportunity in the Asia Pacific region alone.

In India, Byju Raveendran capitalized on his popularity and brand to transform a stream of content into the most valuable edtech company in the world at $5.4 billion. This brand and content-driven approach stands in contrast to edtech unicorns in China, where services are tied to specific needs of students.

Cross-border teaching services in China led by VIPKid and DaDa offer one-on-one classes with specialized teachers for a premium. Then there are the more AI-driven assisted learning tools like Zuoyebang, where students can cross-check solutions to their homework.

Across the Pacific, most edtech unicorns focus on upskilling through modularized courses on topics that cannot be easily accessed through formal education, with the likes of Udemy and Udacity.

Going Granular in Southeast Asia

Even as investments in edtech globally have increased from $316 billion to $1 trillion in the last five years, the opportunities in Southeast Asia are less about supplementing formal education and creating an edge as they are about lightening the burden on education systems. Except for those in Singapore, many institutions across the region are weighed down by infrastructure gaps, manpower deficiencies, and outdated curricula *vis-à-vis* increasing costs.

Instead of the disintermediation of teachers and traditional learning institutions with alternative platforms, the narrative for edtech startups in Southeast Asia is collaboration down to the granular level. Online solutions will be enablers for teachers, now armed with data and new forms of content delivery, to be more effective mentors for each of their students.

Simply having a platform however will not be enough. Given the traditional nature of education systems that has long focused on en masse service delivery, winning in the edtech space in Southeast Asia is all about building a learning platform catered to each individual student — micro-schools, in short. This involves creating a brand of trust, scaling through personalization, and developing learning experiences on the platform — three approaches to growth which happen not in sequence, but work as components in a well-oiled micro-school.

Building a Brand of Trust is a Must

As Byju's model has proven, a trusted brand lays the foundation to scale across demographics and backgrounds. And the key to a trusted brand is winning over parents, many of whom would rather have their children go to after-school centers than use mobile applications for learning. Setting up such centers would slow down growth. However, simply limiting engagement online in the beginning, while more efficient to setup and deploy, will also eventually hit a tough ceiling to crack as it becomes more difficult to acquire customers, who are usually, in this case, parents or institutions.

A model to address this trade-off is a hybrid of offline and online distribution. Offline presence, usually via a study center, will secure loyal customers, and make it easier for them to adopt online tools. When won over, these parents also become evangelists. This hybrid distribution model brings down customer acquisition cost over time. Eventually, the goal is to depart from the offline channels and maximize online engagements based on the brand that has been built. Needless to say, the content and delivery have to be effective.

Scale through Personalization

Personalization builds stickiness. With adaptive technologies like artificial intelligence (AI) and machine learning (ML), edtech companies can design programs that learn with the user. This is where tech startups have a leg up in terms of distribution. It is no longer about simply getting the best content and translating it into local languages or importing teachers from top institutions.

The best content can be broken down, repackaged, and distributed using pathways, both offline and online. This gives each individual student their own micro-school that caters to their specific learning needs and aspirations. These personalized feedback loops set an initial moat against more traditional edtech companies, and reduce customer acquisition costs over time.

One approach to personalized distribution is the constructivist learning theory which, according to Jerome Bruner (1966), is the active process of forming new ideas based on past knowledge and experiences. For example, creating a feedback loop where the learning of a student is then used by the AI to determine what content a teacher should deliver next would create tighter engagements.

Platform as a Venue for Personal Development

Along with the depth provided by personalization, growth also involves breadth of service expansion. Data collected on a macroscale provides insights on what new courses to prepare, better ways of delivering content, and potentially new user bases or age groups.

This is where the narrative of collaboration truly bears fruit. If depth creates stickiness for individual users, breadth creates stickiness for larger groups of people and institutions. This sets a specific moat against purely AI-driven edtech companies, and turns the micro-school into an engine for growth.

When it comes to the value-add for students, more breadth sets up progression for the learning experience, beyond supplementary content and learning engagements. This extends to developing better accessibility to career opportunities, from preparing for college interviews to connecting students to competitions and summits for exposure.

Investing in Education Means Investing in Talent

For parents and their children, an education is never about itself. There are aspirations behind every 5 pm after-hours class, behind the effort parents make to secure such opportunities, and behind the hours the students put in. The opportunity for tech startups is to make these efforts and hours clocked in worth it, by bridging the gap to learning opportunities, whether it be to learn a new skill or apply to a university that best fits the student.

Investing in the edtech space in Southeast Asia means investing into the local talent and the next generation of leaders who will influence and shape the region. The model that will truly reshape the region's education landscape is one that can consistently develop a future-proof workforce.

More than providing an edge in education, edtech startups in Southeast Asia have the opportunity to enable education systems with technology at the granular level, deepening student engagement.

Given the traditional nature of education systems, winning in the edtech space in Southeast Asia is all about building a personalized learning platform catered to each student: micro-schools, in short. This involves creating a brand of trust, scaling through personalization, and developing a learning experience on the platform. The model that will truly reshape the region's education landscape is one that can consistently develop a resilient and future-proof workforce.

(21) Irreplaceability Factor

Based on "To change the tide, go with the flows" by Paulo Joquiño. Published 21 February 2020.

Effective personalization has the potential to create what we will call "the irreplaceability factor". The irreplaceability factor signifies that the platform not only retains customers, but simultaneously creates network effects that bring in other customers into the platform. Say Customer A has its transactions radically improved by the platform. Customers B, C, and D who transact or even compete with Customer

A see that their business partner, customer, or even competitor is benefiting from the platform and try it out.

Ideally, this ripples out, strengthening the reservoir a company is building by making the platform more defensible within the industry it operates and thickening the ties it has with customers. If Customers B, C, and D are already active on the platform, and these customers are key business partners with Customer A, there is even less incentive for Customer A to drop out.

There is the saying that "birds of the same feather flock together." This extends also to the network effects of irreplaceability, as the kinds of demand and supply players the platform attracts and retains heavily influences the overall quality of the platform.

Below are interview excerpts with Indonesian logistics SaaS startup founder Iman Kusnadi on how his company, Ritase, is achieving this irreplaceability factor in the logistics industry.

***

Iman begins with his approach to the logistics industry in Indonesia. "In order to get into the logistics or supply chain sector in Indonesia, you have to look at where inefficiencies in flows come from. If you just want to do cargo matching or Uber-ize trucking, it doesn't really solve the problem, because the inefficiencies in cargo matching begins with processes on the shipper side — order management, processing, and communication."

Addressing these inefficiencies is a two-sided problem. "Even then it's not just a question of getting shippers like FMCGs to use digital solutions, but also trucking companies. How do we get trucking companies to go digital and use transport admin systems and driver applications? If you talk to the trucking community, we're dealing with many truckers who have never used banking or tech services. Sometimes they don't even have proper warehousing."

Iman emphasizes the impact of a platform-approach and importance of market education to addressing supply chain inefficiencies in Indonesian logistics. "Before, information flows would just be done through Whatsapp, email, or phone broadcasts.

Now all that can be consolidated into one platform. It's difficult to change because our customers have been in business for many years. It all begins with market education. While there's a lot of problems we can solve in the sector, and our company is tackling only a small portion of it, we believe it's an important place from which to solve inefficiencies in Indonesian logistics."

He shares an example working with one of the biggest F&B companies in Indonesia. "Before working with us, their goods have to be ready for pickup by 3 am in the morning, but they could only dispatch information to the trucking companies six hours later by 9 am."

He continues, "By enabling the shipper to automatically transmit information and allowing the trucking companies to do their pickups earlier, we can reduce inventory turnaround in the warehouse by a day. With faster stock turnaround, shippers can increase cash flow and reduce overall logistics cost — not just your trucking cost because it includes the inventory management stock inside the warehouse."

Having built his career working at multinationals, Iman explains that these kinds of companies view the value-add of digitalization through the lens of price rather than technology. "For the larger multinational shippers, getting their buy-in is really all about price. Technology is only a nice-to-have for them. If you can give them a very competitive price, then they will be more willing to do the trial. Many FMCG multinationals are already using SAP, an ERP system with high level technology. They don't really pay attention that much to the product itself, simply how much it could save them."

Irreplaceability Factor

Addressing these inefficiencies takes more than selling software and educating the market on how to leverage digital solutions. There has to be a ripple effect. For Iman, that means becoming irreplaceable for their customers. "For example, we own every single order in Jakarta for a multinational FMCG because they use our SaaS product. Now every shipper and trucking company who wants to service this FMCG will automatically make use of the Ritase platform. This strong point is why our SaaS product is our backbone."

With Ritase's SaaS product as foundation for their company's own reservoir, Iman sees many other ways users can benefit from the platform. "Then because truckers are on our platform, when they need new trucks our marketplace can easily support them, even providing financing for these purchases through our group buying service. We also provide trucking companies financing to alleviate the pressure on cash flow from shippers' terms of payment. For individual truckers, we built an e-wallet on our platform that truckers can use to buy food or even cigarettes."

"What we're building here aims to cater to the trucking ecosystem around the country. We want to make sure shippers, trucking companies, and even drivers using our platform benefit fully from the platform we built."

Network Effects of Irreplaceability

Iman shares two different stories of trucking companies that now use Ritase's platform. "The first one wanted to close down their business and sell their trucks because they weren't getting orders and didn't have enough cash flow to run on, with up to 35 trucks but only five or seven shipments a day. When they joined Ritase, we helped them with working capital and gave them more orders with a dedicated feed. They could activate all their trucks right away because we also provided financing."

"In contrast, there was a trucking company in Surabaya where they initially turned down our offer because they already had customers and had been running the business for 15 years. Six months later, they came to us because one of their own customers was already using our platform."

According to Iman, these two stories show how Ritase, as a solution for the entire trucking ecosystem, utilizes network effects both in terms of supporting the sector's growth and lowering customer acquisition costs.

(22) Platform-Driven Growth

Based on "Revisiting the rural economy" by Paulo Joquiňo. Published 16 March 2020.

The third goal of a retention strategy, as outlined in this chapter's introduction, is to eventually enable data generated on the platform to be enriched over time. This enrichment allows the platform to cost-effectively host more services that retain users on the platform. It becomes a self-evolving loop where the platform powers its own growth into a reservoir.

This platform-driven growth is an expanded version of the personalization approach tackled in a previous essay. The platform does not just learn to curate user experiences, but also provides the company with options for how to deliver more value to users.

In the rural economy, where digitalization remains fresh in many areas, this platform-driven growth is critical to retaining customers without draining the resources of the startup. Initially, the focus of the rural economy startup would be to create a new market (acquisition), but to drive sustainable growth, the platform must incorporate a focus on retention as well.

There is less competition for irreplaceability compared to more urban areas, but the path to achieving irreplaceability is costly. Developing creative ways to collect and translate data into growth will be critical to making up for the early stage costs with long-term customers.

***

At the start of this year, we published a piece about how tech startups in Southeast Asia are taking on a distribution-first approach to digitalize the region's rural economy, projected to double in GTV over the next five years.

As the essay discussed, counterintuitive to how startups have normally progressed from product market fit to distribution, establishing a strong distribution network in an environment with relatively low internet and digital native activity enables faster adoption of digital products and services. This distribution network is cost-effective because it involves resources and infrastructure already functioning in the community. Technology then serves to boost the capabilities of these people or infrastructure.

This essay continues where the last one left off, this time moving past distribution into the question of growth in the rural economy. This wave of startups tackling the rural economy have been targeting basic services and industry-specific problems, but sustainable growth goes well beyond capturing users. And as recent events strain traditional supply chains, the race to bridge the gap to better products and services to the rural economy is becoming more important than ever before.

Got 99 Problems, Data Ain't One

While the distribution-first approach is a cost-effective way to drive tech adoption, simply aggregating this network on a tech platform would not be enough to retain either supply or demand. For a tech platform in general, the ideal strategy would be to venture into new use cases and value-add services for users, capturing as much lifetime value as possible from every user acquired.

The rural economy presents a number of challenges to this approach. First is the vast amount of inefficiencies in supply chains and processes that present a variety of entry points for a startup. Second is the high cost of initial customer acquisition cost (CAC) and building the distribution network, which means startups will be hard-pressed to spare more cash to enter into other revenue streams or other use cases. Third is the unpredictability inherent in a lot of these markets.

Overcoming these challenges begins with revisiting the distribution network and looking at it not just as a distribution network but as a reservoir of data. Depending on the kind of data the network generates via transactions on the platform, the entry point into adjacencies and prioritization of value-add services become clearer. This reduces the risk and cost of growth.

We have seen this data-driven approach to growth among some of our portfolio companies working in financial services, logistics, and agriculture:

Indonesian SME financing startup AwanTunai began with financing, digitizing supply chain transaction data to underwrite inventory financing loans for micro merchants. This allows them to tap into Indonesia's offline FMCG retail sales and bring in trusted financial institutions into the picture.

Back in Vietnam, LOGIVAN tapped into truck, route, and driving behavior data generated by matching truckers and shippers on their platform to power an instant pricing model for the next-day deliveries of shippers. This is strengthening retention not just with shippers, but also the truckers, who are able to receive personalized pricing offers.

When it comes to agritech Sayurbox's farm-to-table approach in Indonesia, data *is* what retains consumers. They have found that consumers value visibility on their items, and so they inform customers where their produce comes from. From farmers, they utilize data coming out of sourcing hubs across the country to manage the flow of stock and reduce wastage along the supply chain. Reducing this wastage strengthens farmer retention, as farmers ultimately want to be able to sell as much of their crop as possible.

Platform-Driven Growth

Throughout our discussion of the rural economy, it has been common to cite technology as enabling the rural economy. When it comes to growth however, it is the communities and users enabling the technology to develop further.

This ties back to the distribution-driven approach to retention. If we scale this process of using data to beef up the value of the platform, it becomes clear that from a broader perspective the direction of the platform's growth in capability is driven by the user activity. This not only builds retention, but more importantly, loyalty and trust. This self-sustaining cycle is particularly important to

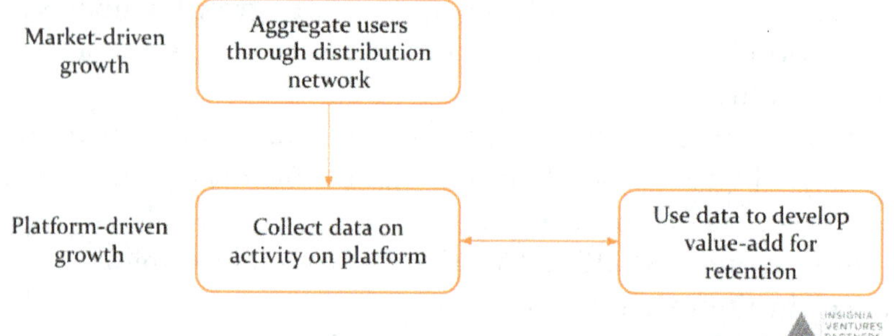

Figure 1.   A framework for growth in the rural economy

	Distribution Network	Type of data	Platform-driven growth
AwanTunai	Micro-merchants + wholesalers	transactions	Financing for micro-merchants
LOGIVAN	Shippers + Truckers	truck, route, driving behavior	Instant pricing model for shippers Personalized pricing for truckers
sayurbox	Farmers + Customers	supply and demand	Visibility for consumers Managing flow of crops to reduce wastage

Figure 2.   How some of our portfolio companies are tackling growth in the rural economy

growth in the rural economy, where the costs can run high to introduce new services or tackle a new geography.

Because of the potential to build such a cycle, many startups addressing the needs of the rural economy are less focused on growth across the region as they are with growth around their core distribution. By focusing on core users and relationships between supply and demand, these startups are able to go beyond market-driven growth and develop a platform that can drive growth on its own. This makes their business models more resilient and enduring.

Exhibit A Platform-Driven Growth: Trucking in Vietnam

Based on "Why you don't want the APPLE to fall far from the platform" by Linh Pham. Published on 19 March 2020.

This and the following three essays will exhibit three companies leveraging on platform-driven growth to explore new ways to innovate customer experience beyond their core service, retain customers, and even onboard more stakeholders from the industry onto their platform. This essay, written by Vietnamese founder Linh Pham, focuses on her company LOGIVAN.

***

Since I founded LOGIVAN roughly two years ago, our team has been constantly exploring how we could further accelerate and better curate matching on our platform. At the same time, we still want to remain asset-light and cost-efficient in our operations, but still provide immense value to our users.

In this regard, we have kept to our roots of working closely with the truckers and shippers. When LOGIVAN was still just a website MVP, we initially went out and spoke to truckers, from the ones we knew to the ones at parking stations, to get insights and feedback. Matching efficiencies needed to be improved, so more of the time could be spent driving and earning. It was from this perspective that we developed LOGIVAN further into a tech platform that could drastically reduce the time spent finding and securing trucking jobs.

Over time, with the accumulation of transactions, the platform gathered data on matching behavior, trucking routes, and pricing. With these data points, we have also been able to upgrade the way we learn from truckers and shippers, and strategically target pain points that persist among our users.

Platform-Driven AI Models

Last year, we launched APPLE (Auto Pricing Project for LOGIVAN codE), an instant pricing model based on market demand and supply catering to all possible routes, truck, and cargo types. For the shipper, the model offers a faster and more reliable alternative to the time consuming and labor-intensive booking process, which often poses a challenge when they have to book trucks last minute for deliveries the next day.

When SME shippers need a truck the next day, they usually call multiple brokers and truckers today to ask for quotes. After waiting an hour or more to get quotes back, the SME shipper has to negotiate for different brokers, which takes a couple more hours. The booking process is very time consuming and very labor-intensive. If you do not finish the negotiation process before 5 pm, then the price increases sharply, because the brokers and truckers know that you are desperately in need of a truck.

Getting instant pricing changes this process entirely for the SME shipper. They can decide on the spot whether their cargo can make it the following day or not. For corporate shippers, while the spot market only occupies 20% of their needs, LOGIVAN also lends a lean and efficient alternative for managing internal operations. Centralizing information and documents can reduce the difficulty of reconciling different truck suppliers that serve them on different routes.

While APPLE gives out an instant price to shippers, it also delivers personalized price offers to truckers as well. If the "instant" aspect of pricing is highly valuable for shippers, the "personalized" aspect of the price offers is just as important to the truckers. Factors such as the type and model of truck, fuel efficiency, the reliability of the truck driver, and the bidding behavior are collected as data points that generate price offers personalized for each trucker. This has also allowed us to see whether a trucker is going to accept a lower price, and thus increasing the margin and spread on our platform.

While the pricing model improves the speed and reliability of matching, we have also found that our marketplace does not

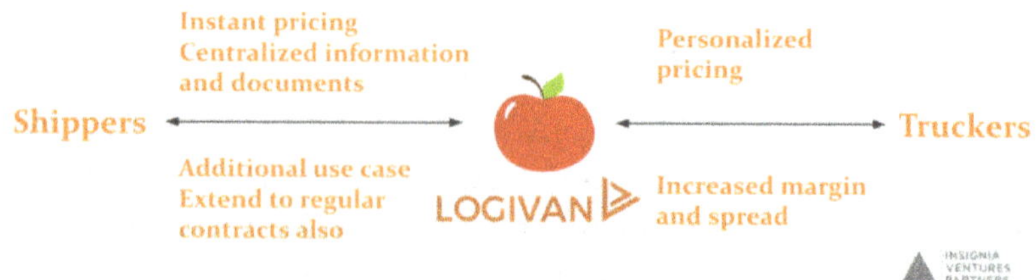

Figure 3. Value exchange on LOGIVAN's platform with APPLE

necessarily translate the aggregation of offers into wins for truckers. Typically, we would send out offers to truckers by the thousands, which actually keeps the chances of winning any particular job low. With that in mind, we built a REcommendation Engine for Logistics (REEL) that predicts when and where the truck is going to be empty and available to take the job at the pick-up location rather than their absolute location at the moment. For the truckers, there are less notifications and job offers but more quality offers, and more importantly, higher chances of winning more of the offers they receive.

The APPLE does not Fall Far from the Platform

Technology platforms thrive on their ability to radically change the way supply and demand find each other. Looking back at my time working with the 10 trucks at my family business, the impact of technology is clear. At the core of the progress we have made thus far has been the ability to work closely with our truckers and shippers.

In the beginning, we talked to them and were able to better define their pain points. As we brought them onto our platform, we listened instead to the data based on their behavior on the platform to create these models that target specifically the areas that would create a better user experience. This allows LOGIVAN to be strategic and cost-efficient with our products and service offerings when it comes to speed and reliability. In that sense, we did not want the APPLE to fall far from our platform.

As companies are diversifying their operations across the world to respond to the trade war and the volatility of the global economy, we are seeing significant positive impact on the logistics sector of Vietnam over the next few years. It is more important than ever to continue listening on the platform to our users and create more avenues for them to generate feedback we can work with. That way, we can grow with Vietnam's logistics industry, our core focus in the years to come.

Exhibit B Platform-Driven Growth: Agriculture in Indonesia

Based on "Planting seeds of digitalisation in Indonesia's agriculture" by Paulo Joquiño. Published on 1 April 2020.

This second exhibit of platform-driven growth focuses this time on an agritech startup from Indonesia, Sayurbox. CEO and Co-founder Amanda Susanti shares her take on the local agriculture industry and how the platform they started in 2016 has been developing to address supply chain inefficiencies and turn farm-to-table into a reality for Indonesians.

What was interesting is finding the similarities between Sayurbox and LOGIVAN in terms of how they approach platform-driven growth. Both have had first-hand experience of the problems in their industry, which comes into play as they create the critical "offline networks" for acquisition. Then there was the flexibility and optionality created by data collection from the activity on their platform.

***

Since Sayurbox started in 2016, Indonesia's agritech space has since gained a lot more interest. It has been hitting headlines and was more recently dubbed as reaching an "inflection point". The country's agriculture market is estimated to be $140 billion and accounts for roughly 13% of GDP — a huge market that remains technologically untapped.

With the impact of the coronavirus, this inflection point is taking on new meaning. Demand is expected to increase for fresh produce like fruits and vegetables. People and businesses are avoiding wet markets but still want to stock up on essential, healthy food items. However, the problems Sayurbox Co-founder and CEO Amanda Susanti discovered in the fresh produce supply chain when she started a farm five years ago still persist. Now, they are straining under the weight of the demand.

We sat down with Amanda to talk about these long-standing supply chain inefficiencies and learn how Sayurbox has been slowly cultivating a farm-to-table culture in the country.

Miles to go before Indonesia Reaps Change

With the lack of transparency and excess of middlemen across the supply chain, it is no surprise that only around 10% of the value chain goes to farmers. This results in supply chain wastage. The fragmentation is such that farmers often do not know where to sell their produce. They also do not have direct access to the logistics facilities that will enable them to turnover their crops. As a result, they end up not being able to sell 30% of their harvest.

The crops they do sell are not subject to price transparency. Middlemen take advantage of this. For a vegetable to go from the farm to the consumer in the traditional supply chain, it can cost upwards of an additional $2 per kilogram. This is a burden on end consumers and businesses that rely on fresh produce for their goods and services. The presence of a grossly unnecessary number of middlemen across the supply chain also produces food wastage of up to 50%.

Because of these deeply rooted problems, Indonesia is still miles behind markets like China and India. The growth of companies like NiceTuan, Meicai, and Ninjakart in those countries is a promising sign that Indonesia can head towards that same direction.

Uprooting Farmers' Pain Points

Tackling these problems need a localized approach, given the unique infrastructure, logistics, and culture of Indonesia's farming sector. Luckily, Amanda had been able to build experience and connections over time, having worked in agriculture for the past five years. In that time, she has realized how valuable it is to have an understanding of the local farming culture, how farmers think, and what consumers value when it comes to fresh produce.

In particular, when it comes to building a presence in farm areas and setting up sourcing hubs in those areas, there is quite a lot to take into consideration with the uncertainty of supply and demand. Amanda and her team work around the reality that farmers want everyone to take their harvest whether it is good grade or bad grade produce.

With this in mind, Sayurbox has taken a multi-demand approach to distribution, covering both B2C and B2B customers. It is easier to forecast B2B demand but in case there are external factors that influence the supply side — for example, if there is an over-harvest, they are able to flush out excess supply to B2C customers because the demand from that side is easier to influence from the pricing. By getting all the harvest from farmers, they are able to secure the produce at a better pricing and reduce waste down to 5% along the supply chain.

Meeting Consumer Demand for Speed and Transparency

Understanding what the end consumer values has also been critical in setting up distribution and operations; that is convenience and transparency on items that customers are getting. With the company running a tight ship on their supply chain, they are able to show exactly which farms the produce is coming from so they know it has gone through quality control — that it is clean and safe.

Harvest and delivery are done within 24 hours, keeping turnover to a bare minimum, with one day for vegetables and two to three days maximum for fruits. Quality control (QC) checks and QC stocks are lined up throughout the supply chain in the sourcing hubs, so the delineation is clear between good grades and the lower grades. Essentially, the aim is to give to consumers what they are paying for and give transparency over that.

Now with the coronavirus issue, customers are also looking for more transparency, they want to know where their food is coming from. Through the app, consumers are able to know exactly which farms the produce is coming from; they know that it is checked, clean, safe.

Fruits of their Efforts

The fruits of their efforts can be told through the avocado. It is one of the best-selling produce on the platform, considering that it can be relatively expensive to procure with the traditional supply chain. However, the reality is that Indonesia has a variety of good avocados from Flores and other areas. Sayurbox is able to source such a large amount that they can sell stock cheaper than wholesale markets.

What they have seen with the avocado is the result of a more efficient distribution network versus the traditional supply chain. Once this network scales with more hyperlocal farm deliveries, Sayurbox plans on achieving faster fulfilment times and distributing more types of produce with fewer barriers. Along with built-in products, they can designate more precise grade types, ensure better food safety, and also cater to a wider variety of fresh produce grade preferences.

While there is certainly still a long way to go in eliminating supply chain inefficiencies, Amanda and her team have clearly planted seeds of change in the industry — ensuring both the pain points of farmers and needs of consumers are addressed with tight, technology-enabled operations.

Exhibit C Platform-Driven Growth: Southeast Asia's Automobile Marketplace

Based on "How to be the Alibaba for cars in Southeast Asia" by Joolin Chuah. Published 19 September 2019.

This third exhibit takes platform-driven growth cross-border and cross-industry with automobile marketplace Carro. The same data-driven approach that enables Sayurbox and LOGIVAN to explore adjacencies within their industry has also enabled Carro to crossover verticals and markets.

Even then, the platform-driven growth of Carro remains tied to the car purchasing experience — this is key. Platform growth, especially for a startup, is more efficiently achieved when based on a central experience or core transaction. Of course, as the company gains more resources, there is more room to experiment and add entirely separate experiences, but focus is important (call-back to Chapter 2).

***

The Singapore Grand Prix is just around the corner, and while the F1s have yet to hit the streets, another race in Southeast Asia has long been ongoing and shows no signs of stopping — the race of consumer platforms to dominate the region.

When it comes to Southeast Asia's automobile industry, Carro has further cemented its lead across four markets as it invests into MyTukar. With MyTukar's strong founders, extensive dealership network, and vision for the digital experience of Malaysian car dealerships, Carro saw the opportunity to accelerate the digitization the country's automobile industry, projected to contribute 10% to GDP by 2020.

The Lifetime Value of Hyper-Vertical Platforms

This push into Malaysia is Carro's latest in a string of successful market entries across Singapore, Thailand, and Indonesia. Its growth is not limited to expansion across geographies. Since 2015, the platform has raised more than $100 million, enabling vertical integration across business models from C2C to B2B, and horizontal integration across services from subscription to hire purchases.

Their growth is a localized hybrid of vertically-integrated unicorns like Uxin running multiple lines of business from C2C used car marketplace to B2B auctions and more horizontally-integrated models like Carvana offering full-stack services for car owners. In Southeast Asia, where regional expansion means navigating vastly different markets, plying along multiple lines of business and aiming for the biggest slice of the pie will not be enough to grow sustainably.

Beyond evolving proven models for the region, Carro has geared its platform to be hyper-vertical, where the focus is on maximizing the LTV of every car owner and partner dealer using the platform. From purchase to maintenance, selling, and repeating the cycle, Carro's users never have to leave the platform. With vertical and horizontal integrations covering multiple use cases and catering to both car owners and dealerships, Carro is able to establish its ubiquity in the markets it is in.

Data Fuels Efficiency of Hyper-Vertical Platforms

If hyper-vertical is the vehicle, data is the fuel, enabling Carro to deepen their integration into the automobile industry. In particular, data amassed over transactions across four markets in the region, from car inspection to bidding, coupled with the performance of their financing platform Genie, has made Carro best positioned to underwrite risk. This enables more efficient transactions across their services and lines of business, from insurance to pricing for subscriptions.

Financial Services Ecosystem Play Accelerates Hyper-Vertical Growth

> With data as fuel, financial services is the high-performance engine that accelerates the growth of consumer platforms. With Genie powering our hire purchases and underwriting capabilities, Carro is able to create more stickiness not just with customers but also merchants on the platform — the foundation of a financial services ecosystem for the automobile industry.
>
> — Aaron Tan *Co-founder and CEO of Carro*

As with tech giants like Alibaba and its Ant Financial, the foray into financial services has proven to open up a plethora of opportunities to build on hyper-vertical growth. Ultimately, the ability to make financial transactions tied to core services on the same platform reduces friction for both merchants and customers, making it easier for them to stay onboard and adopt other value-add services.

Unlike the Grand Prix, however, winning the race to dominate the region is not about hitting the fastest time on the finish line, but about staying the longest on the tracks. With a hyper-vertical platform running on an unsurpassed volume of industry data and the engines of a financial services ecosystem, Carro's race car is marking its lead, and has the edge in the laps ahead.

Innovators do not Grow Platforms; they Engineer Platforms for Growth

Takeaways on retention and growth:

(1) *Finding the right industry partnerships (external) and curating the user experience (internal)* improve matching efficiency.
(2) *The goal is to be irreplaceable for the customer.* Achieving a level of irreplaceability does not help retain customers, but also leverages on network effects to acquire more customers, which then deepens the incentive to remain on the platform.
(3) *Retention requires a shift in approach from market-driven growth to platform-driven growth.* This involves developing a self-evolving loop where data can:

   a. open up insights into new services that can be developed to retain existing users and acquire new users.
   b. provide greater flexibility and optionality for customers.
   c. directly power new services.

Chapter Six

Settling in the Reservoir

Innovators build ecosystems that are both focused and flexible.

*"Better learn balance. Balance is key. Balance good karate, karate good.
Everything good. Balance bad, better pack up, go home. Understand?"*
— Mr. Miyagi *The Karate Kid (1984)*

As expeditions become frequented trips, exploration takes on new forms and meaning beyond the initial journey. Scientists and researchers go on these routes to study flora and fauna, among many other things that can be new sources of knowledge. Businesses are set up in outposts and people settle in areas that were once unknown. Reservoirs are built in these settlements to support activities like agriculture. Railroad tracks are laid down to allow for faster transportation across these once inhospitable frontiers.

From the spice trade routes to the Silk Road and the International Space Station, explorers have paved the way for the creation of infrastructure and systems that sustain travelers for the years that followed these initial journeys.

In the same way, the technology platform company, by setting in motion a self-evolving loop to power growth, is opened up to new forms of business beyond the initial core product or service. This expansion into adjacent business lines boosts the acquisition and retention engines already in place. When these business lines are linked together in an ecosystem — in the same way that banks link services through a savings or checking account — it holds the potential to be self-sustaining.

While this playbook is not limited to Southeast Asia, this trajectory offers defensibility amidst the thickening competition. It also offers a way to secure newfound markets in previously uncharted territory. Finally, it holds the potential to chart a clearer path to profitability.

The fourth chapter introduces the Reservoir Principle and strategies for acquisition. The fifth takes off from product-market fit to securing a place in the market and growing into adjacencies. This chapter focuses on the third element of an enduring reservoir — the ecosystem.

These ecosystems are necessarily complex, and involve many layers of operation. However, these products and services are ultimately hinged on a core focus. Counterintuitively, in order for platform businesses to grow effectively and sustainably, they have to settle in their reservoir. It is less a North Star that directs, and more a foundation that defines the company's growth trajectory.

***

The essays in this chapter explore definitions of reservoirs in various industries, how the reservoir principle enables startups to keep up with industry shifts, the opportunity for platforms to start out as ecosystems (as opposed to growing into one), and the startup holy grail of ecosystems: the super app.

Essays in this Chapter

Defining the reservoir. Ecosystems are complex systems linking various products and services, but stem out of a core focus that ultimately defines the reservoir being built, and this is covered in essays (23) to (27).

(23) **The supply chain reservoir.** *Based on "Cross-border logistics scaling Southeast Asia's Export Potential" by Paulo Joquiño Published 23 August 2019.*

(24) **The learning reservoir.** *By Bill Roosman.*

(25) **The gamer reservoir.** *Based on "Southeast Asia stepping up its esports game in 2019" by Teng Jen Ang, Yinglan Tan, and Paulo Joquiño, 8 February 2019. Also published 12 March 2019 on Business Times as "Esports streams into a new chapter."*

(26) **The relationship reservoir.** *Based on "Going social: The changing landscape of ecommerce" by Joolin Chuah and Paulo Joquiño. Published 1 March 2019.*

(27) **The smart access reservoir.** *Based on "What smart access means for the urban organism" by Paulo Joquiño. Published on 1 August 2019.*

(28) **Keeping up with innovation.** Industry shifts present both opportunity and challenge for startups, and the reservoir principle provides a framework for how to keep up. *Based on "Insurtech in SEA: the big pull" by Joolin Chuah and Paulo Joquiño. Published on 22 March 2019.*

(29) **Building ecosystems from square one.** Platform-first fintechs are setting the stage for a new kind of reservoir growth trajectory, one that begins with the ecosystem. *Based on "Platform-first: fintech's next destination" by Samir Chaïbi. Published 9 March 2020.*

(30) **The ecosystem of ecosystems.** The super app model saw great early success in China. Southeast Asia has since sprouted many aspiring super app platforms from horizontal super apps to vertical/industry-specific super apps, but the region has its own unique challenges. *Based on "Super Apps in Southeast Asia," by Yinglan Tan. Published 20 May 2019. Excerpts from the article were published as part of a Straits Times piece, "Uphill battle for South-east Asia's super apps," published 20 May 2019.*

(31) **Building flexibility in a growing ecosystem.** Grab and Gojek have set off the entire discussion in Southeast Asia regarding super app viability in the region, and the rivalry is far from over. *Based on "Grab and Go-Jek must show flexibility to survive" by Yinglan Tan and Paulo Joquiño, as published on Nikkei Asian Review, 11 March 2020.*

(23) The Supply Chain Reservoir

Based on "Cross-border logistics scaling Southeast Asia's Export Potential" by Paulo Joquiño Published 23 August 2019.

Digitalizing logistics, as we have seen in previous essays in this book on the industry, not only requires deep knowledge of the sector but also connections and strong networks. This essay explores how enabling flexibility and optionality in supply chain management with software that links supply chain components can become a reservoir for businesses of all sizes from e-commerce SMEs to multinational brands.

***

Innovation in Logistics Shifting Upstream to Asset-Light, Cross-Border Services

Logistics has emerged as an important vertical for innovation in the Asia Pacific. Startups in the space took a lion's share of Softbank's $100 billion Vision Fund deployment. E-commerce retail fueled this logistics boom, with an increasing mass of transactions and demand for more convenience requiring more efficient warehouse-to-doorstep infrastructure.

Initially, innovations covered low-hanging fruit like the first and last mile delivery space, but it has since crowded and become a price-driven battlefield with thinning margins and consolidation by marketplaces, as with Lazada's heavy investments into logistics. Momentum in innovation is now shifting upstream to more asset-heavy cross-border logistics services like transshipment management.

Given the heavy infrastructure costs associated with providing logistics services, startups cannot afford to build from scratch. Instead, they take an asset-light approach, implementing digital solutions that reduce costs and information asymmetries for companies extending their logistics network across markets.

This momentum towards asset-light, cross-border solutions stems from a new wave of foreign retail and logistics companies looking to pave more inroads for imports into the region's demand-driven economies. This comes on the heels of macroeconomic uncertainties arising in more mature markets, shifting the gravity well of innovation towards Southeast Asia.

Cross-Border Logistics Scaling Southeast Asia's Export Potential

At the same time, this same shift to cross-border logistics also comes from local marketplaces looking to expand within and beyond the region. Motivated by expansion, these online platforms are taking on a regional approach to growth.

There is only so much that can be done within their home markets. True growth means Southeast Asia and beyond. For the merchants on these marketplaces, this means more export opportunities. It also means more options for sources of inputs to boost production of export goods or cheaper sources of goods for resellers.

> "While Southeast Asia is predominantly demand-driven, there is potential for countries like Indonesia and Malaysia to start exporting out. They're exporting to places like the Middle East, going from Indonesia to Turkey, and from Indonesia to the Philippines as well."
>
> *— Junkai Ng, Janio Co-founder and CEO*

One such opportunity lies in cosmetics, especially for halal products, as most cosmetic products have alcohol content. This creates a huge market opportunity for countries like Indonesia to start exporting halal cosmetics. Another is modest fashion, where Indonesia broke into the top 10 biggest spenders and its overall textile shipments forecasted to reach $15 billion this year, thanks to more active participants on global runways.

Dominating the competition to acquire more merchants are the unicorn marketplaces like Bukalapak. Through BukaGlobal, the unicorn is beginning to target the Indonesian diaspora across the Asia Pacific, where there are pockets of demand for Southeast Asian products.

Digitizing Corridors of Growth for Local Marketplaces and Merchants

The challenge for these marketplaces and merchants is setting up the logistics infrastructure to support this expansion. Logistics companies address this by creating corridors of growth for these marketplaces. However, these corridors are not always efficient, transparent, or cost-effective.

With digitization, technology startups in this space can bring the entire supply chain onto one platform. Capabilities of key components along that chain can also be upgraded, from more optimal routes for truck drivers to monitoring the movement of products across multiple vehicle types.

With logistics startups resolving information asymmetries through digital-first tools and ecosystems, these marketplaces are able to build their own pathway of logistics and fulfilment partners. For example, one combination could be bulk freight streamlining, 3PL management, and last mile fulfilment.

Unburdened by what would have been heavy logistics costs, platforms like Zilingo, Blibli, and Zalora are able to focus on utilizing these corridors to grow their seller base, creating more options for the customer and reducing customer and merchant acquisition costs over time.

As local marketplaces and merchants gain more access to markets and suppliers outside of Southeast Asia, exports will play a stronger role in the growth of the region. As Junkai says, "It's only a matter of time."

(24) The Learning Reservoir

By Bill Roosman

The gaps in Southeast Asia's formal K12 education systems are not new, but the growing adoption of internet services in the region is opening doors for edtechs to offer a compelling proposition for students and teachers to change the way they learn and teach. This essay tackles a reservoir built around a K12 student's learning cycle, where the key to building an ecosystem is striking a balance between distribution and monetization.

***

Edtech in Southeast Asia is entering a golden age. Opportunity for tech startups to cash in the sector has reached its inflection point with the convergence of three key factors: (1) a broken K12 general education system, (2) increased spending on the part of parents for learning supplements and after-school classes, and (3) more consumers familiar with ecommerce, digital payments, and other online services.

Combined with the accelerated, forced adoption of online learning due to COVID19 response measures, there is a strong case for an edtech unicorn in Southeast Asia to be the primary provider of standardized, trusted, accessible and localized education to the K-12 population it serves in the region.

Many edtech founders and investors have questioned, argued and pondered upon what this winning model would look like in Southeast Asia. It doesn't matter which entry point you choose; the winner will be one that captures the complete learning cycle of K12 students. In this essay, I share what capturing this learning cycle means in Southeast Asia's emerging markets and how edtechs can think about their go-to market strategies.

Assessing the Knowledge Gaps

Unlike developed markets where the general education system is mature enough to be the primary source of learning for students, the education systems of most emerging markets of Southeast Asia have yet to play this role. Many emerging markets in Southeast Asia show similar structural issues in the education systems:

(1) Low education attainment especially towards tertiary education
(2) Teaching is on par in terms of man-hours but suffers from quality issues especially outside Tier 1 cities

(3) Skills gap arising from a shortage of homegrown talents especially in engineers.

To make up for these gaps, parents have traditionally resorted to subscribing their children to extra classes from a young age. For the wealthier family, children will get one-on-one attention from private home tutors. For the middle class, group tuitions are common and are typically conducted in highly fragmented private tuition centers across the country. These extra classes are geared towards reinforcing concepts taught at school, assisting students with homework, and preparing for upcoming exams.

Over the years, we have seen branded regional tuition centers like English First and Kumon gaining ground in local markets by leveraging on their home brands and the universality of the subjects they specialize in and providing standardized quality teachings. At the same time, unstandardized offline home tutors or small tuition centers continue to take a significant share of the pie, living off the value proposition they provide in terms of trust, accessibility and localization.

However, these supplementary classes remain limited in reach and scope. Rapid internet adoption and increasing familiarity with digital solutions (especially among the student demographic) offer a way not just to fill in the gaps of education systems but also do this at a scale with which offline tuition centers will not be able to compete. This is the opportunity ushering in edtech's "Golden Age" in Southeast Asia. Class is in session for edtechs to make this "Golden Age" happen.

Mastering the Learning Cycle to Strengthen Gaps

The edtech that emerges at the top in the region will be one that captures the complete reinforcing learning cycle of K-12 students. The cycle is as follows (with no specific initial stage):

(1) **Knowledge Gap Assessment:** Students in the region typically leverage on tools or mock exams to access their knowledge gaps.

(2) **Strengthening Knowledge Gaps:** Then they seek learning materials either in the form of video or texts to strengthen those knowledge gaps.

(3) **Practice and Application of Concepts:** As students climb higher in the Blooms Taxonomy hierarchy, they seek avenues to practice questions and apply concepts learned.

(4) **Reinforcement of Concepts:** While live tutoring could step in at any point of this learning cycle as a facilitator in the journey, its true value is realized in reinforcing concepts of students.

Then the cycle repeats.

The beauty of this cycle lies in its openness for multiple entry points into the student's day to day learning behavior. In China and India, we have seen unicorns starting off at various entry points in this learning cycle.

YuanFuDao, for instance, entered the market with question banks (stage 3) and has since then built out other products that complete the cycle. India's Byju entered the market with eLearning content (stage 2), ZuoYeBang with homework solutions (stage 2), GSX Techedu Inc with live tutoring (stage 4), and 17ZuoYe with study tools and analytics (stage 1).

In one way or another, all these unicorns have launched products that capture a larger part of the learning cycle by the time they hit unicorn status.

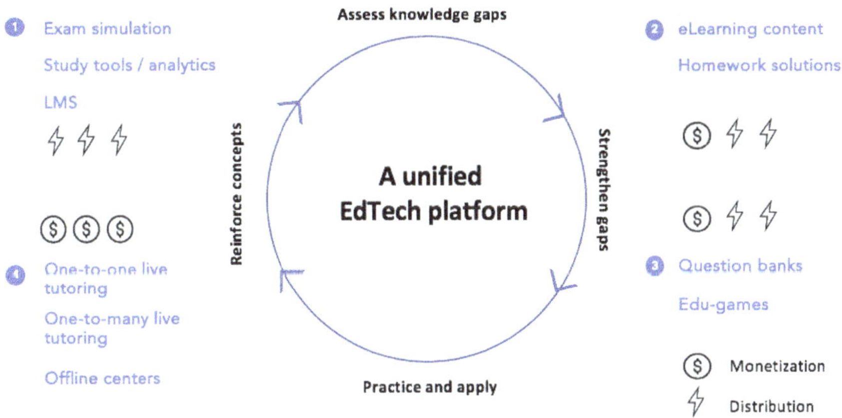

Figure 4. K12 Learning Cycle in 4 Stages Rated According to Distribution and Monetization Capacity. A Unified Edtech Platform Captures this Entire Cycle.

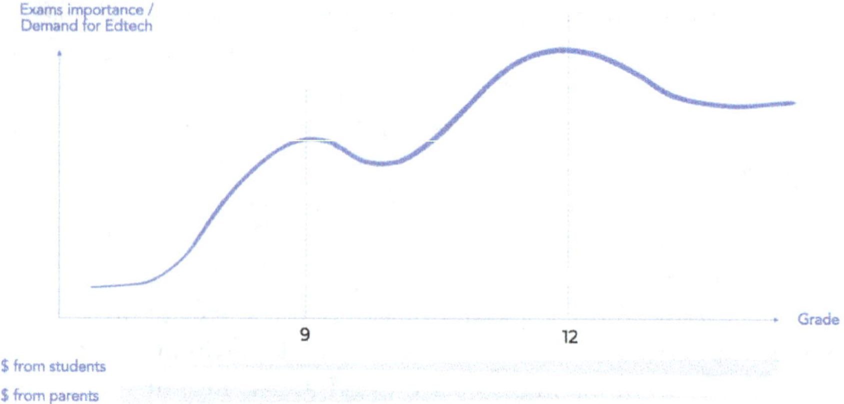

Figure 5.   Unlocking Monetization by Gearing up for Test Prep use Case.

These models also all gear towards test preparation, which reflects the culture and paying habits of the China and India markets. This is similar to Southeast Asia, where test preparation has been key in pulling students towards edtech platforms and unlocking the first out-of-pocket spending.

That said, in Southeast Asia's relatively young edtech market, the challenge facing founders in deciding a point-of-entry into the learning cycle lies between distribution and monetization. At the beginning of the learning cycle (stages 1 to 3) is where mass distribution happens, and monetization kicks in as the student progress towards the end of the cycle (stages 2 to 4).

The general rule of thumb for any edtech player is to be the category leader in one of the stages of a student learning cycle before moving on to the next. The winning model is able to eventually strike the balance in both distribution and monetization, while staying top-of-mind for students for anything education-related. In order to do this, the edtech needs to become a unified edtech platform.

Applying the Unified Edtech Platform Approach to Southeast Asia

With increased ecommerce and digital payment penetration rates in Southeast Asia, the concept of learning online has become more

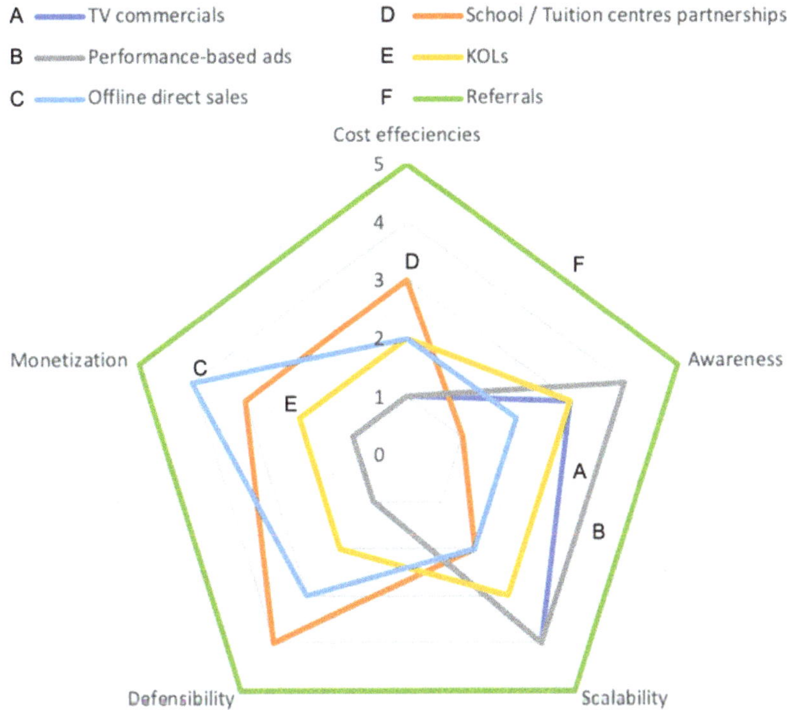

Figure 6. Comparing Go-To Market Strategies for Edtechs in Southeast Asia.

familiar among students and parents in the region. When it comes to gaining awareness, performance-based ads have been effective in reaching students while TV commercials have been effective in generating buzz amongst parents. COVID19 has also certainly driven users to look for these online platforms.

While barriers to adoption have lowered, the trickiest part in Southeast Asia's edtech landscape is monetization. Student behavior has been well-entrenched in going to offline tuition centers or superstar tutors. The key to converting free adoption to sustained out-of-pocket spending is trust, which parents and students place on brands. That means edtechs have to think creatively how to build their brands without draining too much on marketing. Offline direct sales appears to be the most effective in unlocking large out of pocket expenditure of parents, something which Byju in India did successfully. Meanwhile, referrals by an army of satisfied students can be the most effective in owning a recurring share of the student's budget.

Reinforcing Changes in Learning and Teaching

Even with edtech entering a golden age, the traditional K-12 schooling system is here to stay in Southeast Asia. Students will still go to school, be taught a standardized curriculum and undergo a form of assessment to graduate. What will change is the way students learn and the way teachers teach.

As unified edtech platforms gain more adoption in the region, students will spend a substantial amount of after-school learning time on these platforms, and teachers will deepen their integration of platform solutions into their teaching curriculum.

Reinforcing these changes in education will be a matter of developing data-driven feedback loops and scaling a tech layer beyond the limitations of traditional education.

Over time, more customized solutions will emerge from these platforms as both students and teachers become more data-driven in their learning and teaching. Beyond the geographical barriers and human capital limitations posed by traditional K12 schooling systems, especially outside Tier 1 cities, edtech platforms can provide accessibility to learning beyond the four walls of the classroom.

(25) The Gamer Reservoir

Based on "Southeast Asia stepping up its esports game in 2019" by Teng Jen Ang, Yinglan Tan, and Paulo Joquiño, 8 February 2019. Also published 12 March 2019 on Business Times as "Esports streams into a new chapter."

Esports, as with any sport, are defined by their talents. Talents do not only win competitions; they gain massive following, which can then be leverage for sponsorships. Then their success becomes a draw for more enthusiasts to explore an esports career. As the number of esports fans increases, especially in Southeast Asia, technology platforms have an opportunity to support the growth of esports talents. A reservoir in this industry is built around the gamer, as this essay explains.

***

The Platform Play

With institutional backing already in full force, what will enable platforms to win the esports game in Southeast Asia, and eventually scale beyond the region, is the platform play. It is not just about creating a live streaming platform and leveraging partnerships with competitions to drive adoption. The platform play involves consciously integrating what the big leagues are doing right with team development and what streaming platforms are doing well with mass adoption in a conscious effort to scale.

Stage One: Keep Key Talents and Influencers Onboard

The first step is to create a platform that will attract key talents, game publishers, and influencers in the industry.

Twitch did this to great effect for Respawn Entertainment's Apex Legends by drawing in top streamers like Michael 'Shroud' Grzesiek and Tyler 'Ninja' Blevins, who won the platform's first Apex Legends Tournament. With the record-breaking attention this breakout game drew in — 31.73 million hours watched in its first week, knocking out close rival Fortnite (which continues to rule YouTube and younger audiences) by around 18 million hours — the platform hosted the tournament's second run on February 19, 2019.

Key to the success of Apex Legends was the more than 30 hours spent by Twitch's top influencers on the game, even beyond the initial draw of advertising slots. This shows the power of an esports platform to generate adoption by matching key talents and influencers to the right games.

Stage Two: Develop the Talent to Win

With key talent and influencers onboard, the next step is making the platform an environment to develop their skills and community reach through an array of tools, which could involve integrating AI-based features to better monetize esports fans, producing original esports content to raise exposure, or designing reward infrastructures for top streamers.

Aside from player development, what will make the platform competitive long-term is closing the market gap in proper talent management, ranging from addressing early player burnout to furnishing more professional gaming facilities for teams. Partnerships, like the multi-year sponsorship sales deal between Team Liquid and Twitch, can be leveraged to connect the platform to needed infrastructure for players and expose teams internationally. As talents grow and reap in the wins, it becomes easier to draw in more players, sustaining growth on the platform.

Stage Three: Adapting to the Gamer, Games, and Growth

What will seal the deal for esports platforms in Southeast Asia is developing for the Southeast Asian gamer's experience. Infrastructure needed to support services like streaming and payments remain latent across the region, with LTE and 4G speeds plateauing and credit card penetration only at 5% *vis-à-vis* COD predominant in countries like Indonesia and Vietnam. Making game features more accessible will enable more gamers to go pro and compete globally, and this means working with local payment gateways and internet providers to boost platform usability.

Product-market fit also goes beyond the gamer. Fortnite's Southeast Asian launch saw Epic Games successfully introducing sub-region matchmaking. Games entering Southeast Asia are also leveraging on mobile, with the new wave of gaming phones like Razer Black and Xiaomi Black Shark and the mobile gamers projected to be more than 250 million by 2021. What games are being played, how they are being played (localized), and where they are being played (mobile) affect user acquisition and gamer interactions on an esports platform, and working with these dynamics is crucial to scale.

(26) The Relationship Reservoir

Based on "Going social: the changing landscape of ecommerce" by Joolin Chuah and Paulo Joquiňo. Published 1 March 2019.

Just as esports talent are able to garner a huge following online and influence consumption of their following, e-commerce sellers have also emerged to be an influential force in the industry. E-commerce has since evolved to go beyond high profile influencers to tap into agents and sellers are centers of influence. These reservoirs are built on more authentic social relationships rather than discounts and subsidies, which can make a huge difference especially in the rural economy where trust is a key hurdle to driving adoption.

***

The next chapter for e-commerce is going social. The ability to influence consumption en masse by facilitating social interactions and engagements makes social commerce powerful.

Social commerce platforms have already been gaining ground in the e-commerce space. In China, Mogu, Meilishuo, and Pinduoduo have been chipping away at e-commerce giants Alibaba and JD. com's local market share. Core features built into the platform like live video sales, purchase sharing, and group buying accelerate transaction growth.

On the other hand, e-commerce and social media platforms transitioning into social commerce are also making headway. They are able to leverage on an existing user base and battle-tested features that facilitate e-commerce transactions or social interactions. For example, this year Amazon rolled out content and community-based platform Spark in India, and partnered with Snap to create purchase journeys on the platform.

Capitalizing on the E-Commerce Boom in Southeast Asia

In Southeast Asia, there are three key trends powering the shift to social commerce: (1) the growing usage of mobile and social media bringing down the cost of user acquisition, (2) the growth of platforms like Lazada and Tokopedia opening up e-commerce opportunities in the region, and (3) more funding being poured into driving the growth of these big players. With the worldwide social commerce market expected to reach $5.23 billion by 2022, social commerce platforms in the region can capitalize on these three forces.

Social Commerce Platforms Create Influencers

With Southeast Asia's mobile and internet penetration boom widening the exposure of online personalities, influencer marketing has become a go-to approach for e-commerce platforms to support brands and resellers. The problem is that it would not necessarily bring down the cost of customer acquisition. Influencer marketing at scale tends to favor big brands that can capture most of the activity on the platform. This pulls in middlemen like agencies, which not only racks up costs but also distances influencers from consumers.

Social commerce does not go down this path. Instead of getting trapped by the pressure and costs to pull larger and larger influencers, these platforms leverage on the niche sphere of influence their users already have. Instead of following influencers to grow the platform, they set up the platforms so users can become influencers themselves. This way, it is the communities that drive purchases rather than all the burden sitting on the shoulders of the platform.

In the case of Meesho in India, they enable sellers to capitalize on the effectiveness of families and friends as influencers. This lowers the barriers to purchases and increases repeat purchases, with more trusted recommendations and reviews. This also cuts down customer acquisition cost and discount dole-outs.

Winning Customers for the Long-Term with Seamless Consumer Experience

The growth of heavyweight e-commerce platforms in the region have paved the way for platforms to acquire users faster. This means simply building a platform will not be enough to sway customers over and keep them on the platform.

The race now is to develop more seamless consumer experiences. Employing a data strategy can help platforms better understand the breadth of consumer behaviors and preferences and provide the right services and features to increase retention.

For some platforms, this results in horizontal integration into payments or logistics. Line poured in more than $180 million into mobile payments earlier this year, allowing merchants to drive purchases faster using the chat app's already existing social commerce features like multimedia broadcasts, consumer polls, and coupons.

Building a Moat Against Bigger Players by Localizing into Niche Areas

Pouring in cash to create an ecosystem of services and drive transactions in spite of heavy short-term cash burn is a long-term bet not all tech startups can make.

With big e-commerce platforms dipping in the red to cast big costly bets on growth, emerging players in the region have the opportunity to build moats by localizing into niche market segments. For example, placing a special focus on halal cosmetics can secure a considerable portion of the growing market. This specialization can potentially flip the competitive scenario into one with opportunities for partnership with bigger players.

Making Social Commerce Work in Southeast Asia

Shifting to micro- and nano-influencers, developing seamless consumer experiences, and capitalizing on niche market segments are key to making social commerce platforms thrive in Southeast Asia. This next chapter of e-commerce opens up more opportunities for platforms to extend access to online marketplaces deeper into the region.

(27) The Smart Access Reservoir

Based on "What smart access means for the urban organism" by Paulo Joquiño. Published on 1 August 2019.

There is an argument to be made for the most successful software companies being built with a strong hardware foundation. This is most certainly the case for IoT companies driving the smart city vision into reality. In particular, the ubiquity of smart access across industries and use cases opens doors for even more smart city applications, as this essay explains.

***

Each city in Southeast Asia — Singapore, Kuala Lumpur, Manila — is an urban organism living in a unique environment differentiated by culture, infrastructure, and policy. Given the region's disparate urban spaces and needs-based economy, bespoke solutions for individual cities and clients dominate the smart city industry.

However, the trajectory of smart city solutions in the region will be one of convergent evolution. Localized solutions will integrate into unified systems integral to cities across the region — a Smart City OS, as industry players like to call it. And the catalyst for this shift is smart access.

Smart Access as Catalyst for Convergent Evolution of Smart City Solutions

This goes beyond a keyless world. If the city is an organism, its entirety (i.e., borders) and components (i.e., buildings, roads, power grids) are spatially defined by membranes, or surfaces through which other components or organisms make contact. Smart access makes interactions with such contact surfaces seamless, and they do not necessarily deal with doors.

Consider the manhole. Manholes serve as access points for telecommunications companies to maintain their lines. As manhole covers are cast iron, anyone armed with crowbars can open up these covers and damage the lines. Having smart manhole covers can easily save telcos millions of dollars in maintenance costs, and ensure less service disruptions.

The challenge here is that manholes in a city have different owners. This points to the importance of designing and implementing solutions for and with people, the DNA of the urban organism.

"The smart city industry is growing to be $400 billion by 2025, with APAC taking up 42% of this. Smart access can easily take 10 to 20% investment from all of this and the rest will be waste management, data integration, street parking, among others. But smart access forms the core foundation of anything you are trying to build in the city."
— Anthony Chow *Co-founder and CEO, Igloohome*

Ecosystems and Experimentation Drive Smart Access Technology Adoption

If smart access is the foundation for the smart city, what will drive adoption of smart access technology? Two things — ecosystems and experimentation. More accessible APIs allow enterprise and governments to tap into a software ecosystem like Iglooworks. This widens the coverage of smart access solutions. More use cases can be tested and refined. These are opportunities to make existing and untapped data more efficient.

Think of data as oxygen, and these open source platforms as the red blood cells carrying oxygen throughout the rest of the organism. How can more oxygen be delivered to the rest of the organism? For humans, it is exercise. For the smart city, experimentation. This leads to discovering more use cases for data.

Take medicine cabinets, for example. Medicine cabinets are one of the more valuable spaces in the hospital. With keys, which are easily misplaced, it is difficult to track supply. Smart access not only replaces the keys but presents an opportunity to know exactly which nurse has gone to which cabinet at what time to procure which inventory.

The data here not only benefits the hospitals, but also pharmaceutical suppliers and even governments once more hospitals are connected. Data flows better throughout components in the city with more use cases explored. In this way, rather than replacing jobs, smart access solutions enable work to be done smarter.

Survival of the Fittest is All About Integration

The inflection point for smart city solutions is finding model use cases with technology integrations that can be adopted across cities. The challenge is managing the long product development and sales cycles. Startups need a strong runway and network of partners to support growth.

This is where investments and partners come in. While the innovation gravity well bends toward Singapore, increasing support from governments and the private sector are creating pockets of investment and driving adoption in other Southeast Asian cities, as with Sansiri, one of the largest real estate developers in Thailand.

The condition of these urban organisms dictates investment priorities. For example, a city with an ageing population may focus on smart elderly alert systems, or a city beset with waste problems on materials reprocessing or smart packaging. Startups looking to scale from city to city need to stay abreast of development trajectories, and work like enzymes, catalyzing changes from an inside-out approach.

As smart city solutions evolve from custom builds to platforms and complex systems, survival of the fittest is all about integration. This means building systems that can easily cater to different contact surfaces and use cases, from cross-border logistics to street-level parcel delivery.

This evolution begins with smart access.

(28) Keeping up with Innovation

Based on "Insurtech in SEA: the big pull" by Joolin Chuah and Paulo Joquiño. Published on 22 March 2019.

Building a reservoir never happens in a vacuum. Instead, the building of reservoirs is possible for technology platforms precisely because of the rapid changes brought about by digitalization (i.e., everything that happens outside of the reservoir).

Industry shifts inflict some kind of gravity that can make it easier or more challenging for platforms to grow. On one hand, these shifts can open doors for these platforms to expand into new services and new ways of looking at the customer experience. On the other, they can also throw a platform's trajectory into chaos. This essay explores the evolution of insurance platforms and how insurtechs can tap into the reservoir principle to align itself with the new value of insurance.

***

Gravity Shifting towards Insurtechs

Custom-tailored policies, on-demand coverage, fractionalized premiums, and underwriting in a matter of seconds — all these done on a smartphone. The insurtechs behind these innovations have shaken up the insurance industry, and the reaction of an incumbent has been to heavily invest in or acquire an up-and-coming insurtech to boost its technological capabilities. Insurtech deals with an incumbent or its strategic venture arm jumped from 3% in 2014 to 14% in 2016.

With this approach incumbents continue to dominate ownership of the customer relationship, as with AXA's acquisition of Maestro Health last year closing digital gaps in their customer channels. While M&A activity of incumbents will not slow down, the next few years will see the industry's center of gravity shifting towards insurtechs, as more economic pricing strategies, convenient platform services, and technological developments will enable more scalability on the part of insurtechs *vis-à-vis* traditional insurers.

This comes with the evolution of the insurtech value proposition from disruptive technological solution to user-focused value provider. Traditional insurers will have to deal not only with the positioning of these startups but also transforming within to remain competitive long-term. For consumers, the shift will see less "push" strategies for them to use products and services and more environments and communities that will cater to their needs.

Evolution of Insurance Platforms

This shift is evident in both hemispheres. In the West, while investment has slowed down since 2016's record $12.3 billion, startups running on the heels of recent funding rounds are evolving their business models to scale across insurance options, beyond home markets, and along the value chain. Online insurance marketplace LendingTree successively acquired QuoteWizard in 2018 and ValuePenguin in 2019 in an effort to scale their portfolio.

While aggregators are consolidating options through acquisitions, direct-to-consumer providers are entering more markets, like car insurance platform Root Insurance's target of 12 new states in the first half of 2019, fueled by successive Series C and D rounds last year. More insurtechs are going beyond specific verticals and into end-to-end solutions. Berlin-based WeFox raised $125 million in Series B funding to power One, their all-in-one ecosystem for insurers, brokers, and consumers in Europe.

In the East, China is an emerging powerhouse, seeing 20-fold growth in insurtechs, from $1.6 billion in 2013 to $26.5 billion in 2017. The mass adoption of e-commerce and social media platforms paved the way for this growth, opening up the floodgates for insurtechs and online insurance services to reach many uninsured and first-time buyers.

It comes as to no surprise then that the country's tech giants are leading the way, like Tencent with Zhongan, the first insurtech unicorn from Asia, and Alibaba with Taobao Insurance. A key factor that allowed China's insurtech industry to grow rapidly *vis-à-vis* the West is the absence of legacy systems with investments in AI technologies, allowing insurtechs to take off unencumbered by pre-existing infrastructure.

With insurtechs in the West growing across multiple fronts and those in China maturing locally, the industry's compass is pointing towards Southeast Asia as a hotbed for the next generation of insurtechs, and the stars are aligning. Low-insured populations — around 3.4% of GDP versus 6.8% global average last year — as those in the Philippines (1.9%), Cambodia (0.3%), and Vietnam (1.7%), along with high e-commerce and social penetration in the region present an opportunity like China did.

Unlike China however, cost and infrastructure constraints are higher, which will drive innovation as regional players race to capture these markets precisely to develop solutions for these challenges. They will not be alone as China insurtechs (as with many of their peers across industries) like Ping An and ZhongAn, following heavy injections from Softbank, are moving into the region, posing not only competition but collaboration as well. Finally, countries in the region like Malaysia, Singapore, Indonesia, and Thailand have been developing sandboxes for insurtechs to grow in recent years, allowing startups to test out new business models in looser regulatory environments.

The Big Pull

There is clearly a shift in the value of insurance, and the industry compass is pointing towards insurtechs as the North Star. Insurtechs should lead the way, especially in Southeast Asia, where the environment is perfect (challenging enough) for growth. What will it take for insurtechs and even insurers to be competitive in Southeast Asia? The key is to evolve beyond existing business models and cross-pollinate with other sectors, capitalizing on the "pull" effect towards more convenient, usable, and cost-efficient insurance platforms that will attract users, partners, and investors in Southeast Asia. This strategy involves three steps: (1) setting up a distribution platform, (2) developing more personalized value propositions across segments, and (3) leveraging on platform and industry linkages to deliver more value to consumers.

Setup: Platform Entry

When it comes to scaling in insurtech, becoming an accessible distribution platform is key. Considering the region's high e-commerce and social media usage and community-oriented cultures, distribution has a strong case as a value chain gateway for a Southeast Asian insurtech. Globally this has been the case as well. Creating a platform through distribution goes beyond aggregating policy options, providers, and brokers, and this is where differentiation happens. For India and Singapore-based Symbo, going beyond means streamlining services from search to reinsurance; for India-based Acko, it is digitizing end-to-end for transportation-related use cases, like transport-intensive platform services.

Regardless of the approach, upscaling distribution capabilities involves creating a community, and this may require the help of integrating existing platforms, like WeChat in the case of Shuidihuzhu, or tapping into familiar models, like Lifepal's B2B services for SMEs and crowdfunding for retail consumers. Once enough scale has been reached, the next step is to work on consolidation of use cases and verticals, as Ping An did with its One Account. The end goal is to create a low-cost, highly scalable environment where the consumer's insurance needs can be facilitated.

Proposition: Aligning Platform with Shifting Value of Insurance

As the nature of insurance shifts from aggregation/evaluation to prevention, insurance is evolving to become a lifestyle product — usage-based and on-demand. When the product has evolved in terms of delivery (a matter of seconds), channel (online), and nature (flexible, cost-efficient), product-market fit becomes less definitive and more exploratory. With personalization as an approach to PMF, unit costs can be reduced and more economic pricing introduced. Beyond cost and pricing, however, what personalization really brings to the table are value propositions that have an even stronger pull for consumers.

The first step to personalization is leveraging data to understand PMF. Key to this is having an efficient feedback loop that ensures fast time-to-market. Aside from product testing and scaling, data can also be a core part of the business, like data-based eligibility comparisons for financial product matching. With data in the bag, the next step is to align user experience and redefine distribution models with the platform's PMF. The alignment can range from incorporating familiar platform features (e.g., reviews, booking) to coming up with new interactions to ensure consumers realize the value being offered by the platform.

Growth: Leveraging Linkages to Scale Platform Value

Even with the internal gears in motion, the role insurance plays for consumers does not happen in a vacuum — insurance is part of an ecosystem. Leveraging ecosystem linkages scales value (especially data) across niches and creates more touchpoints for consumers. These linkages can happen between insurtechs and other platforms, incumbents, and financial institutions. The proposed rollout of customized insurance products and fractionalized premiums on the Grab app under the Grab-ZhongAn JV illustrates the benefits of cross-platform linkages through unbundling, upselling, and cross-selling policies.

Product segmentation makes insurance more approachable while generating multiple revenue streams spread over time. Aside from platforms, linkages can also be formed with incumbents by speeding up their digital transformation with end-to-end digitization services, which means having to secure the necessary licenses to roll-out these in specific markets. Finally, working with banks and financial institutions rather than disrupting them has been key to the success of insurtechs (and fintechs in general) in the region.

(29) Building Ecosystems from Square One

Based on "Platform-first: fintech's next destination" by Samir Chaïbi. Published 9 March 2020.

So far, we have explored how businesses *become* ecosystems. This essay takes a look at how industry shifts in fintech are ushering in the platform-first fintech — in other words, a business that *is* an ecosystem from the get-go. This vastly compresses the reservoir growth trajectory, and has its benefits for the customer, but also presents its own risks.

***

Fintech in Southeast Asia is entering a new chapter with digital banking. This new chapter brings with it the reduction of costs and dependencies. It also attempts to answer the limitations in services that often cause friction in the growth and adoption of fintech platforms. At Insignia, we have invested in several fintechs across the region and have seen how consumers are looking for ease and convenience from their banks, while at the same time demanding an ever-widening range of offerings from fintechs.

Recently, through TONIK Bank, the region's first fully-fledged digital bank in the region, we are investing in a fintech play that aims to do both. To better understand the undercurrents that brought this model into fruition, this piece runs through the evolution of the fintech model over the past decade and how it has led to TONIK's approach.

Unbundling: Delivering a Better Customer Experience

In 2015, CBInsights published its now famous "Unbundling the Bank" picture showing how newly-minted startups were going after brick-and-mortar banking incumbents in the US and around the world.

The thesis could be summarized simply — a large number of consumers were growing increasingly dissatisfied with the relationships they had with their banks. Taking a page out of the digital native playbook that e-commerce giants were offering to change how consumers shopped, the likes of Venmo, Acorns, Wealthfront, Betterment, LendingClub, Funding Circle, Transferwise, and Lemonade introduced digital products over the last decade in the US and Europe that enabled consumers to engage in cost-efficient, customer-friendly financial services.

Figure 7. Unbundling of a Bank by CBInsights (2015).

In China, the fintech revolution began earlier, in 2004, when AliPay spun out of Taobao to create a payment system catering first to its own needs and over time to millions of external merchants. AliPay rapidly became the payment network of choice, rivalling Visa, Mastercard, and Union Pay domestically.

These fintechs tackled specific banking services better than traditional banks did. While these "single product" approaches disrupted banking activities across the board, they were limited by the small share of the consumer wallet they could win. The increasing competition within each segment also pushed CAC to unsustainable levels. This threatened the economics of startups relying on an already narrow set of revenue streams. It also placed additional burden on users who had to manage multiple apps and optimize among them.

While "unbundling the bank" helped save consumers time and money, consumers did not completely do away with traditional banks. Hungry for growth, fintech players broadened their offerings with one goal in mind — be the figurative and literal consumers' wallet of choice.

Rebundling: Leveraging on Data to Become the "Wallet of Choice"

Acorns' move to open checking accounts for its clients, Wealthfront's breakout into lending, and Sofi's launch of investment and debit accounts are all examples of the more recent rebundling era where fintech startups want their users to consider them as their primary financial services partners.

AliPay followed a similar strategy. With a high frequency, high volume use case in hand and a wealth of consumer data in its commerce payment product, the company launched its Ant Fortune wealth management platform in 2015 with its now famous Yuebao (余额宝) money market fund. At its peak, Yuebao held more than US$250 billion in assets-under-management (AUM) and displaced Fidelity's and JP Morgan's money market funds as the largest in the world. Underpinning its product strategy is Sesame Credit, a behavioral credit scoring system based on the consumers' purchasing history on Alibaba and Alibaba partners' websites.

The ability to extract credit scoring data from user behavior on high frequency use cases (e.g., payment, ride-hailing) to offer broader product suites is the leverage that a number of other consumer-focused startups used to build up their own financial stack including Southeast Asia's Grab and Gojek. The recent US$1.7 billion acquisition of Credit Karma by Intuit confirms the treasure trove that represents customer credit data at scale.

En Route to the Multiverse: A Similar Story in Southeast Asia?

Southeast Asia's fintechs have broadly followed a similar unbundling — rebundling strategy over the past few years from single product to multi-product, multi-usage platforms. Our very own Aspire, Ajaib, and Payfazz broadly reflect this trend.

From lending to one-stop shop

Since 2018, Aspire has been catering to the 39 million underbanked MSMEs across the region. They initially started with lending powered by their in-house risk assessment engine. The accumulation of these loan transactions, as well as key partnerships with local banks, have allowed them to create a comprehensive digital banking product for MSMEs covering deposits, FX, cards and credit, extending the LTV for each customer well beyond loans.

From investment to personal finance

Launched early 2019, Ajaib's online investing platform began with more affordable and accessible stock trading for middle-class Indonesians, especially those with no prior experience and low starting capital. Since its inception, however, the founders have seen the huge potential for the platform to be used for other wealth management services, and have since been developing other features for their growing base of both retail investors and fund managers.

Company	User base	Origin	Destination
蚂蚁金服 ANT FINANCIAL	Taobao/Alibaba merchants and users, banks	Payments	Tech infrastructure geared towards fintech
aspire	Underbanked MSMEs	Lending service	Banking platform for MSMEs
ajaib	Middle class retail investors	Stock trading app	Personal finance platform
PAYFAZZ	Unbanked merchants	Money transfer, Bills, Loans on single app	Multi-software/app ecosystem of services for merchants and unbanked

INSIGNIA VENTURES PARTNERS

Figure 8. How Southeast Asian Fintechs are Creating Ecosystems vs Alipay Model.

From inclusion to diversification

Since 2016, Payfazz's offline agent network approach to banking the unbanked has allowed it to reach more than 30 million unbanked Indonesians. At the core of this approach is the merchant or agent who not only serves as a high frequency touchpoint for the unbanked to access financial services, but also benefits from the services available. In fact, it is these merchants, according to co-founder and CEO Hendra, who drive Payfazz's diversification from a financial inclusion platform into a full stack of services for consumers and businesses alike. In 2018, Payfazz launched Sellfazz, a POS and store management system for their merchants.

What is interesting with how these fintechs are taking the route to financial services platforms are the vehicles that are driving them on this path. For Aspire, it is the many banking needs of underbanked MSMEs. For Ajaib, it is the rising middle class's propensity to invest and convenience with which they can do so. For Payfazz, it is the neighborhood retail stores and restaurants' feedback and network effects.

Platform-First: Surpassing the Limits on Capital and Innovation

As with the unbundling approach, the ongoing rebundling efforts of most consumer-focused fintech startups also has its limits. Taking the example of lending startups, which have been prone to jump on the rebundling bandwagon globally, they have had to rely on (expensive) external sources of funding originated from traditional banks, multi-finance companies, credit hedge funds, etc., constraining their margins, especially as compared to banking incumbents. Going to other ancillary services does not solve their fundamental unit economics problem even if it (theoretically) increases their customer LTV.

On the consumer side, while access to credit is a key pain point for subprime clients in both developed and developing markets, fintech players despite their rebundling efforts have not yet been able to displace traditional banks to access the consumer fintech "holy grail" — checking accounts constraining their ability to finance themselves at lower costs and cross-sell.

In order to break away from these limits, some fintech players are choosing to become fully-fledged banks. In the US, Lending Club acquired Radius Bank, a FDIC-regulated, retail deposit-taking bank, last month. Varo, a digital bank that was relying on third party licensed community banks to acquire depositors, also announced that it became the first fintech in the US to obtain a retail bank charter. In both cases, a cheaper and more stable access to capital as well as the ability to cross-sell and innovate without relying on partners were cited as key decision factors.

The past decade also saw fintechs going platform-first, redefining the bank as a store of value holder. Starting with checking accounts or better yet market-leading savings accounts, neobanks licensed to take retail deposits such as N26, Chime, NuBank, and Monzo catered to different segments of the population from mass-affluent travellers (Revolut/Niyo) to SMEs (Atom/Qonto).

This platform-first approach generates better unit economics than the single-product approach by drastically reducing cost of capital. It also created enough margin to release products covering liabilities aside from pure asset-focused products, catering to a wider range of customer needs.

Fintech approach	Unit Economics	Strength	Weakness
Unbundling	High CAC LTV limited to product	Focused (quicker to launch)	Limited wallet share, either low margin or low frequency
Rebundling	Short term CAC > LTV Long term CAC < LTV	User-driven growth (tied to high frequency use cases)	High cost of capital Innovation constrained by 3rd party and regulation (no access to consumers' main accounts)
Platform-first	Short term CAC > LTV Long term CAC < LTV	Access to consumers' main accounts Low cost of capital	Short-term licensing efforts Long-term capital requirements

Figure 9.   Comparing the Different Fintech Approaches.

Embracing the Platform-First Approach in Southeast Asia

In Southeast Asia, TONIK Bank is the first to embrace this platform-first approach. Based in the Philippines, as the first stand-alone, fully-licensed neobank in the country, the bank will cater to retail consumers across the entire credit spectrum from prime to unbanked segments of the population.

While there has been a lot of coverage recently on Singapore's efforts to open up the local retail and wholesale banking market to new players, the Philippines was the first country to pull the trigger on the neobank model given how much pent-up demand exists locally.

There are indeed close to one million mass-affluent households in the country frustrated by their experience with brick-and-mortar local banks (e.g., slow and analog processing, high fees). More importantly, close to 20 million households are currently underbanked or unbanked. For the latter, the frustration over the years manifests in their unsustainable financial situation. Many of them turn to local loan sharks and pawn shops as their only sources of access to credit. TONIK will be offering both segments of the population a clearly differentiated proposition on both financing and deposit products.

(30) The Ecosystem of Ecosystems

Based on "Super Apps in Southeast Asia," by Yinglan Tan and Allen Chng. Published 20 May 2019. Excerpts from the article were published as part of a Straits Times piece, "Uphill battle for South-east Asia's super apps," published 20 May 2019.

The super app has evolved into a holy grail in the technology platform space, in the same way that unicorn-hood has for tech startups in general.

In essence, these super apps demonstrate the reservoir principle in action — from acquisition through high frequency verticals to higher margin adjacencies and monetization strategies across an entire ecosystem of products and services.

This essay traces the evolution of the super app play — how it took off in China and has evolved in Singapore and Southeast Asia.

***

Super apps will definitely have a future in Southeast Asia. In fact, we are already seeing different startups extending a multitude of services on one single platform (e.g., Payfazz, Carro), albeit using a different approach from Gojek or Grab.

Meituan-Dianping and WeChat started in China with group buying and messaging services, both being high usage frequency mass services. They expanded quickly into super apps because of several key factors. Emerging markets, like Indonesia and Vietnam, that share similar traits with China would be the perfect breeding ground for such apps in the region.

Super App Growth in China versus the US

Internet penetration in China was undeveloped in the early 2010s. With the first launch of the iPhone and subsequent availability of cheaper Chinese phone brands, most of the population skipped the desktop era and their first access to online services was through the smartphone. This created a market of emerging middle-income consumers who were mobile-first.

The result of the undeveloped internet ecosystem was that many consumer services such as leisure and entertainment, health and beauty, and bill payments were largely offline. There was pent up consumer demand for such services to move online. Hence, the evolution of super apps was a natural result of Meituan-Dianping and WeChat moving into adjacent consumer services.

Unlike China, the West already had a developed internet ecosystem when the smartphone era started with the launch of the first iPhone. As such, consumers were already accessing online services through multiple providers primarily through desktop. Examples of this would include e-commerce (i.e., eBay and Amazon), payments (i.e., PayPal), travel (i.e., bookings.com), and the list continues. With the transition into the mobile era, each competing service had their own standalone app.

In addition, the move into super apps was necessitated by a need for Chinese tech platforms to monetize through a transaction-based business model (i.e., earning commissions from transactions facilitated through the platform). In the US, however, the advertisement-based business model was the primary monetization model for many tech platforms like Facebook and Google.

With the exception of Baidu, business models for major technology platforms in China were very different from their comparables in the US. The relatively lower consumer spending power in China meant that monetization through advertisements were less viable. The only way for technology platforms to monetize was through a transaction-based model where they expanded into multiple verticals and took a commission from every transaction they facilitated through the platform.

The growth of super apps was aided in part by the concept of privacy and personal data protection among Chinese consumers, and hence, the level of data collection and usage they were willing to hand over to developers. Chinese consumers are most willing to sacrifice privacy with convenience — 94% of Chinese consumers were willing to let businesses share or reuse their personal data. This lies in stark contrast to the West where tightening privacy requirements and the Cambridge Analytica scandal have shaped an environment where consumers demand control over their own privacy and information that they were willing to share.

The widespread adoption of WeChat in China was propelled by the social context of sending money based on the established tradition behind sending red packets. With the adoption of a mobile wallet on the primary messaging platform used across China, it paved the way for WeChat to layer other e-commerce offerings and services on its platform.

In the West however, social and commerce do not mix, at least not to the same degree of success seen in China. Amazon remains focused on expanding its e-commerce offerings, including groceries, while Facebook's Marketplace has seen limited success and it has yet to integrate financial and payments services through its platform.

Super Apps in Singapore

Super apps start by providing a high usage frequency basic service before increasing user stickiness by layering other adjacent services. The basic services are the core product of the platform and serve as the entry point to acquire users and build important data. However, it is difficult to monetize such services, including mobile messaging and ride-hailing, due to the razor thin margins. Thus, super apps require massive scale in order for the unit economics to work. Given the small market size in Singapore, super apps here have to begin with a large vertical.

Singapore is a highly competitive market with sophisticated users who can easily switch loyalties if a particular platform is able to provide more value. The ecosystem here is diverse with multiple competitors within each vertical. For example, besides GrabPay, every other major bank has their own digital payments app. In food delivery, there is GrabFood, Deliveroo, and Foodpanda. Within the shopping deal discovery space, there is ShopBack, Burpple, Entertainer, Chope, and others.

Thus, increasing user stickiness and retention is key. This includes strategies such as Grab's newly-introduced subscription plans which bundle discount plans and incentivize users to return to the app, maximizing the value of the discounts.

Mobile payments in Singapore have been around for quite a while but they have struggled to proliferate. This is due to the well-developed banking infrastructure existing in Singapore. Consumers are accustomed to using physical cash and cheques, supported by the convenience of using easily accessible credit cards and ATMs. The success of super apps in Singapore depends on whether they can educate consumers and encourage a shift in consumer habits.

Southeast Asia at an Inflection Point

Southeast Asia is at an inflection point where the combination of a rising middle income group across countries like Indonesia and Vietnam, and increasing mobile penetration make for perfect breeding ground. There is an opportunity to tap into a new customer base of mobile first and unbanked consumers who were previously inaccessible to the traditional offline incumbents. This represents a huge addressable market for the first super app that will use technology to solve entrenched problems posed by the existing infrastructure and provide the best services to consumers.

The Super App Play: Key Verticals + Data

The super app playbook is to start with a high usage frequency core product and move into adjacent services, attracting new customers and increasing the time existing users spend on the app. This progression further entrenches users into the ecosystem and makes it hard for them to move. In the early 2010s, China witnessed the war between group-buying websites where multiple competitors eventually consolidated into the O2O consumer services giant, Meituan-Dianping. This is essentially a winner-takes-all-market — the first competitor to expand into a core range of key verticals can build a moat against competitors.

Steep discount wars are unsustainable in the long run as they push thin margin services into negative territory. Before they move away from discounts, companies must ensure users can extract similar value from the platform and stay entrenched in the ecosystem. Margins of the core services are likely to remain paper thin but the key lies in how data around high frequency daily transactions can be utilized to learn about users and recommend higher margin services such as financial and insurance products.

Hyper-Vertical Super Apps

While current super apps in the region (Grab and Gojek) are mass horizontal platforms across verticals from ride-hailing to logistics and O2O services, future super app platforms would be hyper-vertical. These platforms solve entrenched inefficiencies in a specific vertical and innovate on end-to-end solutions to service customers throughout the entire customer lifecycle. For example, Carro started as a used car marketplace to help car buyers make more informed purchase decisions before expanding into after sales support (roadside assistance), and financing and insurance (Genie Financial Services). It recently launched car subscription plans to service a separate set of customers — short-term car owners.

With a 73% unbanked population in Southeast Asia, there is a huge opportunity to bring financial services beyond just mobile wallets and bill payments. This is especially for the emerging middle-class populations in third- and fourth-tier cities where trust is a critical factor. Traditional financial institutions lack distribution here and transactions remain hyperlocal and mainly offline. Companies like Payfazz in Indonesia utilize a network of offline agents (i.e., local resellers and mom-and-pop stores) to overcome these issues. Starting from high frequency transactions like bill payments and money transfers, these companies move into different financial products like unsecured loans, insurance products, and investment plans, and evolve to become a financial super app — the next digital bank in Southeast Asia.

Pitfalls on the Road to Super App-Dom

The biggest danger for companies is to dilute focus away from their original core product. It is the DNA of the company and the quality of this core product should never be compromised in the midst of the company's expansion, especially when barriers to entry are low and it is easy for users to switch between apps. Although WeChat has morphed into a super app today, it has never deviated away from its core as a mobile messaging app and social network. WeChat has always refrained from introducing advertisements to the platform and has consistently focused on ecosystem development (mini-programs), user experience, and core social network features.

Another great danger lies in misjudging the market and expanding into the wrong vertical. The natural evolution of a super app should follow a systematic expansion into adjacent verticals based on trends and user behaviors. For example, consumers were already using Meituan's group-buying platform when they were dining out. Meituan subsequently moved into food delivery so that it could capture the remaining scenario when consumers decide to takeaway.

Similarly, Gojek launched food delivery (Go-food) and on-demand parcel delivery (Go-send) services. This was a natural expansion given that users were already booking ojeks (motorcycle taxis, a common form of transport used in Indonesia) to deliver food or send parcels.

Conversely, an expansion into the wrong vertical would waste resources and fail to increase user stickiness when it does not leverage on existing user behaviors.

(31) Building Flexibility in a Growing Ecosystem

Based on "Grab and Go-Jek must show flexibility to survive" by Yinglan Tan and Paulo Joquiño, as published on Nikkei Asian Review, 11 March 2020.

The most prominent tech companies gunning for super app-dom are Grab and Gojek. A comparison between the trajectories of these companies shows how building an ecosystem can be approached from multiple angles. Regardless of the approach, it is important for the business to nail down market entry and initial acquisition, and have the flexibility to shift sights to be sustainable in the long run.

What this means for the ecosystem is that while having a singular focus is important, the composition of the ecosystem will inevitably change. The services that help a platform build its user base may not be profitable in the long-run, and so other revenue streams need to take center-stage as the company grows.

This is why building a reservoir to support an ecosystem of products and services is all the more ideal for a platform. It creates optionality for the business as it grows and competes in a region like Southeast Asia, where the service that wins in one market may not be the best approach in another.

***

The headlines often dub Grab and Gojek as the rivals locked in Southeast Asia's super app race. While neither have yet reached the level of ubiquity Tencent's WeChat has in China, both demonstrated the power of entering the right market early on and outlined equally compelling growth strategies for technology startups in the region.

The Final Lap?

Recently, the super app race has entered a new chapter. Tech unicorns are under pressure to show profitability, and the growth-at-all-costs strategy is rearing its ugly head in light of the recent global outbreak. In response, both contenders are adjusting their trajectory to changing investor expectations and user behaviors.

Grab is securing its position into financial services (i.e., microinsurance, digital banking bid) and setting up food delivery as its poster boy for profitability. On the other hand, Gojek has been cutting down on its business lines to the ones critical to landing in other markets, a campaign that it began in earnest last year.

It remains to be seen whether this is the final lap in a race that began with Uber's exit from the region in 2018, as both platforms continue to break ground in new verticals and markets, albeit more cautiously.

The Rise and Fall of Ride-Hailing Economics

This race all began with ride-hailing. Ride-hailing was a key service to drive the technology market in the region, as it brought users onto a technology platform in an unprecedented way.

It was a high-frequency activity and met a compelling market need (i.e., traffic with a lack of mass transport options in urban areas). Back then, venture-backed startups could afford to set aside the high costs of operation as long as it allowed them to build the user base they needed to pull in more cash to grow bigger. With this confidence, companies like Uber landed beachheads in the region.

The entry of more players into the market, like EasyTaxi in Vietnam, weighed down on the already low margins of the business as the market became locked in a cash and subsidy-driven battle (as is still the case). Regardless if these platforms won or lost, it was clear that the once blue ocean of opportunity was reddening with the thinning margins. Players still in the race realized that ride-hailing services cannot be the long-term play for the business.

Gojek played to their strengths from the beginning and focused on a motorbike ecosystem of services, rather than cars or ride-hailing per se. Grab optimized matching efficiency and rule setting on their platform, while at the same time experimented with other services, eventually hitting gold with food delivery.

The End of Ride-Hailing?

While Grab and Gojek started out focusing on mobility, ride-hailing continues to play significant, though different, roles for both ecosystems.

Though Grab looks to food delivery and financial services as key drivers to profitability, ride-hailing remains a substantial moat and retention point for its users, given their competition. For Gojek, ride-hailing is but one in an array of services they have been entering markets with since last year, having focused on building an ecosystem around motorbikes early on in Indonesia.

Ride-hailing seems to have taken a backseat in the playbook, but its role as the key jump-off point in terms of business and user experience means it cannot be simply taken out of the equation. Even though competition continues to flood the space, both platforms have established near-indelible brand equity and leadership with the service in the region, and that bears significant value.

Verticals in the Driver Seat

Though ride-hailing was foundational to bringing in users and generating retention for both Grab and Gojek, the difficult economics of ride-hailing and the shift to a more sustainable bottom-line requires a change in vertical focus. Given their different approaches to growth, the verticals they will focus on will be different as well.

Grab's early rapid expansion means that the key verticals for the platform will be those that will bring better unit economics and profitability to sustain this scale.

For Gojek, as they have only recently gone into regional expansion, their focus will be more on the verticals that will establish a strategic presence in each market, while at the same time maintaining their leadership in homecourt.

A Good Beginning is Half the Journey

What founders of technology platforms can take away from the super app race is the need for a strategy to achieve self-sustaining value extraction. In other words, a plan for users to stay engaged on the platform for the long-term.

One can focus on a particular vertical and extend into the various use cases around it to secure more long-term users, or focus on rapidly expanding a particular service then leveraging on the accumulated user base to move into more high value verticals.

Regardless of the approach, it is important for a technology platform to start the journey right. Tech startups need persistence and focus to pursue a singular vertical or market early on. If the market does not turn out to be "right" or sustainable later on, these companies should also have the flexibility to make strategic pivots.

Innovators Build Ecosystems that are Both Focused and Flexible

Takeaways on building ecosystems and the reservoir principle:

(1) *Ecosystems are complex but hinge on a singular focus* that defines the reservoir being built.
(2) *Building reservoirs enables flexibility amid industry shifts.*
(3) *Startups can start out as ecosystems from the get-go,* which can be potentially more cost-effective for customers, but does not come without its own risks, which range from the potential regulatory "backlash" (i.e., a response to a completely different system of doing things) to long-term capital costs.
(4) *No matter the approach, an ecosystem must be built with focus and flexibility in mind.*

Chapter Seven

Unlocking the Treasure Chests

Innovators do not raise money; they grow the company so the money finds them.

"It's obvious that you have to plan for a major life event like a launch. You can't just wing it. What's less obvious, perhaps, is that it makes sense to come up with an equally detailed plan for how to adapt afterward."
— Col. Chris Hadfield Astronaut,
from *An Astronaut's Guide to Life on Earth*

Explorers prepare a lot to face unfamiliar environments. Mountain climbers undergo a lot of endurance training in order to hold out in the high altitudes. Astronauts train for at least two years of basic training before ever having the chance to step foot in a spacecraft. South Pole pioneer Amundsen sharpened dog-skiing skills from living with the Eskimos.

Aside from training and gaining skills, explorers often have backers (or savings) to spend on resources for the journey. Especially for the pioneering expeditions, it is impossible to plan perfectly for how much resources will be needed. The most similar expeditions in the past are used as benchmarks, but the successful explorers make sure to have room for the unexpected.

This combination of becoming "fit" and "fueled up" for the journey does not assure success, but reduces the risk of failure borne solely by the explorer.

Startups also become fit and fuel up for growth through fundraising. These fundraising rounds dominate the headlines of startup publications, as they signify a certain milestone that has been achieved and/or plans of the company to double down on growth. At the same time, fundraising headlines also open up the discussion on the fitness of a startup to venture further.

***

Startups are often fueled by venture capital firms. Venture capital investments are often made on the general presumption that the company is well-positioned to multiply the dollars put in by investors. This belief in the possibility of reaping exponential returns come from the benchmarks set by tech companies to rapidly scale and massively impact millions of people. By investing an X amount to develop software program, that X could become 100X or a 1000X if that program becomes a household necessity across the world — and that is a big "if."

And not all companies are suited to take every kind of fuel. Venture capital in particular is like jet fuel that propels companies into space at high speeds of thousands of kilometers per hour. In the tank of the wrong business model, the company could explode. At the same time, venture fuel is not the only fuel out there, though it is the preferred fuel of choice for startups simply because startups aim to grow fast.

Even with venture capital rocket fuel, because of a combination of factors, from the startup's tenuous position itself to changes in the market, only a small percentage of startup investments eventually make it into space and land on the moon. This is not to say that the business inevitably closes shop, but that like a startup "Apollo 13", the moon landing had to be aborted.

***

The startup investment landscape in Southeast Asia is not as populated as Hangzhou, or as minted as Sand Hill Road, but thanks to the region's potential uncovered by early investors, more and more are looking for these "fund-making" startups to back.

However, this rise in Southeast Asia's startup investments also comes at a pivotal point for the global landscape as well. As one of the essays in the first chapter described, a slew of IPOs that punched below expectations and aborted exits have shifted investor confidence towards the "fitness" of the business model and the founders rather than "fuel capacity" (i.e., how much money they can attract).

Being able to pack in a large fuel tank does not necessarily mean that the business is "fit" to use it. This is not to say as well that the mechanics of venture capital investments are becoming obsolete. The nature of investing in startups is tied to the odds that startups face and the kind of impact founders (presumably) want to have. The odds are stacked against these ventures because — in a word — they are new and the kind of impact startup founders want to achieve is on an exponential scale relative to their starting point.

***

This chapter explores startup fundraising through various lens. It argues for a fundraising dynamic where fit companies are fueling up rather than companies fueling up to be fit.

Essays in this Chapter

(32) **Through the lens of a venture capitalist.** Venture capitalists have a variety of philosophies when it comes to funding startups and approaches when it comes to managing a portfolio. This is one out of many. *By Paulo Joquiño, based on excerpts from interviews featured on 7.5 degrees, TFA Geeks (Published 3 June 2020), and Business Times (Published 21 March 2020)*

(33) **Through the lens of LP–GP relationships.** The relationships between VC fund managers and their limited partners in Southeast Asia are evolving. *Based on "From betting on the future*

to charting its course: venture building with LPs" by Yinglan Tan and Paulo Joquiňo. Published on 13 December 2019. Also published on informaconnect 5 December 2019.

(34) **Through the lens of corporate venture.** There are a lot of ways that startups and corporates can help each other out, but these partnerships thread a thin line of balancing interests. *Based on "Corporate venture capital landscape in Singapore" by Yinglan Tan and Allen Chng. Published 29 March 2019. Excerpts appeared on Business Times.*

(35) **Through the lens of unicorns.** Unicorn-hood is coveted but becoming a unicorn is less about reaping the rewards of billion-dollar valuation and more about facing the harsh realities of growth. *Based on "Demystifying Southeast Asia's tech unicorns" by Paulo Joquiňo. Published 18 November 2019. Excerpts published on Nikkei Asian Review.*

(36) **Through the lens of a crisis.** Crises change the game for fundraising, and bring companies and investors back to basics. *Based on "Prudence and Perseverance" by Paulo Joquiňo. Published on 20 March 2020.*

(32) Through the Lens of a Venture Capitalist

By Paulo Joquiňo, based on excerpts from interviews featured on 7.5 degrees, TFA Geeks (Published 3 June 2020), and Business Times (Published 21 March 2020).

As Southeast Asia has been relatively late to the startup boom, compared to neighbors China and India, the region has the advantage of attracting talent that has seen several market cycles in these more mature ecosystems. This extends to the venture capital profession, with many seasoned GPs either "returnee" investors from the US or China or ex-founders who landed successful exits.

The venture capitalist (VC) industry in the region has only reached its inflection point, with early funds starting to scale operations and more funds being set up to bridge the varied interests of capital from outside markets or traditional spaces to the growing supply of founders and companies. Even with belts tightening in these current global macro conditions, this trajectory will see more outside investment talent gain interest in the space, especially in the long-term. It is a matter now of how GPs will find and grow the right talent for their firms.

While the kind of talent VCs look for intersects with corporates and family offices, the VC environment is still far different from a professional standpoint. Thus, it is not necessarily a tug-of-war over the best investment professionals. The draw for many to venture capital, and arguably what sets this profession apart from an investment perspective, is the opportunity to truly work with companies early on and be a part of their story.

When it comes to tapping into the opportunities in Southeast Asia and working with startups in the region, VCs have a variety of philosophies and approaches. This piece tackles one view in particular on what makes great companies and investor-founders relationships work.

***

A Matter of Conviction

Venture capitalists need conviction. It is difficult to make high stakes, high-risk decisions without it, just as it would have been difficult for early navigators back then without the stars guiding their way.

For Yinglan, founding Insignia Ventures Partners back in 2017 was a matter of following through with a conviction in Southeast Asia.

This conviction comes from a career spent participating in the region's startup ecosystem, which he often compares to roles on the football field. "My time in government was akin to being a referee laying down the rules and making sure they were followed. Then my tenure at Sequoia was like being a coach guiding founders. With Insignia I've gone into the pitch with a team committed to playing side-by-side with startup founders in the field of Southeast Asia's technology market."

It is a confluence of venturing out to make something for himself, and giving something back to the region. "I always thought of creating a firm from which I would be able to see personal returns, and at the same time, one which is dedicated to helping Southeast Asian founders build companies which stand the test of time."

Since the start of his career, the direction of the ball may have changed several times, and will continue to change, but the goalposts remain unmoving. "Insignia calls Southeast Asia home and the future, and it's a future that wakes me up every morning."

Riding the Waves of Innovation

How this conviction and motivation translates into investment decisions is something often asked from investors — "What do you look for?"

"In a fragmented region like Southeast Asia, where local industries have long-standing inefficiencies, platform companies are best positioned to bridge these gaps digitally and create impact while remaining asset-light and agile." This focus on platform companies originates from his time spent leading Sequoia Capital investments in Asia, including Tokopedia, Gojek, Carousell, Appier, Pinkoi, and 99.co.

Yinglan explains why platform companies are highly attractive. "On the surface level, platform companies optimize matching between demand and supply. But through data-driven growth on top of a solid user base, these platform companies have the capacity to create entire ecosystems of products and services, and this is the part that gets investors truly excited. Gojek for example initially began connecting people to ojeks for ride-hailing, but that has since evolved to a whole gamut of services from food delivery to even video-on-demand."

"Being able to create and monetize an ecosystem does not only result in scale but can also lead to sustainability for the business. That platform-to-ecosystem growth trajectory, driven by unstoppable founders and A-teams, makes platform companies enduring, like Alibaba, Netflix, and Airbnb," he continues.

His time at Sequoia was an epiphany. He saw the emergence of platform companies in the region, from horizontal marketplaces to vertical-specific platforms and enablers. Setting up Insignia Ventures in 2017 placed him right at the cusp of a new of wave of companies emerging at the heels of marketplaces like Gojek and Tokopedia. "It's what I like to call the 'third wave' of technology companies in Southeast Asia. We began looking for founders who are unstoppable in their quest to reimagine technology adoption in the region."

"We see ourselves as counter-cyclical investors in the ecosystem. For example, in times of crisis like these, we see the opportunity to make more investments. That said, this opportunity is also a call to be more selective and thorough with our analysis. Ultimately, regardless of the season, it is our goal to build great companies in the region, and in times like these, that means seeing things differently and perhaps taking the road less travelled."

Insignia has since raised two funds, which represents a "doubling down" on the region's waves of innovation. "Rather than a progression from one market to another or one industry to another, the difference between Fund I and Fund II is a progression through time. Southeast Asia is a rapidly changing region. When we started back in 2017, we were focused on how new ventures were coming up to support marketplaces that had dominated the region's internet economy."

"Now we are seeing a myriad of new areas being opened up to digitalization, including more secular sectors like healthcare and education and largely untapped markets like the rural economy. We aim to capture the continuing evolution of Southeast Asia's internet economy, while also doubling down on the evolution of our existing portfolio's businesses."

Understanding Unstoppable

Apart from looking at the market and waves of innovation, Yinglan also pays close attention to the founder. When asked what kind of founders he looks for to invest in, Yinglan always distils his answer into a single word: "unstoppable."

"Unstoppable" is best captured in the age-old fable of the Turtle and the Hare. The eager hare starts the race ahead, but the persistent turtle wins in the end. Unstoppable founders are neither hare nor turtle. Instead, they translate the early-stage eagerness into long-term persistence.

Unstoppable founders are sustained by an obsession that keeps them on track. It is not an obsession that clouds judgment, but clarifies and reflects in their work ethic and business decisions. "If you had gone to Singapore's Blk71 a few years back, you would have seen the founders of Carousell hard at work, and I daresay that has played a role in where they are today. We back founders and teams who will always choose to be the company that has the greatest impact in the market and have the mettle to commit to that choice."

The race to have the greatest impact in the market is shaped by a vision the founders have for the region's future, five, 10, and even 20 years down the road. Southeast Asia has been through several waves of innovation over the past decade, from marketplaces to enablers to more vertical-specific technology platforms. There are more to come, and the founders Yinglan looks for are already riding the incoming waves.

Even though the unstoppable founder can be game-changing for a market, it has become critical to find founder-market fit as well, especially in secular sectors or industries where connections and expertise can boost one's position in the pack.

"One of the more critical things we look for is a founder-market fit — a market that is on a great trajectory for growth and unstoppable founders equipped and hungry to build a fast-growing business in that market. We've invested in Sayurbox, an agritech cofounded by Amanda Susanti, a former farm owner who became a founder to solve inefficiencies in the fresh produce supply chain. We've also invested in logistics startups like Janio and Shipper with years of experience and connections in their founding team."

"That said, the founder-market fit isn't just about having experience or expertise. Counterintuitively, a better fit to tackle problems in the market can be found by having a fish-out-of-water perspective. Sometimes the founders can have a compelling, non-obvious view on what the market needs or more importantly, what it can be in the future, that garners our support."

Fostering Strong Investor–Founder Relationships

Apart from finding unstoppable founders and great companies to invest in, VCs are also involved in portfolio management. This has become a point of differentiation across firms, and effective portfolio management is ultimately built on strong investor–founder relationships.

A strong investor–founder relationship is built on trust. This kind of trust cannot be generated with cookbook precision nor can it be manufactured overnight. It is the invaluable fruit of consistency and results cultivated over time, inside and outside of the boardroom. Nevertheless, there are some key ingredients that are needed for a GP to be valuable as an investor and board member:

(1) pace
(2) market sensitivity
(3) founder–investor fit.

Founder–investor fit is all about matching the GP skills with what the founder needs at a particular stage in their growth. This can range from optimizing decks for fundraising to making critical executive and country-level hires as the company expands. This is not a fixed constant determined at the beginning of the relationship; it is a function that has to keep evolving, as the cap table expands and the company grows.

In order to keep up with this founder–investor fit, GPs need to be in touch with the market just as much, and ideally even more, than the founder. This market sensitivity is a mindset rather than any particular action. Founders highly value market connections and information, but these results are themselves fruits of relationships built within the industry and the habit of staying in touch with the latest market developments.

Finally, even with the founder–investor fit and market sensitivity, it would be difficult to have a quality relationship on the board if GPs are not keeping pace with the founder on a regular basis. Even before board meetings, the best GPs already have an idea of where the founder is and where the company is headed to ask deeper questions and push forward valuable insights during the meeting itself. Ideally, this culture of "running with" the founder 24/7, in and out of the boardroom fosters more valuable collaboration.

The ability to resolve conflict is ultimately rooted in the kind of relationship the GP has with the CEO. A weak relationship is easily eroded by tension and conflicting views, leading to misalignment. A strong relationship fosters objectivity and turns tension into productive decisions. If founders know that you are backing them the whole mile, they will be more likely to trust your input and be open to your recommendations.

In this dynamic, getting a board seat should be more an effect rather than a cause of a strong relationship with the founder. Yinglan shares, "I often tell my team that being on the board of a company is earned. It's not a privilege but an opportunity and responsibility to influence the direction of these organizations. The top venture capitalists are those who have been able to grow and position themselves as people who founders would want to have on their board, rather than expecting founders to hand a board seat in a deal."

From the founder's perspective, there is more to capital than fundraising, and one significant and sometimes overlooked piece of that is who gets on their board. "Having the top venture capitalists as board members not only brings more insight and expertise to the table but also has network effects in terms of fundraising and even business sales down the road."

"Because the VC industry and startup investment community operate on trust and reputation, the top VCs have the connections to unlock doors to more capital and revenue streams that would otherwise have been difficult to access alone." This is something that can make a huge difference especially in times of crisis.

For Yinglan, digital technology (and data) has an important role to play in facilitating founder–investor relationships. "While the input of an investor depends on the output the founder and the company needs, what I've found is that technology can be invaluable in expediting many of the processes in between, from facilitating meetings, recording information, and monitoring cap tables and talent pipelines. Bringing technology in the equation ideally saves on time and effort across the board, especially as the firm grows and there are more moving pieces all working to support the founders."

Being able to effectively meet the needs of the portfolio is a constant learning experience. "One piece of advice I give, even to my team, is to always keep learning. The crisis we are experiencing these days shows us that things can turn 180 degrees on the fly, and at times it can be impossible to fully prepare for what is ahead. Instead, it is more practical to learn how to be flexible and resilient amidst uncertainty, and that often means constantly learning what is new."

For a venture capitalist working in the technology market, this piece of advice is all the more relevant, given how fast the sectors VCs operate in evolve, and the huge advantage there is to gain by understanding more of what is happening. "Building up this propensity to learn is useful not just in finding deals but in supporting founders as they themselves try to grapple with an everchanging landscape."

Winning as a VC

This "propensity to learn" enables foresight as well, important for the early-stage VC to be competitive. "Because early-stage venture capital is the business of finding the future in the present, success is less a factor of firepower than it is of foresight. The founders who lead the unicorns we know today likely did not have a smooth ride fundraising their early rounds. Markets that are now populated with competitors today were unimaginable or at least seemed unlikely a decade ago. Having the largest fund doesn't necessarily equate to sealing in the best deals."

"The best way for a VC to be competitive is not to compete at all, and all the more when the landscape seems to be limited and finite, being able to look beyond what is apparent in the present can be needle-moving for a fund. Fortunately, in Southeast Asia, we don't necessarily have to start from square one. In our LP base we have several founders from tech unicorns in Silicon Valley and China whom we work with to spot opportunities and advise companies based on their insights and experience."

Ultimately, success is in the long play and reaping the returns of long-term value creation. "Underlying this broad shift in focus from backing growth-at-all-costs to supporting more sustainable models is greater clarity when it comes to balancing value creation and rapid growth. Enduring venture-backed companies were able to strike a balance between value and scale. They developed their business so that rapid growth engineers true value creation, instead of the latter being forsaken in pursuit of the former. Venture capitalists certainly win with grand exits, but true success is being able to support enduring companies that are valuable, not just to their investors, but also to their customers and the larger community."

(33) Through the Lens of LP–GP Relationships

Based on "From betting on the future to charting its course: venture building with LPs" by Yinglan Tan and Paulo Joquiño. Published on 13 December 2019. Also published on informaconnect 5 December 2019.

Most funds that back startups are often managing the money of other investors. Funding to startups comes through capital calls general partners (venture capitalists) make to their limited partners (investors in the venture fund).

Investor-startup relationships focus on the venture fund and the startup but limited partners also exert influence on the larger direction the fund takes. It's important for founders to realize that this LP–GP dynamic exists and evolves, though it is often undisclosed.

***

The seafaring thoroughfares of Southeast Asia in the 1500s were plied by all manner of vessels — junks from China to galleons from Spain — carrying not only precious goods but people, many of whom would never return to their homeland in pursuit of greener pastures and bluer seas.

This human desire for opportunity that brings many an adventurer well beyond the comfort of familiarity extends to venture capital, as the growing ubiquity of digital innovation deepens its transformation of industries and markets. Global innovation has seen several fund and market cycles in more mature markets, and so the question is no longer whether to invest or not in innovation, but where innovation is driving market growth and industry transformation next.

Funding the Captains of Innovation

Ferdinand Magellan's expedition proved to the Western world that the world is round and ushered an era of exploration. The expeditions of Admiral Zheng He expanded China's reach far beyond what the scholars of the Forbidden City could have ever imagined. Neither expedition would have reshaped human conceptualizations of the world without adequate resources. However, neither would have also gotten those resources without indomitable leadership.

LP interest is similarly focused on finding these groundbreaking ventures that will not only result in high magnitudes of returns, but also drive long-term impact across the board. That ultimately means finding the right decision-makers, both VCs and founders, who will be steering the fleet and navigating the uncharted.

In an article by Kauffman Fellows, Chris Douvos from Ahoy Capital emphasizes the depth of the relationship that goes into these partnerships. "[LPs] are investing in people as an asset, as we don't have the luxury of products or business plans... We're investing in people that make decisions — we need to understand the decision engine, an amalgamation of their behavior footprints, where they are most comfortable, and uncomfortable."

Shifting the Course of the Conversation Beyond Capital

The continuity of exploration was driven largely by the painstaking work done documenting earlier expeditions and collating such knowledge in maps and compendiums, as Antonio Pigafetta did for Magellan. This same knowledge transfer can drive global innovation. Having seen or perhaps even participated in the miracles of Silicon Valley and Hangzhou, LPs can translate lessons from past cycles into great businesses in emerging markets.

At Insignia, conversations with our partners, 20% of whom come from 55 tech unicorns across Asia, Europe, and the US, do not only cover capital allocation. Instead, it is all about what fast-growing technology businesses can be built in Southeast Asia. Interestingly, 80% of our ideas for growing the portfolio come from 20% of our capital base. This exchange of ideas brings to the table what our ecosystem partners have seen and experienced as a starting point to navigate innovation in emerging markets.

This shift in conversation between LPs and VCs from investing capital to building ventures makes it clearer what value the LPs can bring to the portfolio and enables them to become more pivotal in the portfolio's growth. For example, one of our partners comes from the board of a well-established logistics company in China. He provided the wisdom that helped incubate now two very fast-growing logistics companies on our portfolio.

In Southeast Asia, the right talent and capital continues to elude many founders, in spite of the widening of options and increasing flow of both into the region. This is not unique to the region, and many LPs familiar with this narrative are able to step in and provide clarity and broader perspective to decision-making.

For some markets in the region as well, the digital infrastructure reflects that of China's several years ago, and the presence of seasoned China founders and investors as LPs provides relatively close case studies of how innovators capitalized on infrastructure gaps to bring the market where it is today.

This relationship is not about replicating proven models, but rather, equipping companies in the portfolio to deal with market uncertainties and industry challenges.

As Uncertainties Grow, the Partnership Deepens

Oftentimes, exploration is driven not just by the pull of the unknown, but the push of the untenable. Famine, persecution, and depletion of resources drove many expeditions just as much as, or even more than, the allure of what was beyond the horizon. This not only raised the stakes for such ventures but also pushed greater collaboration among those involved.

As global economic conditions abound with uncertainty, the deepening partnership between LPs and VCs in growing the portfolio reflects a more concerted effort to chart a path for fast-growing companies into long-term sustainability, and such effort can come in as early as the founding of the company.

This proactive approach to growing the portfolio lays the foundation for a reservoir or ecosystem of ventures with a unity to it, as opposed to a stream of investment bets on the market. Reservoirs stand to fuel innovation for much longer, as it connects the right talent and capital to drive and make such innovation possible and sustainable.

(34) Through the Lens of Corporate Venture

Based on "Corporate venture capital landscape in Singapore" by Yinglan Tan and Allen Chng. Published 29 March 2019. Excerpts appeared on Business Times.

In Southeast Asia, the rise in venture capital has also reeled in corporations. In order to better position the company for digitalization, corporations are exploring collaboration with startups, of which setting up a corporate venture shop is one approach. For both the corporate and the startup, there are pros and cons to consider *vis-à-vis* more traditional VC fundraising. The piece below examines the CVC trend in Southeast Asia and what CVCs and startups have to look out for entering into these deals and partnerships.

***

Total corporate venture capital funding in Singapore and within the Southeast Asia region has greatly increased over the past five years. Total investments by such funds increased from US$405.8 million in 2014 to US$5.31 billion in 2017 (published on sgsme.sg, original source from SVCA). A few key factors are driving these trends.

Industry landscapes are changing quickly — startups are quicker to respond to changing consumer preferences and are disrupting corporates with cheaper, better, and more competitive services. Corporates are realizing that they need to evolve to tackle the competition from young startups.

The key factor in the tussle between large corporates and young startups is the speed of innovation versus the startup's scale of distribution. The faster the startup scales its distribution network, the faster the corporate has to innovate and respond with a competing product.

This is also the reason why we are seeing more partnerships between corporates and young startups within each industry. Corporates provide startups with the scale and resources while startups give corporates the opportunity to innovate new products and a channel to tap into previously inaccessible customers. Startups can also be tapped into as a solution to solve internal operational problems faced within the corporate.

For example, Singtel Innov8, Singtel's CVC arm, invested in Igloohome, a smart lock startup powering Singapore's smart city charge. Through this investment, Singtel taps into Igloohome's smart locks to remotely manage its telco infrastructure assets through an access management platform.

Strengths of CVCs

CVCs provide corporates with a platform to get a foot into the door amid the disruption which is happening within their industry. Corporates get access to different startups and launch multiple partnerships before deciding whether to acquire the startup if the partnerships work out well.

Aside from the above, there is a case for corporates to set up an external independent venture capital fund (i.e., CVCs) as opposed to funding it internally through their balance sheet. Investments done through the main corporate setup are subjected to slower decision-making processes and corporate budget allocations. Conversely, CVCs have more autonomy to invest into new technologies and business areas. This is especially important in the context of today's competitive venture capital scene where investor allocations in funding rounds favor VCs who can move fast. Faster funding rounds are also preferred during early stage investments because startups are then able to focus on growing the business.

Venturing for the Wrong Reasons

We observed cases where corporates embark on corporate innovation programs without a well thought out process into the objectives and institution-wide changes which are required — cash-rich corporations facing declining businesses and desperately trying to buy innovation. In these cases, the CVC serve more of a PR purpose to the corporate — cosmetic initiatives to give the corporate an image of being an innovative and forward-looking organization.

The decision-making process and measured outcomes of the CVC has to be guided by the intended purpose and desired goals — be it achieving strategic objectives and synergies for the corporate or maximizing financial returns from the investments.

The acquired startups end up becoming puzzle pieces which do not fit into the overall business. This happens when attempts to integrate the startups are faced with internal pushback by middle management who are concerned with protecting their turf.

Pitfalls of CVCs

Every CVC needs to have very clear objectives in place right from the outset, whether the objective is to pursue strategic goals and synergies or maximize financial returns from the investments. In the case of the former, the CVC focuses only on investments that will produce strategic synergies with the corporate and places a priority on connecting portfolio companies with internal corporate divisions. Conversely, strategic synergies take a backseat if financial returns are the main objectives. Sometimes, the CVC might even invest in startups which are trying to directly compete with the corporate.

The success of the CVC depends on how well the decision-making processes are aligned to the desired objectives. CVCs are rarely successful when both objectives co-mingle because it is rare that an investment would be able to perfectly satisfy both objectives. Even if they do, the universe of startups that the CVC can invest in is very small and the startup would have to ultimately make a decision to prioritize one objective over the other.

In addition, the incentive structure of the fund managers has to be appropriately aligned to the objectives of the CVC. If the CVC objectives were to achieve strategic synergies, performance-based stock options in the corporate become an important compensation tool. Conversely, a CVC pursuing financial returns would have to adopt the carried interest incentive structure more commonly seen in traditional venture capital firms. In both cases, the incentive structure also has to be aligned with the overall compensation structure adopted by the corporate.

CVC Landscape Shaping Up

We can expect to see more CVCs being set up. The first wave of CVCs in Singapore has been pushed by Singapore government-linked companies (GLCs) and blue chips in certain sectors like fintech and real estate. Moving forward, we can see this progressing into other sectors like healthcare, logistics, and the legal industry.

Corporate investments (both co-investments and lead investments) have grown more than 2.5x from 2014–2017 (source from "Southeast Asia PE & VC: Investment Activity" report published by SVCA). With mega deals such as Alibaba's investment into Tokopedia, we will see more foreign CVCs entering the scene to tap into local startups with significant presence in the region.

Over the years, we have seen the first wave of unicorns emerging such as the likes of Gojek and Grab. The next wave of startups is likely to be vertical champions that will push the digitization in specific industries. As these startups grow in scale towards Series A and B, we will increasingly see more partnerships that will serve to supplement the goals of corporates.

To this end, we can expect that CVCs will increase the scale of corporate innovation initiatives such as accelerator programs and hackathons. The goal here is to build a community which can further bridge the corporate to startups and innovation.

Tech Companies Venturing into CVCs

We are positive about such a trend to the extent that the strategic and financial objectives have been clearly identified, and the purpose and desired synergies have been well thought out. Also, the managers heading the CVC have to be scouted and key incentives that align the managers to the CVC's objectives have to be set in place.

Many new-age tech companies raise mega rounds based on the potential behind the large untapped markets in the region. CVCs are a good way to pursue inorganic growth to expand into new markets (new distribution channels, new segments or new business areas) without spending time to incubate a new division from scratch. It is also a way for new-age tech companies to acquire new disruptive technologies from the younger startup.

(35) Through the Lens of Unicorns

Based on "Demystifying Southeast Asia's tech unicorns" by Paulo Joquiño. Published 18 November 2019. Excerpts published on Nikkei Asian Review.

Unicorn startups have been cast unto a class of their own, with the billion-dollar valuations signaling to investors a potentially valuable exit in the making, and to founders a milestone to achieve. However, the unicorn optics can easily run surface deep. This is becoming more apparent with companies having mega rounds and less impressive exits to show for. There is much more to be said about how investors arrive at such valuations and how these companies utilize their war chests for sustainable growth.

***

The Lengthening Road to IPO

While it is taking less and less capital to start a company, it is also taking more and more capital to scale globally. The road to IPOs for technology companies has become longer, with the likes of Tiger and Softbank raising the tickets for later rounds. The resulting abundance of private capital has enabled the region's unicorns to take longer to go public, with megafunds essentially taking the place of public market investors.

For companies, this has become an opportunity to focus on growing even further across the region and expanding their portfolio of services. For private capital, especially the megafunds, there is a concerted effort to create new markets and scale technological niches globally. This reflects the strong belief many investors have in the region's potential to continue producing more fast-growing, highly valuable companies, even amid the global headwinds.

Such global events are reflective of how the capital markets view unicorns which have raised unprecedented amounts of private capital without a viable business model. In the end, however, a sustainable financial model, profitable business, and fast growth are still well received, as seen with B2B SaaS companies like Zoom.

In particular, the gaps in Southeast Asia's market infrastructure have also given rise to business models different from US counterparts, spelling better financial sustainability leading up to IPOs for these unicorns. While Uber and Lyft are purely on-demand transportation platforms, Grab and Gojek have managed to build strong payments platforms as part of their ecosystem.

Justifying Valuation

Tied to this trend of companies raising larger and larger rounds is the ballooning of valuations. Valuation is ultimately a question of supply and demand, rooted both in the confidence of investors in the entrepreneur and the entrepreneur in the venture. With the gravity well Southeast Asia has created in the global economy in terms of capital and talent flows, investors in the region have always been optimistic with the growth of companies in the region.

At the same time, the more money has poured into the region, the smarter this money has become. Both sides of the deals have gained more prescience when it comes to the implications of funding at different stages of growth. This means that while there is healthy competition among investors to unearth value, this is less likely to boil over, especially if the companies are unable to deliver financial performances that justify their valuation at subsequent stages. Funds in the region are also taking a more active role in helping their portfolio companies grow, going beyond the capital and offering hiring and tech services to address the toughest challenges founders in the region face.

Striking a Path to Profitability

The abundance of private capital may present a buffet of options for the fast-growing startup, but this trend makes it more important than ever for a company to have a clear path to profitability at an early stage. Growth and profitability do not have to be on opposite ends of the spectrum, and smarter money is making it possible to do both at the same time. Doing both means looking at growth not just as a function of market share and transactions, but also of value exchanged across a product or service — how much more value can customers derive from the platform?

For unicorns, answering this question has led them to acquire, invest in, or partner with smaller players to incorporate more services that could boost usage on their platform. Gojek, for example, has acquired many fintech players to tap into payment gateways more accessible to specific markets. Grab, on the other hand, is speculated to be in talks to merge OVO with Ant Financial-backed DANA to dominate the Indonesian online payments market.

Scaling value in Southeast Asia is burdened by infrastructure and logistics costs that come with a wider distribution of product, but tech companies are in a position to take on an asset-light and cost-effective approach to growth — without needing the war chest to invest or acquire. Janio, for example, works with localized logistics partners across several countries to cover the variety of logistics needs clients may have to export goods.

Comparing Unicorns' Paths

Given the megafunds and heavyweight tech companies backing unicorns Grab and Gojek, the question will not be whether or not these companies will continue to grow but in what direction will the growth be. While both are mass horizontal platforms, the future of tech platforms is hyper-vertical growth. Instead of spending runway to capture basic services across verticals, the focus will be on extending services across entire customer lifecycles. This will prove to be more cost-effective as it plays into the existing customer base and increases retention.

Ultimately, both Grab and Gojek will have to prioritize certain verticals over others, as well as certain markets over others. Where they place their bets will determine their growth trajectory, and who will win in specific markets and verticals.

The Role of Unicorns in the Startup Ecosystem

Unicorns have become vehicles for investors, both private capital and large tech firms, to tap into the region, given the massive customer bases these platforms already have. For example, Masayoshi Son recently committed $2 billion through Grab to invest in AI and green vehicles for Indonesia. This trend will continue as more global investors take interest in the region, and more unicorns emerge across specific verticals and markets.

At the same time, some startups are pulling away from larger players, establishing themselves in underserved verticals. The unbanked still comprise a majority of Indonesia's population at 66%, especially in second- and third-tier cities. Traditional industries like healthcare, property, and education are still at the cusp of disruption. These startups on the frontiers of innovation are developing unique capabilities and their own distribution networks, reducing dependencies on unicorns.

*Given that the larger the company the more capital is needed for it to grow, *vis-à-vis* less capital needed for each startup at early stages, it is also not as surprising that unicorns have captured the majority of startup investment.

(36) Through the Lens of a Crisis

Based on "Prudence and Perseverance" by Paulo Joquiño. Published on 20 March 2020.

Crisis is part-and-parcel of the startup journey. The very nature of introducing a new way of doing things (innovation) in an industry or to the consumer creates external tension that can result in crisis moments in the company. The desire to generate massive impact in a relatively short period of time also creates internal tension that can also result in crisis.

Then there are crises that are not directly the result of the startup's existence or growth. There was the dotcom bubble at the turn of the century, the SARS epidemic three years later, the 2008 financial crisis, and the COVID19 pandemic. The resolution of these crises are beyond the grasp of the company, and so adaptation must be prudent and focus on perseverance.

Even as a crisis calls for certain measures such as cost-cutting and conserving cash, there are takeaways from fundraising in a crisis that are better applied as a general rule rather than an exception.

***

As the impact of COVID19 ripples throughout the startup ecosystem, investors, publications, and consulting firms are advising startups to buckle in this year. This piece tackles the overarching theme of prudence and preservation (company culture, cash, relationships), and when it comes to dealing with the difficulties in fundraising and exits during this period.

Not Just a Cash Shock

While cash conservation is practical advice for any business during this time, startups in particular have to be more cautious as this is not just a cash shock, but a psychological/culture shock as well. We have seen a wave of startups dependent on heavy capital expenditure or subsidies — they will have to rethink their business model and the company culture.

This has also affected how startups operate and grow their teams. As markets undergo a dry spell, early fundraising and cash conversation are strategies that will affect not just the balance sheet, but the company culture as well. Founders need to take these effects into consideration.

Depending as well on the market the startup is in, founders may be more conditioned to adapt to this situation. Startups that have already been operating with tightened belts given the nature of their industry will be better prepared to adjust. Startups that have grown accustomed to spending heavily on marketing and hiring in the last year will feel the weight of the shock more than others.

Keeping Warm with Cash in this Capital Winter

While there is pressure among startups to secure a warm supply of cash before the winter deepens, startups should still be strategic when it comes to investors. Founders should still align themselves with investors who can provide commensurate long-term value, and for the larger pockets, perhaps even participate in rounds down the road.

Convertible notes in particular can be a beneficial choice early on if the business can safely expect a subsequent round in the works or accumulate enough follow-on interest. However, as the current situation has rendered the next few months highly unpredictable, founders need to work under the assumption that it will be more difficult for investors to commit. Regardless of the approach, the situation calls for more strategic fundraising, rather than panic-raising and taking anyone's cash.

Keeping the Relationships Warm as the Exits Cool

When it comes to exits in a capital winter the pressure builds up on all parties to ensure that the exit will be a win-win situation. Founders need to be clear on what the exit means for them at this point in time in their company's growth, if their expectations can be met by interested parties and if their market position likewise meets the expectations of buyers. From the buyer side, belts are tightening but there is also the upside of making a valuable purchase at this time in markets that are receiving more business and consumer demand.

Even though less exits can be expected this year, activity around them will likely remain high. After all, these deals are not overnight affairs and evolve over time. So even with the short-term uncertainty, building relationships and well-grounded confidence in potential buyers even through these conditions will be critical.

At the end of the day, if the company is on the path to profitability — making good gross margins on top of a sustainable business model — the opportunities for quality exits will come. To that end, founders will want to put themselves in a good position and maintain healthy financials and operations throughout this winter.

Technology Emerging from the Crisis

The current macro conditions will be a definitive moment for business models that have emerged over the past decade. Business models dependent on a regular supply of outside capital to scale will feel the strain more than those that have been designed to grow on the economics of their platform. The latter will prove to be more enduring, as we have seen with tech companies that have gone through several market cycles. For VCs in Southeast Asia, this is an opportunity to have more scrutiny when it comes to deals as business models are put to the test.

Even then, the current conditions will not necessarily mean tighter belts and slower growth for all sectors. If there is anything the social adjustments taking place around the globe has proven, it is that technology is critical to supporting business operations, day-to-day activities, and even supply chains straining under the stress of lockdowns and social distancing. Business support software like conferencing tools and online education platforms are in demand more than ever. Platforms that are able to digitalize supply chain transactions will see higher activity as people find more convenience in doing business online. This is an opportunity to double down on companies digitalizing Southeast Asia's industries.

Innovators do not Raise Money; they Grow the Company so the Money Finds them.

Takeaways on fundraising and working with investors:

(1) *Fundraising begins with clarity on the company's financial fitness.* It will be difficult to raise, much less utilize, funding if the business is not on top of its financials (from cash burn to accounts receivables and payables, etc.).

(2) *Fundraising has to be done with a clear business goal in mind (that does not involve only becoming a unicorn).* It can be hiring, product launches, or market expansion.

(3) *Finding the right "fit" with an investor when fundraising is important to gaining the best value from having them on board.* Any deal always involves something more than the cash and equity exchange, especially with CVCs. This is important to keep in mind in a crisis when the desperation can lead to lopsided deals.

(4) *The best investors can open doors to even more sources of financing (and even business).* It is important to always communicate with investors and have clarity with what the business needs.

(5) *Fund LPs also play a significant, though broader, role in investing in startups,* which affects how GPs or fund managers approach investments.

Chapter Eight

Weathering the Storms

Innovators do not just weather crises; they see opportunity amidst the storm.

"When fisherman can't go out to sea, they repair their nets."
— *Nabil Sabio Artist and author*

No matter how "fueled up" or "fit" the explorer is for the journey ahead, the odds of success still remain stacked against the exploration. It is not a coincidence that those that reach their destination are celebrated and go down in history. Before Roald Amundsen led the first expedition to reach the South Pole, many expeditions tried and failed to do so (which ironically helped Amundsen succeed). The success of the Apollo 11 landing did not guarantee that those that followed them were going to be successful as well. The failure rate is tremendously high, and that is in good times.

Crises deepens the uncertainty, and tests the fitness and fuel of the explorer. Bad weather has shaken off many Mount Everest hikers from risking the peak. However, the expeditions of Rob Hall and Scott Fisher in 1996 chose to proceed to the Mount Everest peak with bad weather conditions, which then combined with ill-prepared hikers, resulted in tragedy.

For startups, surviving (and even thriving) in a crisis can spell the difference between success and failure in the long run. This means that crisis management is critical for startups, especially in a crisis that is external and cannot be controlled.

Many of Southeast Asia's startup founders are facing their first economic crisis (at least as founders in the region), and it is exacerbated by the reality that this crisis is not just economic in impact. COVID19 will be a defining period of time for tech startups in Southeast Asia. Some will not make it through, and many will only get by, but there will be those that take the opportunity to lead the region.

This chapter on the COVID19 crisis is divided primarily into two parts. The first is a coverage of various tactics, approaches, and perspectives from founders and investors on how to survive through a crisis, prepare for recovery, and make sense of its impact on industry and the region. The second revolves around digitalization as an impact of this particular crisis.

Essays in this Chapter

(37) **Crisis response 101 for startups.** Responding to a crisis is a holistic affair. *By Paulo Joquiño, based on a webinar on COVID19 strategies for tech startups organized by Insignia Ventures on April 2020, with Linh Thai, former head of Vingroup Ventures and DFJ VinaCapital, and Aaron Tan, CEO and co-founder of Carro as guests alongside Yinglan.*

(38) **Preparing for the upturn.** It is no use conserving cash if the business is not making moves to prepare for what happens after the crisis. *By Paulo Joquiño, based on a webinar on COVID19 strategies for tech startups organized by Insignia Ventures on April 2020, with Linh Thai, former head of Vingroup Ventures and DFJ VinaCapital, and Aaron Tan, CEO and co-founder of Carro as guests alongside Yinglan.*

(39) **Making sense of the impact.** COVID19 has made the future more uncertain than ever before, but great companies are able to spot the short-term impact and translate these into long-term

opportunity. *By Paulo Joquiño, based on a webinar on COVID19 growth opportunities organized by Insignia Ventures on April 2020, with Zhang Tao, founder and CEO of Dianping.com, and Chih Cheung, co-founder and co-chairman of global sportswear manufacturer JAMM Active Limited, as guests alongside Yinglan.*

(40) **The Learning Curve.** Edtech is taking off across markets in lockdown; we look at the experiences of two startups, one in Indonesia and one in Vietnam. *Based on "Responding to Vietnam education's wake-up call," an interview with Edmicro founders Linh Dang Bao and Que Nguyen (Published 6 May 2020) and "Acing edtech in Indonesia," a podcast conversation with Pahamify CEO and co-founder Rousyan Fikri. Published 8 June 2020.*

(41) **Beyond the first-order impact is second-order opportunity.** Digitalization is a clear impact of the crisis, but how will this affect the way tech platforms do business and compete on the internet? *Based on "Embrace the Vujade" by Paulo Joquiño. Published on 29 April 2020.*

(42) **Considerations for digitalization.** As many traditional businesses head to the internet for customers, it is important to consider that digitalization is not just about putting up a Facebook page or a website. *Based on "Making the exodus to online business" by Joolin Chuah. Published on 22 April 2020.*

(43) **Data as building blocks.** One of the second-order effects of digitalization will be data's greater role in the Internet economy, from facilitating day-to-day connections to business operations. *Based on "Data in a post-COVID world: Highways of the digital economy" by Paulo Joquiño. Published 16 April 2020.*

(37) Crisis Response 101 for Startups

By Paulo Joquiño

The insights here are based on a webinar on COVID19 strategies for tech startups organized by Insignia Ventures on April 2020, with Linh Thai, former head of Vingroup Ventures and DFJ VinaCapital, and Aaron Tan, CEO and co-founder of Carro as guests alongside Yinglan.

"Cash is king." This adage has been echoed many times as it became clear just how impactful COVID19 would be for businesses. This essay looks into a holistic approach to keeping cashflow healthy in a crisis, from cost-cutting to exploring new avenues of revenue generation and fundraising.

***

Assessing Impact

When crisis strikes the first thing to do is to assess the impact, specifically on cashflow, the lifeblood of a business. Startups need to conduct scenario planning based on several possibilities of how long it will take for the crisis to resolve. In the case of COVID19, the timeline being floated around has ranged from 12 to 18 months, the approximate time it will take for a vaccine to be developed.

With this benchmark, startups can then look at how long their cash will last for several scenarios *vis-à-vis* how revenue will be impacted by the crisis in its current state (as the impact of a crisis can evolve).

When it comes to forecasting impact on revenue, staying conservative is best. In a global crisis like COVID19, everyone is hurting. Accounts receivables and NPLs are likely going to be paid later than expected, especially in hard-hit industries.

Scenario planning is key to laying down strategies to survive in the crisis. A company with a six-month runway and a 80% to 90% drop in revenue during a crisis that will optimistically take 12 months to resolve needs to take a serious look at cutting costs and look for ways to get additional financing to make it through to the following year. Meanwhile, a company that is seeing revenue increase (or even more activity on its platform) with a 12-month runway can leverage that to consider a bridge round with existing investors.

Preserving Healthy Cashflow

The shorter the runway, and the worse the impact on revenue, the more cash has to be conserved and stretched out over the duration of the crisis. Even then, whether the business has a healthy cashflow or not, it is more prudent in an unpredictable crisis to find ways to reduce unnecessary expenses and keep a safe distance from the red.

There are many ways to go about it, and below are some advice from investors and entrepreneurs:

(1) "First cut off the things that can be reversed," advises Linh Thai. "For example, digital marketing [is] easy. You turn off Facebook, turn off Google and then later on, you [can] turn [them] back on. [These are] things that you can do with very little repercussions. And then once those are cut, you look at the more serious ones like rent, labor and HR."

(2) Do not overestimate the business's capacity to pay off accounts payables like rent and capital expenditure. In the same way that accounts receivables are difficult to collect in a crisis, it is also wrong to assume that accounts payable will be an easy expense to clear out. It really depends on the supplier or service provider and the contract, but in general, working out a more flexible payment schedule is the ideal outcome.

(3) Reducing operational inefficiencies can also lead to cutting down on cash burn. Ironically, these inefficiencies are more likely to be found in well-funded startups. Investment-fueled growth in a bull market can easily lead to shaky foundations, and if they do not give way in a crisis, every opportunity should be taken to strengthen them.

(4) Changing behaviors because of the crisis can also be a source for savings. In a viral pandemic like COVID19, people in tech jobs will likely be encouraged to work from home, so office expenses can be cut down while the team is working remotely.

(5) Instead of laying off, introducing top-down pay cuts, issuing equity, and furloughing can ease the burden on the business without having to fully let go of employees. However, if laying off is inevitable, it is best to be strategic, do it all in one go, and do it with sincerity and respect.

A holistic approach to cost-cutting is the most effective. Looking across the board from the P&L line items to workflows for cost-cutting strategies can result in more creative decisions that do not necessarily handicap the business coming out of the crisis.

Growing Sideways

Aside from reducing costs from all possible angles, startups can boost their cashflow health by looking for opportunities to continue growing as much as possible. The COVID19 crisis opened up greater demand for online products and services, with has worked to the advantage of tech startups, at least those with purely online platforms like esports or edtech.

The more cashflow positive companies, with around 18 or more months of runway, are better positioned to pushing their product even if slower than normal, especially if competitors are less equipped. Lower crowding in the market may mean also lower cost per acquisition (CPA) which helps with onboarding new users to the platform.

Aside from doubling down on acquisition strategies, another approach is to grow "sideways", as Linh Thai put it. Growing sideways could mean repackaging products and services for the internet (e.g., a yoga center offering classes on Zoom) or making online sales and marketing channels (e.g., a virtual showroom for properties or cars), given that the COVID19 crisis has forced many offline businesses to close shop.

Growing sideways could also mean tweaking the business model (or at least user acquisition) from B2B to B2C, which is something that online communication and collaborative tools like Zoom have done with increased demand on their platform.

The opportunities for these pivots in reaching out to or engage with customers can be found within the value chain as well. With public markets closed down to prevent community spread of COVID19, e-commerce marketplaces and logistics enablers have been supporting farmers and fishermen to get their goods direct to consumer.

What Investors are Looking for in a Slowdown

Investors also become more cautious in a crisis, with all the uncertainty. For COVID19, the crisis came at a time in the year when fundraising is supposed to pick up, and on the heels of a year when investor sentiments had been shifting.

As Carro CEO and co-founder Aaron Tan put it, "I think the landscape has been very, very challenging over the last few months… Coming into CNY that's [when] we start to pick up and move on to fundraising, but in this particular year, it was really slow coming into the year and then this whole COVID situation makes things a lot worse. So in other words, for folks that didn't start fundraising earlier on last year or towards the end of last year, I think life is very, very tough."

In general, crises create a slowdown in fresh investments. This slowdown can be influenced by the fund investors or limited partners with how venture capital investments usually work. As Linh Thai explains, "…when [investors] raise the fund, say US$100 million, they don't get the hundred million right away. They make capital calls when they need the money, and then the LPs send the fund money when they're ready and then the fund makes the investment in a startup… In a situation like this where there are a lot of businesses short on cash, LPs may…be slow to send the money."

It is also influenced by the fund's strategy. Some investors may be more preoccupied with supporting their existing portfolio than making new investments. Those that were able to amass dry powder prior to the crisis have more to deploy but will likely be more strategic given the even more uncertain positions startups are in.

What then do investors look for in the midst of a crisis? It is all about going back to basics and communicating to investors that the company has a plan to emerge stronger from the crisis. As Linh put it, "Fundamentals always win," implying that this is a key factor regardless of the weather. "…I would say [in this environment], investors are actually okay with moderate growth plus profitability. Before, you could say, "We're growing at a ridiculous rate, but we're nowhere near profitability," and that would have been fine and that actually may have been preferred. But nowadays, [investors are] looking for companies that can survive. This is going to be a really tough period, it could last 18 months or more. So a company that's still trying to find product market fit may have a tough time trying to get funding at this time."

Apart from the fundamentals, investors are also looking at "green shoots" and "sunrise sectors" that are gaining traction as a result of the consumer behavior changes. In the same way that the SARS epidemic in China gave the likes of Alibaba and Dianping the opportunity to address the needs of consumers online, COVID19 has also been creating new pain points that technology platforms are suited to address at scale. Sectors like education, healthcare, and logistics are getting digitally transformed at record pace, so platforms that can reduce the friction and deliver on product will be attractive to investors.

Fundraising in a Crisis

So, say the company has already done scenario planning, got its house in order, mapped out a plan for growth, and decided it needs financing to follow through on this plan and stay ahead of the market. How do startup founders approach fundraising in a crisis?

Yinglan advises to apply for government grants first if possible. Once grants options are exhausted, founders can then reach out to two sets of people. The first are existing investors. Founders can have a candid chat with them for bridge financing or introductions to other investors they know would be interested in investing. The second are investors who have been tracking the company over time. They have already been warmed up from previous conversations and have likely done some research on the company, and now it is a matter of communicating that the company is fundraising.

Apart from traditional sources of financing, debt financing can be an option, especially if the government and banks are working to absorb the risks of downside on the part of the banks.

Even a hybrid round with venture debt will tend to be useful in crisis. Then for smaller startups, there is the option to talk to angels. Then there are also the family offices interested in technology investments.

In general, however, the COVID19 crisis is not the best time to make fresh connections. Fundraising timelines are also extended in places that are difficult to travel to due to restrictions. Investors will find it challenging to do thorough due diligence, which often involve company visits and talking to customers. The irony is that investors are more inclined to be more thorough in their due diligence during a crisis because of the untenable position startups tend to be in even in normal times.

Regardless of the kind of investor or source of financing, it is key to get into many conversations/applications early and close in as soon as possible. A crisis like COVID19 is unpredictable in its impact and its development, and it is a better strategy to cast a wide net of introductions and get money in the bank early than not. For some companies, it can be the difference between life and death.

Then there is the matter of valuations, where a healthy dose of realism is needed. In a crisis, it is better to have cash for survival than optimize for valuation. "If the valuation isn't so good, get used to it. Because it's better to stay alive than to shut down. So take maybe a smaller amount at a valuation that you're happy with. Live for the next 12 to 18 months, and then get a better round, when you're the only one that's alive, then your valuation would be really good coming out the other end," shares Linh.

(38) Preparing for the Upturn

By Paulo Joquiño

Like the first essay in this chapter, the insights here are based on a webinar on COVID19 strategies for tech startups organized by Insignia Ventures on April 2020, with Linh Thai, former head of Vingroup Ventures and DFJ VinaCapital, and Aaron Tan, CEO and co-founder of Carro as guests alongside Yinglan.

Even as a crisis calls for prudence and perseverance, it also calls for preparation — preparation for the upturn and recovery. For innovators, staying ahead of the game and waves of innovation are important, and so is staying ahead of the crisis. The essay cites practical advice on how to operate in a crisis by preparing for what happens afterwards.

***

Opportunity for Overcommunication

The implementation of remote work poses its challenges for collaboration, but it also presents an opportunity to build a culture of overcommunication.

This overcommunication is important especially in managing cross-border teams. In the case of Carro, Aaron "tends to empower the local CEOs to do what they need to do," but at the same time, "has daily calls, if not at least two days or so, I have an understanding of whatever that's happening in various countries."

Having this clear sense of what is going on across, especially considering the differences in how governments respond to crises, is critical to decision-making.

Bringing together Capabilities for the Future

Apart from ensuring the team remains tight-knit albeit distributed, it is also important for the founder to consider what kind of capabilities their team has and needs for the future.

As Yinglan put it, "Talent is much cheaper. So I would say you should freeze hiring to cut burn, but I think [you should] always be open for exceptional candidates that are available. And try not to cut your engineers because in Southeast Asia engineers are a scarce commodity."

"You want to make sure that you are prepared for the upturn when it comes, right. So you got to make sure that you are not only surviving the downturn, but you also have capabilities. You don't want your capabilities to be really affected when the upturn comes."

Testing and Forming Relationships

The strength of partnerships is truly tested in the midst of the storm. According to Yinglan, this crisis is as much a test of commitment for investors as it is of endurance for founders. "Most people choose their partner in not knowing how they'll behave in [bad] times. And it's easy for VC funds to invest in companies that go right into hockey stick, but I think it is in a downturn you see whether your partners will be there for you. And whether they spend the time to help you through a crisis in it."

And sometimes, crisis may also be an opportunity to work more closely with other startups to help each other out in a difficult time. Linh gives a scenario. "I know of a company that has production, but their sales team is all offline. So now they can't really go out and talk to people and try to make their pitch and so it's really hard to sell their product."

"So then what if they find another company that's very strong online, but then this [company B] just can't sell their product. Maybe [company B] sells travel products which nobody's really buying right now. So then they each take what is strong [from each other] and work together… The goal is to continue to stay alive until after this period… And you'll see, I think a lot of companies, a lot of your competitors will go under… [It's better] being super creative and trying to find any way you can to keep your doors open."

Having strong partnerships, be it for investment or the business, to ride out through recovery can also bring in returns long after the crisis has passed.

Building Resilience

Managing an ecosystem of services in a crisis forces the platform to look at what the customer really needs and what lines of business to focus on.

For Carro's secondhand car marketplace, they experienced an expected drop in demand, though it did not come directly from consumers buying less used cars. As Aaron notes, "…And [the drop in demand is] not even because consumers are buying less used cars, but actually because of the fact that customers are buying less new cars. Because when people are buying less new cars, it results in less trade-ins. And as a wholesale marketplace, it becomes tougher for us to get trade-ins of cars."

At the same time, the demand for their leasing product, Carro Leap, leaped through the roof. "What we have seen is the increase in demand for our leasing or our subscription product, right, where we talk about six months subscription or one-year subscription of vehicles."

The demand is so much so that they saw this as an opportunity to work with struggling car dealers. "We don't even have enough cars to fulfill the demand that we actually asked the other companies that were struggling to say, "Hey, do you want to do this [for] your cars on our platform instead, so that we can work together with you to lease your cars out and you just subscribe to the platform."

Carro learned that while demand for trade has decreased, the demand for subscription has risen a lot to the extent that it could negate that drop in business.

For Aaron, moving forward it will be a matter of how they think about business models. "How do we think about what the customers are fearful of? Is it safety or is it because they just want to get the car from the comfort of their home? [Then we can] move on to innovate on different business models that can survive through these tough times. So we're always constantly thinking about how we future proof the business — how do we COVID-proof the business so that at the end of the day, this particular situation that we are all in right now becomes more an opportunity, versus an issue or a trap for a company."

Regardless of how the company COVID-proofs its business, this crisis is a time of reckoning. The best entrepreneurs went through their own near-death experiences and came out of it as leaders and pioneers in their industry. Crises like these are a test of the founder's capability and resilience.

Seeing how resilient founders are in the face of adversity will actually draw more support. So, it is important to be able to help yourself first and stand up for yourself.

(39) Making Sense of the Crisis' Impact

By Paulo Joquiño

The insights here are based on a webinar on COVID19 growth opportunities organized by Insignia Ventures on April 2020, with Zhang Tao, founder and CEO of Dianping.com, and Chih Cheung, co-founder and co-chairman of global sportswear manufacturer JAMM Active Limited, as guests alongside Yinglan in the second.

The impact of the COVID19 crisis has left no stone unturned. All aspects of life from education to healthcare are being transformed, and the resulting shifts are here to stay for the long-term. Tech startups are no exception, as founders are now confronted by the challenges the crisis poses on their finances, operations, and even company culture.

It is during these times that many turn to the advice of those who have seen, survived, and possibly even succeeded in past crises. While the context is different from any past crises, and uncertainty still dominates any analysis of the situation, conversations with veteran founders and investors bring up insights and outlooks that are not necessarily timebound.

*****

The Crisis is Global

Zhang Tao shares Dianping's experience going through the SARS outbreak in 2003 and the financial crisis around 2008, and compares it to COVID19. "[Dianping] started right in the middle of SARS, so there's some parallel there [to what is happening now]. In a major crisis like COVID, there will be big changes to the whole economy and industry, so some will suffer, and some will benefit."

Back then, SARS drove Chinese consumers to use online platforms like Taobao, and Zhang Tao notes the same phenomenon happening with COVID19. "So [when] Ali[baba] was still very small, SARS helped in a way, [because] people [bought] more stuff from home. We see that with this COVID19 [crisis] now. A lot of the online services [are] actually doing very well even during the depths of the stock market crash; you see all these big tech companies actually holding up fairly well. You look at Amazon stock, [it's at an] all time high now. They [are doing] more online education. Zoom [saw] incredible growth; food delivery also [saw] incredible growth. [In] countries outside China the adoption curve has just started, [and now] I think it will just go way over the top."

Zhang Tao recalls Dianping's own fundraising situation back in 2008, and why they ultimately decided not to raise. "We were planning to raise a new round of funding in the next six months before the '08 crisis... We sat down and we went through our finances and we kind of figured out at that time the burn rate is very small. We are talking about, I forgot the exact figures, maybe two hundred thousand a month, US dollars, and we [had] a little bit of income. So we did some financial analysis and figured out if we push a bit harder, actually we can break even with all our capital."

This is scenario planning in action. Apart from the financial analysis, Dianping looked at the investment landscape in China back then. "Then we [looked] at the environment. Obviously, it's very hard to raise money; [it was] always actually even tougher for entrepreneurs in China than I think even now, because when there's a financial crisis it freed up cash and more importantly at that time, there were not many VCs here. This entrepreneur thing was not a sexy thing and a VC was not a big industry in China, so [founders] didn't have a lot of choices."

Ultimately, he calls their decision not to raise a "blessing in disguise" because they were able to survive without having to give away equity or take on loans. Based on Zhang Tao's experience with Dianping back in 2008, the decision to fundraise depended on two factors: (1) where they were geographically, as it determined the fundraising landscape, and (2) where their company was financially.

However, today, looking at the region, things are different, even in Southeast Asia. "This time is different from 2008. There's a lot of VCs, there's a lot of money. A lot of funds raised a lot of money before the crisis. And it's actually hard to deploy in the past couple years. So, money's there; it's just that people are cautious. And so, it depends where your business is. If your numbers and your metrics all show very promising growth then the money will be there then you can start trying. If your numbers are not there, then maybe [be] cautious."

"One thing I do see in Southeast Asia [is that] the valuation will be higher. I think it's a couple years behind China. So, China cooled down already in 2018 and 2019, but Southeast Asia is a couple years behind. So, I would say before the crisis, valuation is too high, like in China early 2018 or late 2017. Now during the crisis, if you are good, you will still be able to make money, but maybe because of the valuation jump, you [need to] be more realistic, because you are coming from a higher level."

For Chih Cheung, crises make companies more disciplined, but this one in particular, compared to the SARS crisis, the dotcom bust, and the 2008 financial crisis, is global in nature. This means more long-lasting effects and changes across the board. "I believe that this crisis is more universal and global than in the past. If you look at what happened in the past, whether it be the tech bubble [burst], or the SARS crisis or the financial crisis, it's limited to either a region, or it's limited to a sector, be it tech or financial services."

"This time it's actually global in every sense of the word. It's not limited to any one sector, and it's certainly not limited to any one region. And the thing that some of the change that's happening right now is very fundamental. So, what I see is that for my business — so as Yinglan mentioned, I'm in a supply chain business, would it be Li & Fung or my own business which does performance fabric for companies like Nike, Under Armour, and LuluLemon — obviously there's huge changes there."

Six Effects of COVID19

Chih Cheung outlines eight of these changes, both in his industry (supply chain) and other sectors:

(1) *Digitalization of supply chain as a result of demand shocks and supply restraints.* "One of the things that you see immediately in the supply chain area is the fact that there's a huge push to digitization that you otherwise would not see, especially in a traditional industry like supply chain... So one of the things that's actually happening in real time right now in the industry is, for example, 3D sampling of design. In the past, people or the customer wants to see the physical sample now they are willing to see 3D samples virtually. In some way [even when] demand comes back, it's actually more efficient."

(2) *Supply chain diversification as an opportunity for Southeast Asia.* "I think what most countries have realized is that they cannot depend on just simply a global supply chain; it's too complicated. So during a crisis, for example...a lot of the masks are not made in the US. And in the country where even if it's a US company, like 3M...they have a factory in China that makes N95 masks, the Chinese government will not allow them to ship [these masks] from their factories in China to the US. What's going to happen is that the supply chain will shift from globalization to regionalization. And I think that actually goes well for Southeast Asia... Now, the trend of moving away from China was already happening because of the US China trade war, and I think the COVID-19 just accelerated that dramatically."

(3) *(Short-term) shift in consumption from experiences to goods.* "In terms of what happened in the past ten years, there's been a shift of consumption of goods to experiences. Now, the question is, is it going back to goods over experience, because people are afraid to travel, at least short term. Obviously, the natural thing is delivery versus inside experience with visiting a store or restaurant. More people are prone to delivery now... Frankly, I'm actually not surprised by the bounce in terms of sales for

Hermes. It's a premium brand. If you think about it, people feel good when they consume. And in the past, [Chinese consumers] could have taken the same amount of money and gone on a luxury trip somewhere in Africa or Europe. They're not doing that anymore. They could go to a fancy restaurant and buy a nice bottle of wine. They can't do that anymore. So in some way, I would argue that short term, there actually might be more opportunity for people to consume physical goods as opposed to experiences."

(4) *Increasing healthcare awareness.* "The other big thing that's happening that's universal and fundamental, is just a general awareness of healthcare. I think biotech and areas like that are going to do very well... If you have to look at one area that is going to do well in the next three to five years and find the right company, that would be the one area we'll definitely look at, because people are just a lot more aware about [healthcare], and people willing to spend money on that."

(5) *Rethinking work and collaboration.* "...we're all learning how to do remote collaboration and working. And for a company that knows how to do this, they've actually increased their efficiency. One of the things that is interesting that I see is that the way people conduct business has changed. Whereas in China in the past, right, everything needs to be done face to face — *ren-ching* (人情); it's critical. Now people realize that it's actually not so critical. You still should meet people face to face; it's important, but does it have to be every night going out to dinner meeting with your people? Not necessarily because it's not very efficient, frankly."

(6) *Digitalization of customer experience.* "I'm involved with a company that sells cars in the US, and also another company that actually sells housing properties in the US. And one of the things to see is that customers actually don't actually need to go to the site and actually physically see the product to buy. The property company Redfin is basically a public company in the US. What they've done [is] they've actually developed a video platform a couple years ago, but it wasn't very popular. And what they're

doing now is that the agent still goes to the property, but instead of doing an actual showing with people, they are actually doing a virtual showing and then posting it. Over time, that's just obviously going to be more efficient. If people get used to it, they change their buying behavior. So, what's really important is that the quality of the video broadcasting. Whoever knows how to use it right is going to end up winning."

Focus on the Micro Environment Instead of the Macro View

The global nature of the crisis that Chih pointed out makes it quite difficult to predict what the world will look like coming back. Although at the time of the webinar, China had just reopened after three months of lockdown, and became a time machine of sorts for the rest of the world under lockdown at what recovery might look like, Zhang Tao points out that the complex tensions in geopolitics and social structures make any crystal ball or time machine impossible to read.

"In the short term, for a country like China, they have a little bit under control now. So the business is kind of going back to normal. So consumption is coming back a little bit. But are we [experiencing] very strong consumption to make up what happened last? We haven't seen that in China yet. You go to restaurants and they're still half-empty."

"And so I think it really depends on this kind of wealth effect, and how people feel how much money they still have left. Maybe people are [going back to their] jobs, even though the virus is conquered, but they're still very cautious to consume or how optimistic they are with the future, with their future income coming in… I think the crisis is not a one-time shock; it will linger for some time."

For the entrepreneur, this macro view is too complex to be useful for the business decision-making, except for the reality that things will be uncertain. "The best thing is to keep yourself alive. Whoever survives will become great, but you need to survive. I know it's not just half a year, but the two or three more years [in] uncertain times in terms of financing, in terms of valuation, in terms of metrics. So be a little more cautious in terms of your planning."

Instead of macro, Zhang Tao advises founders to look at the micro environment instead. "It doesn't really matter, the macro view. It is really more about the micro environment you are in and that could be a different story."

And part of this micro view is looking at how each government is handling the crisis. As Chih puts it, "I will caution the founders in Southeast Asia is that you can certainly look at China as a playbook in terms of what potentially could happen. Like, for example, how Nike, Starbucks, and everybody open up their stores, but the recovery rate is different, and actually might be different in Southeast Asia. So I actually would caution you on making too much of the China playbook and just applying it blindly. I will also look at the local conditions because one of the things that I think will have a huge impact on how every country recovers in Southeast Asia is the role of the government."

Great Companies Balance Short-Term and the Long-Term

There is a tendency for entrepreneurs to either focus on short-term survival or long-term growth opportunities. The challenge — and what makes great companies — is the ability to look at both. Zhang Tao says that this is a leadership problem for any kind of company. "I remember 20 years ago at Wharton, Jack Welch gave a talk, and one quote from this talk, I remember still. He said, "As a CEO of a big company, it's easy to manage it for the long term, and it's very easy to manage it for the short term. But the difficult part is always to manage both." So I think it's true for any kind of business."

For Zhang Tao, it is about striking a balance that varies from business to business. "Of course, [say] you're doing a business and your competitors are not having the funding and your business actually benefits [because] of this current crisis, you should take advantage of it. At the same time, if you spend too much cash, and the funding is not coming along because of some situation where the funds have dried up, how do you manage that? It has to be business by business; you have to look at your own business very carefully and make a kind of trade-off."

An example would be balancing the long-term opportunities of a M&A versus the short-term uncertainty. For a company with a strong business model, management team, and capital base, a crisis presents an opportunity to buy for cheap. However, Chih warns that consolidation should result in greater scale and efficiency, and that depends on the industry. "I think certainly in industries where consolidation does benefit, you're going to see more of that so scale benefits certain types of industry, for example, you kind of mentioned hotel, right. I think having a bigger scale makes you run more efficiently. Given what's going on in the supply chain, I'm not sure having a bigger scale really helps. For example, if all your factories are in China, it's not good for you to buy more factories in China, because your customers actually want to diversify sourcing things. So it really depends."

Crisis is a Time for Youthful Passion and Change

Dianping started in the middle of the SARS epidemic, and many more companies also found their footing and launched into the stratosphere in the midst of a crisis. With the cost of starting a business decreasing with services like AWS and Shopify, and the adoption of online products and services increasing, young people are in a better position more than ever before to work on their passion and start a company.

As it is difficult to predict what skills will be necessary in the future, Zhang Tao advises to direct skill-building with passion. "That cannot be a better bet. Because if you like it you'll be better. It's very hard to predict what kind of skills will be useful, what kind of maybe entrepreneur ideas, industry, and sector will do very well in the future. It's not easy. If it's good, so many people already do it and the opportunity is gone. So I think it's a much safer bet to focus on what you really like to do, same with your knowledge base, your skill sets, and also in particular with the company you want to start in the future. It's much safer and the process will be much more enjoyable. You will have a lot more insights with the thing you are doing; you will find real needs instead of what other people tell you…I think with COVID especially it's going to be more online. So anything to do with digital and online, I think that's where the future is. So if you can combine your passion in that kind of arena, if possible, I think that would be the best…"

Along the lines of going digital, Chih sees the opportunity in digitalizing traditional industries and rethinking how businesses can reach their consumers. "I actually think that there is incredible opportunity in a lot of different industries, particularly traditional industries that may need to be digitized, that might have a new way of selling. I would really just focus on, you know, one industry that you have some sort of experience in, some sort of expertise, and some sort of passion or interest. But then think about the industry in a slightly different way. How can you take advantage of technology and the current prices to kind of offer a better service or better product at a cheaper cost to a greater group of people, because you still fundamentally have a model that is slightly different than what's out there today? Because you're going to be able to change and pivot because you don't have a lot of the legacy issues that a lot of traditional current leaders have."

(40) The Learning Curve

Based on "Responding to Vietnam education's wake-up call," an interview with Edmicro founders Linh Dang Bao and Que Nguyen (Published 6 May 2020) and "Acing edtech in Indonesia," a podcast conversation with Pahamify CEO and co-founder Rousyan Fikri. Published 8 June 2020.

As most economies went into lockdown, schools, teachers, and students were forced to come up with new ways to continue their schooling while at home. In this piece, we compiled interviews with edtech founders from Vietnam and Indonesia on their own experiences. This way, we can compare and contrast the "learning curve" education systems had to go through to go digital and how these startups responded to these new needs.

***

To give better context to their experience and response to the COVID19 crisis, these excerpts from the introductions they gave in these interviews are included.

Edmicro Introduction

"In Vietnam and all over the world as well, people tend to focus more on the instruction side of this online learning saga. But instruction can't go alone. Teachers need to keep track of student progress. That's what we do: provide online tools and question banks so that teachers can delegate and collect assignment results automatically and then organise online assessments. Students can track their own results and practise with our question bank too. It is important not only in this period but also in the long run. In Vietnam, teachers and schools have extremely little data to rely on to decide instruction strategy. At the same time, class size is huge, with 50 to 60 students per class in the cities. It's almost impossible to do anything like personalised instruction. We can certainly help with that."

Pahamify Introduction

"With Pahamify, we are helping students to pass the most important exam in their lives which is the college entrance exam. Because in Indonesia only 10% of the population holds a bachelor degree. We build our service based on this end in mind. We offer a set of test simulations where they can track and analyse their performance. And it's integrated with other services like the concept videos, talent mapping test, ask teachers, and also counseling sessions with psychologists."

The Wake-Up Call

In Vietnam, the government imposed their lockdown after the Lunar New Year holiday. "No one was prepared for that. At first, everybody hoped it would last only one or two weeks. But then, as the situation worsened, school closure lasted until the end of April," shares the Edmicro founders.

Several actions were pursued by the Ministry of Education and Training, including encouraging long-distance learning (as online learning was not officially recognized before), officially recognizing online formative assessment results, and reducing the number of lessons and assessments in the curriculum.

Although Vietnam is often lauded as a rising production and manufacturing economy in the region, majority of the country's 100 million people still work in agriculture, Edmicro pointed out. "Internet broadband and 4G are well-covered even in rural areas, everyone has a smartphone but personal computers are less popular. Most teachers and parents are not familiar with educational apps whereas students are more tech savvy."

This means COVID19 became a wakeup call for teachers in Vietnam. "On a normal day, they would have few incentives to change the traditional way of teaching with paper and blackboard. But then they caught up quickly. After modest instructions, they were able to move their classes to the cloud fairly quickly, except for the few zoom-bombing incidents. Teachers [had to] transition to using Zoom, Google Meet or Microsoft Teams as online teaching tools, Onluyen.vn for online assignments and assessments, and Zalo and Facebook for classroom communications."

For students, there was also a shift, but it varied across school levels. "To secondary and high school students, online learning is more natural as learning via free video lectures on social media platforms like YouTube or Facebook has been a norm in the country, even before the pandemic. It's more difficult with elementary students since most of them need parental supervision and support. Thus most elementary classes could happen only in the evening, when parents were at home."

Meanwhile, Indonesia's online instruction shift started later, in mid-March as schools shut down. "Everything moved to online. But of course, doing online teaching is a totally different animal compared to offline teaching... So after schools shut down, schools and offline tutoring institutions tried to do online teaching and online test prep. But they were clueless. The ministry of education endorsed several edtech platforms to help. Pahamify is one of them and we opened the access of our concept videos for free," shares Fikri.

In Indonesia, not only did schools shut down, college entrance exams were also postponed. The options for online alternatives were not convenient for students. Fikri points out, "The thing in edtech is, students just want to use the best product. Product that is reliable, has a good UX and offers good content."

That is where both Edmicro and Pahamify show the opportunity for their products, expertise, and technical capabilities to be of greater value to the market as schools remain closed in their countries. As the Edmicro founders put it, "In general, online learning has been a welcome alternative in this time of crisis. The pandemic has accelerated the digitalisation process in education years ahead."

Social Distancing Brings Edtech Closer to Students

With governments encouraging the use of online learning platforms, both Edmicro and Pahamify experienced a spike in growth over their lockdown period.

Even before the lockdown, Fikri shares that adoption on their platform had already been on the rise. "As a new player in town, we've been seeing double growth in the beginning of this year. And we mostly grew through organic channels. So students told us that our platform is the most caring education technology platform. It is the rookie online platform of the year because even if we're new, we've offered them with complete content, the best UI and the best UX."

Now, social distancing measures multiplied this exponential growth even more. This allowed them to hit record growth with minimal marketing spend. "These [social distancing measures] are serving as a catalyst for our product growth which already speaks for itself. We were trending quite frequently in Google Play Store, Social

Media like Twitter and also top the chart at AppStore without spending a lot of marketing budget."

Once the students are onboarded, Fikri says they were hooked. "For students, learning becomes fun and addictive for them once they know Pahamify… Because right now they use our app for around one hour a day. They said it changes the way they learn. That's why even though we've been seeing tremendous growth in the number of users, our play store rating is increasing."

In particular, because of the entrance exam postponement, test prep has become a popular service on Pahamify. "So the content related to School Aptitude Test such as reasoning test and math, they became trending videos in our app. In terms of features, we see students sharing our test-prep performance tracker in social media a lot, because they like to see their progress so they share it on social media. This feature is heavily used periodically and intensely during this COVID [crisis], because we are the only edtech platform who focuses on performance improvement in the Indonesia market. And clearly, it resonates with what the students are looking for."

For Edmicro, they had already been in talks to pilot their personalized learning platform in several provinces pre-lockdown. The COVID19 crisis sped things up significantly. "It took us a little time to realize this was a unique and rare opportunity for us. We had been in talks to pilot in several provinces before the crisis. The pandemic cut a lot of time in negotiation and paperwork. We got approved quickly as there was almost no other viable alternative. Then more and more schools and provinces asked to be included in the pilot."

Keeping Up with the Class

One challenge for platforms experiencing sudden spikes in demand is being able to keep up both on the technology side and the operations and customer experience side.

Edmicro did not face this problem on the technology side. "One of the right things we did from the beginning was building the products based on microservice and cloud infrastructure. Even though the number of active users increased tenfold within a few weeks, we were able to adapt quickly without any major disruption."

In terms of operations, they had to quickly expand their capabilities. "In just two to three weeks, we doubled the team. Since it was a lockdown, all interviews and onboarding for new employees were conducted online too. It was a "wartime" period for our company but the result was rewarding too. We successfully deployed in 250 schools in 11 provinces. 15,000 teachers and 300,000 students were onboarded."

For Pahamify, they have been working round-the-clock to serve users. "Due to the COVID situation, it's mandatory to quickly adjust our content production framework to be able to produce and conduct live streaming remotely. While our engineering team continuously optimizes the platform, the marketing team also needs to be responsive to see what's been going on from the users' perspective. Sometimes we couldn't fulfill all of their requests. Sometimes we even make mistakes and we have to admit it. And this is where having an intimate relationship with users matters the most."

Keeping Up the Good Work

Moving forward, both the Edmicro founders and Fikri expect online learning platforms to play a greater role in education.

The Edmicro founders framed it through three takeaways from their experience.

"We think there are a few lessons here. First, digital literacy should be a must in any national or regional curriculum. We are doing all kinds of things online now, in and out of the classroom. Thus governments and online learning platforms should discuss and implement digital literacy standards so that all students are well-prepared when coming to online learning.

Second, mobile learning should be prioritized more. In a low-middle income country like Vietnam, personal computers are quite rare, and smartphones are more affordable. It's a question of equal access too. What if some students have PCs while others don't?

Last but not least, we should care more about teachers too. What they need is not only online tools, but more guidance on how to switch to data-driven teaching and assessments."

Ultimately, online education will not replace traditional education. "It will be an essential companion. It addresses the core weakness of the current system: one-size-fit-all learning path. Schools and teachers are more ready than ever to adopt these online learning platforms. It is a question now of how quickly we can deploy and build up new ways of teaching and learning."

It is the same weakness present in Indonesia, but Fikri sees these problems being addressed on even larger scale as their local edtech market takes off. Live streaming is one approach. "Seeing the trends recently, I believe live streaming class is one of the things that we should put more effort to experiment with. And we kind of cracked some formula to it, we've been conducting this for the last two months and the [students] feel like this live-streaming session is just as powerful as the offline tutoring session. I believe this is where we can explore the possibilities in the future to improve the interaction between students and teachers online."

Regardless of the approach, Fikri emphasizes that seamless and efficient education should be core to the edtech platform's focus. "At the end of the day an edtech startup should put education first. What matters the most is how the student can learn from the teachers. How to keep this interaction seamless and learning process efficient by using technology. But what works in other countries might not work in Indonesia."

(41) Beyond the First-Order Impact is Second-Order Opportunity

Based on "Embrace the Vujade" by Paulo Joquiño. Published on 29 April 2020.

While it is important to focus on survival, startups in particular are in a position to use the crisis to innovate and prepare for what the world will need beyond the crisis event. The COVID19 crisis in particular has opened up many opportunities for digitalization, and this plays into the hands of many online platforms that are experiencing a surge in demand online. This piece explores what this push to digitalization means for the internet companies and internet experience of the future.

***

It was a comedian, the late George Carlin, who introduced the word, "vujade." It is dejavu flipped around, and according to Carlin, refers to the "strange feeling that, somehow, none of this has ever happened before" — a direct opposite of dejavu.

With the COVID19 crisis, this feeling is all too familiar. In webinars on business strategy, panelists are often asked to identify what is dejavu and vujade about our current situation *vis-à-vis* past crises, with questions like, "What lessons can be learned from previous financial crises? How is this crisis different?"

While this certainly has predictable economic effects, and there is much to be learned from the past, this current crisis is fundamentally different in its nature. Its nature as a fundamental threat to our physical well-being make its impact far more widespread than any financial crises.

Even among viruses, its virulity and our globalized world have made its spread more rapid and intense than previous epidemics in this century.

All in all, the crisis invokes less dejavu than it does vujade. The feeling forces radical shifts in perception and opinion.

One immediate example of its manifestation is the realization that this virus-induced crisis has been and will continue to be far more commonplace and dangerous than we would like to believe. From an economic standpoint, the bull run of the last 10 years or so was a rare record rather than a norm — and some would even argue that a correction has long been in the making. Due to this shift in perspective, healthcare systems can be expected to change over the next few years, as governments try to prepare for future outbreaks.

For tech startups, assumptions and commonly held perspectives are also being upended by the crisis. In order to adapt to these changes, founders needs to embrace vujade rather than escape it. Below are some of these overturned assumptions on what businesses, and tech startups in particular can do to embrace the vujade.

Go Digital to Keep Up

Digitalization will no longer be an alternative, but a norm for business, as it permeates nearly every aspect of operating in a COVID19 world, from video conferencing to digital storefronts. Even after lockdown measures are lifted and a vaccine becomes widely accessible, the efficiencies (or even delight, in the case of gaming and entertainment platforms) realized from being forced to spend time online may be enough to retain users.

It will be easier to drive adoption as more people will have experience using online platforms. However, setting up a significant moat with a digital solution will lose its novelty or value. Even traditional businesses with physical goods or in-person services are venturing into shifting transactions and specific processes online, as in the case of dark stores for retail or even telemedicine for clinics.

It does not mean that the role of platform companies as outsiders looking in will be rendered unnecessary as industries are forced to undergo change inside out. On the contrary, there is more room for platform companies to enable digital transformation, but it will take more than just setting up a marketplace or Uber-izing an industry.

Battle for the Superior Online Experience

Disruption will no longer be about simply bringing people online, but making these online experiences more refined and curated. With more exposure to various online platforms, consumers and even businesses will have more defined and smarter preferences when it comes to what they want and need from a digital solution.

While the usual route is to take on cash-driven price wars to compete over users, we have seen from the larger players in Southeast Asia that this is not sustainable, nor does it assure the longevity of any user on the platform.

The competition will purely have to be on how well the customer is able to use the product, and whether or not it meets their expectations. This will be crucial especially in the short-term as customers will be stingier given the cash crunch many are undergoing.

This competition on experience may result in the deeper personalization of user experiences. Depending on how inefficient the distribution of these services has proven to be as a result of COVID19, platforms will seek to leverage on technology like AI and machine learning to better curate the user experience and focus on specific user needs. In Vietnam's trucking industry, even before COVID19, LOGIVAN had already introduced AI models and algorithms to better curate shipper offers for truckers in the spot market.

While this approach to curate solutions specific to markets and users is important in operating in a region like Southeast Asia, the challenge with personalization is to still maintain a level of standardization across the platform that users can come to expect.

Operate in Smaller and Smaller Circles

While the online experience will continue to eat up most of our day-to-day activities, many of the gears that allow these online experiences to happen at scale will remain offline. These include manufacturing, logistics, and service industries (e.g., food delivery).

However, because of the varying responses of countries to COVID19, these industries may be operating differently and separately across markets even in the medium-term.

The diversification of the global supply chain, already set in motion by the China–US trade war, will be accelerated. More manufacturing hubs will be set up to serve local market demand, as in Vietnam or Thailand. Service industries will have to come up with localized standards depending on the government response in each market they operate in.

The world will certainly continue to grow smaller with the internet economy, but smaller and smaller circles of operations will be set up within markets. This will be necessary to sustain the flow of goods as countries go on-and-off lockdowns and implement varied mitigation strategies in the foreseeable future.

Data as Building Blocks

In order to effectively operate under these new norms — which themselves are changing rapidly — businesses will need data, not just as a resource, but an integral part of the business operation and culture. From the new oil refined for business growth, data becomes the building blocks of the digital business.

Because platforms will be competing on the superiority of their user experience (i.e., how well do you know your customers?) and markets will be localizing, setting up information flows into the company's operation to stay on top of shifting consumer needs and market developments will be important. For many industries, the data and information are already online, and it becomes a matter of setting up platforms to acquire, process, and communicate that data faster.

Having this kind of data-driven approach to running the business requires not only data, but discipline. Indonesian fintech AwanTunai's Dino Setiawan shares that this mindset towards data needs the discipline to be transparent, even internally, about what is working and what is not working. Information is only as useful as it is interpreted.

Going Back to Building

Over the last decade, especially in Southeast Asia, cash has been chasing after growth. Secure cash, then you could build (or arguably in most cases, subsidize) what you need to grow. This cash-driven growth has resulted in cases of mega rounds and high valuations on top of models dependent largely on subsidies.

With COVID19, as the cash moving around dwindles down, the thought process is reversing. The crisis may have called for businesses to be lean and do some serious house repairs, but it is also calling tech startups back to building. Given the shifts in competition, data, and globalization, companies also need to revisit the kinds of systems and infrastructure that will be needed to face a post-COVID19 world.

It is an opportune time to focus on developing products better suited to the changing market and test them with customers who are actually looking for these products given their situations have changed. It does not have to be an entirely new development — it can be new ways of packaging and distributing existing products and services.

However, building is not just confined to programming and engineering products. Given how tech companies in Southeast Asia have some level of offline component or network, maintaining business relationships and listening to people on the ground is important for the building to be effective.

Building can also be about culture — for some companies that have been through tumultuous internal issues, this is an opportunity to review values and routines that have defined the organization, whether these are necessary or efficient and whether they can be improved.

Building can also be centered around repairing and replacing exists elements in the organization — for example, replacing internal communication channels with more efficient ways of sharing information real-time.

At the end of the day, this kind of growth makes for companies that are better in touch with the value they create and deliver rather than valuations that are continually subject to the ebb and flow of the market.

(42) Considerations for Digitalization in a Crisis

Based on "Making the exodus to online business" by Joolin Chuah. Published on 22 April 2020.

There has been a popular meme going around in the wake of the COVID19 crisis that COVID19 has become many business's Chief Digitalization Officer. Digitalization is not as straightforward as having a website however, especially with many businesses competing for the online attention of consumers. The company must be well suited financially and operationally to take on business online. The business should also be able to explore new ways to engage customers given shifting consumer preferences because of the crisis.

***

Singapore announced on 21 April 2020 that their lockdown, locally termed "circuit breaker," will be extended to the first of June that year after first being implemented two weeks prior. It is the latest in a line of measures meant to stem a second wave of infections coming into a country lauded by the WHO and the media for being one of the countries leading the pandemic response.

Meanwhile, a vaccine is expected to come out in the next 12 to 18 months. This means the recovery timeline in Singapore and other East Asian countries where the pandemic first hit, let alone the rest of the world, will go well beyond 2020.

This drawn out timeline has forced businesses to be much more cautious and conservative. For startups accustomed to accessible sources of outside capital, for example, this means having at least enough runway to last through the next 24 months.

For traditional, offline businesses like restaurants, retail stores, and hotels, the timeline offers no relief in the foreseeable future as revenue dropped sharply and continues to burrow deeper with people staying home and adhering to social distancing guidelines in place across the globe. Even though lockdowns have been lifted in China, the pandemic's first epicenter, social behaviors remain skewed towards caution and safety, and demand has not returned to pre-COVID19 levels.

This new normal of consumers preferring reduced contact and less offline interactions is something that many businesses are now preparing for.

Online Platforms Riding the Adoption Wave

At the same time, while revenues have dropped significantly in businesses heavily dependent on offline transactions, online businesses have been *largely* experiencing a spike in demand.

The rapid change in community needs — and how to meet these needs safely — have caused (if not forced) this spike. It is reflected in the surge in orders for food and grocery delivery, as households prefer the convenience of being able to get essentials to their doorsteps with minimal contact. There has also been a surge in online education and gaming as more people, especially students, spend more of their time on their devices at home.

Internet technology businesses are well suited to meet these needs. The technology is scalable, unbounded by physical stores and the need for foot traffic, and lightweight, with minimum cost and capital expenditures.

Video conferencing platforms have been "Exhibit A" for the positive impact of this "new normal." From 20 million daily active users (DAU) in December last year, Zoom has since grown to 200 million monthly active users (MAU) and a $42 billion valuation today; Teams now have 44 million DAU, up 12 million since the outbreak began.

Not only have these platforms reaped the fruits of massively increasing adoption; they have also responded to it with new features for retention, from virtual backgrounds to more security features and low bandwidth support.

New Normal: A Call to Shift with Consumers to Online Platforms

It is not all magic and rainbows, however. The rapid adoption of these online platforms has put pressure on these businesses to better manage supply chains to meet customer demand (as in the case of Amazon) and deliver on more efficiency (as in the case of streaming and video platforms).

Seeing that even digital-first businesses are facing difficulties at their own game, every business may not be well suited to go online from the get-go. However, the current situation is forcing this option on the table even for those who may not have considered this direction before.

Over last month, economies around the world have been experiencing historic unemployment spikes, with the US tallying more than 22 million unemployment claims — the most in their history. This widespread loss of income means spending power will shift online, and this new normal may not include offline channels of consumption.

It is against this backdrop that businesses face a sudden exodus towards online channels. Internet technology offers efficiency and reach to consumers while the physical world remains safely distanced for the foreseeable future.

How can your business suit up and make the most out of possibilities of internet technology?

Travel Light

In the short-term, it is critical for cost-cutting measures to be in place for your existing business operations. It is hard to stay ahead or even move forward when you are weighed down by business baggage that may not be making the same returns they did before the pandemic struck.

That includes turning offline stores into dark stores, where only curbside pickups or deliveries are allowed, or reorganizing your marketing team towards capabilities for customer acquisition through online marketing. The goal is to enable the business to continue serving customers safely and efficiently and perhaps even capture more customers online.

The business should also aim to keep human resource allocation efficient and non-redundant, and this will result in layoffs, especially for businesses that have relied on high staff count to cater to foot traffic in physical stores.

Apart from operations and human resources, look at the balance sheet as well. Address low grade SKUs, high and recurring capex, accounts payable and receivable.

Ultimately, the goal is for the business to be lean enough, not only to weather out the storm, but also to have the cash and business focus to explore new sources of revenue.

Explore and Unlock New Sources of Revenue

Never put your eggs in one basket. The same goes for businesses moving online. You need to think about how your SKUs or offerings will (1) be valuable and economic for consumers during and even beyond the pandemic, and (2) effectively translate into products or services available online. These will take time and resources, but it is important to develop new insights on the consumer as behaviors and preferences rapidly change.

It is key to rethink assumptions about what consumers need and consider opening up to new SKUs that better cater to the new normal. While consumers are looking to stock up on daily necessities, not all daily goods and services are as necessary now as they were before. US oil prices for example, went negative for the first time in history as oil companies face an oversupply. Groceries are shifting from non-perishable to perishable goods, as consumers look for items like fresh produce.

These assumptions go beyond daily necessities and extend to all aspects of life, from education to investments. Online learning platforms are turning books into online-first, mobile-first content like videos or podcasts. Retail investment offerings are moving from stocks to more long-term savings products.

Even customer preferences towards non-essentials like luxury items need to be reconsidered. Is it the same as in China, where Hermes saw more than two million in sales on the weekend after lockdown measures were lifted? The shifts may be even more varied across markets the less essential these items are.

The shifts will vary across industries and markets, but understanding what consumers value and are willing to spend their (constrained) income on will make it clear what other baskets are out there.

Opening up new sources of revenue is not just about finding new SKUs. It can also be about looking at new ways to bundle and distribute these SKUs. In other words, instead of looking for new baskets, perhaps it is time to switch out the basket for an online shop. Moving online offers low-cost, time-efficient, and possibly even more engaging ways to introduce new bundling and distribution, versus having to refurbish physical stores or coordinate an offline marketing campaign across markets.

For example, with more consumers purchasing essential items as family units (or sometimes entire neighborhoods), grocery and food platforms can offer more affordable family-based packages for delivery on top of regular ala carte.

E-commerce, meanwhile, is merging with online entertainment as brands tap into opportunities to sell products through live streaming platforms. The "lipstick queen" Li Jiaqi, for example, reaches tens of millions of consumers every day, a gold mine for lipstick brands. This live streaming evolution of e-commerce offers a new way to distribute products online at relatively low cost and massive scale — what home shopping television did to store retail back in the day.

Finally, sometimes new sources of revenue are not necessarily a result of introducing new offerings or packages but a result of new segments of consumers being able to access your business. Less cross-border travelling may bode well for more local consumption in the post-COVID world, from snacks to car rentals.

Look for Company Along the Way (if you have Cash to Spare)

During this crisis, transitioning online may need more than cost-cutting measures and new revenue sources. The business needs to be able to work with partners and the larger ecosystem, especially if these partnerships bring more efficiency to the table.

Global supply chains are being diversified as companies protect themselves against the risk of export/import bans and price gouging. COVID19 will see a world that leans more towards more localized and regionalized supply chains. This may be an opportunity to work with local partners at lower cost, especially for smaller businesses that are not necessarily working with resources unavailable in their locality.

For businesses with more than 24 months runway and yet unable to take off with cost-cutting and generating new sources of revenue, cash can be devoted to acquiring a smaller player faring far better. This partnership can set up new lead generation channels and open up new markets.

If there is a player experiencing hockey stick growth online but is in need of more back-end resources and supply chain connections for example, this could be the entry point for larger, arguably slower businesses to move in. It is all about finding the right fit to help both businesses in the deal to thrive online.

This outlook is useful in industries where combining capabilities to reach scale will enable more efficiency during this pandemic.

While all businesses are being heavily impacted in the crisis, the shared impact and shared desire to survive and thrive make it possible to explore collaboration where there was likely no interest or motivation before.

(43) Data as Building Blocks

Based on "Data in a post-COVID world: highways of the digital economy" by Paulo Joquiňo. Published 16 April 2020.

Data plays many roles in the digital economy, from a resource fueling tech giants and multinationals undergoing digital transformation to the produce reaped and grown by tech startups.

In the wake of COVID19, it is now playing a greater role in facilitating more secure, accurate, and transparent connections and communication among consumers and businesses as they move more of their offline lifestyle and operations online.

Oil of the Digital Rigs

In 2006, British mathematician and architect Clive Humbly is said to have coined the phrase, "data is the new oil." These words heralded its value but at the same time pointing out how it needs refining to truly become useful. This phrase summed up the rising value of data — and the need for people and resources devoted to refining it — in a world of rapid digitalization.

Since then, this phrase has itself been refined for various industries and businesses. In particular, technology and software companies, at the forefront of the revolution, have been reaping the benefits of scale when it came to data processing.

It has become part of the tech startup ethos to acquire and leverage on data — be it to tap into network effects and build moats around their user base with this data. In 2017, *The Economist* brought to the forefront the effects of technology companies dominating the economy with the data they had been able to amass.

In a previous piece, we covered how one of our companies, car marketplace Carro, is leveraging data it had amassed over its operation in Southeast Asia. With the data, it expanded its business beyond a marketplace into financial services for car owners and sellers. This not only strengthens incentives for their users and partners to stay on the platform, but has also kept the business running during COVID19 as marketplace demand dropped.

Fruits of the Digital Farms

The "data is the new oil" paradigm stemmed from the idea that a digital economy makes it valuable. In emerging markets like Southeast Asia, data is not just a non-renewable resource like oil, it needs to be made available and valuable with the right technology.

Having seen how digital tools can turn data into firepower, startups tackling largely offline markets are reverse engineering the process — using data to create digital tools and sustainable businesses from square one.

Metaphorically, it has evolved one step further from a non-renewable product to be drilled from the depths of the earth to become a sustainable, renewable resource that is both cause and effect of digitalization. Technology companies have, from one point of view, become digital data farms, not just rigs drilling for data — where data is planted, harvested, and whose fruit are then used to produce more data.

For AwanTunai, data has been a key component of their business from day one. CEO and co-founder Dino Setiawan explains how they worked with FMCG wholesalers to obtain and digitize transaction data on micro-merchants to provide access to financing for the latter. Eventually, the mine they had struck attracted banks, institutions, and other investors to support them with capital.

The data they had discovered in the downstream supply chain was inherently valuable already. What Dino and co-founders did was develop the infrastructure (also known as the farm) to make it valuable at scale, and it has since allowed them to explore other services for micro-merchants and wholesalers. The data was enabling adoption of digital services in a valuable way.

Data also drives retention. Customers value transparency especially in traditionally opaque transactions, and data-driven efficiency can be a reliable way to keep partners and suppliers onboard. Sayurbox co-founder and CEO Amanda Susanti shares how visibility over the quality of the fresh produce they source directly from farms is crucial to the consumer experience.

For Sayurbox's own supply chain, being able to monitor supply and demand data allows them to be more flexible when it comes to distributing the fresh produce across different business lines. This reduces waste and helps farmers get a better return on their produce — key to retaining them on the platform.

Sustaining the Highways of the Digital Economy

In the COVID19 pandemic, the role of data in the digital world is once again evolving. As more business and day-to-day activities are forced to go online, data is no longer simply a result nor a tool of digitalization. The digital economy in the wake of COVID19 will be populated with more individuals and organizations operating online. This presents an opportunity for business in particular to make processes more efficient and secure at scale, especially when it comes to information flows. Leveraging on the ability of data to scale the capabilities of digital technology will be critical to achieving this efficiency and security.

Highway checkpoints

Curation mechanisms will play a larger role in the digital economy, especially now as the world not only battles with a pandemic but an "infodemic" as well. Think of these mechanisms as border controls in the highways of the digital economy.

Social media platforms are being pressured to play a more conscientious role in curation, as many people now locked up in their homes depend on internet platforms for up-to-date information.

Tech companies are also playing a direct role in the pandemic response by supporting governments through real-time contact tracing and quarantine monitoring.

This brings to question the standards with which technology platforms obtain and curate the data they amass from users. This has been a key issue of internet regulation in the past decade, and privacy laws have since been erected, but the years that follow will likely see more action being done to either set up these border controls or take them down.

Highway maintenance and protection

The digital economy also needs to accommodate more activity and this means being able to manage and secure data for an even larger population. Enterprise software applications are facing this challenge as they take in more customers. Organizations, now with the challenge of managing operations online, are also thinking of ways to keep communication flows intact and efficient.

Now, organizations will be thinking more about how they can integrate a data strategy into their operation, or leveraging on digitized data to make once offline transactions more efficient. Think of this data strategy as paving the roads for online communication and operation. The more paved the roads are, the smoother the flow within an organization. One can expect more players in the race to provide tools that can help organizations manage data securely and efficiently.

Increased visibility and optionality

Finally, as more people do their day-to-day activities online or with the help of a digital tool, from exercising to grocery shopping, visibility and optionality features will be a critical value proposition. Adoption will be less about getting people online as it will be making the online experience optimal for them.

Technology platforms will have to be more conscious in helping their consumers make informed decisions. These also play into how they can make an even more personalized experience for each of their users. Faced with criticism for using China data storage centers, Zoom has recently offered the option for paying customers to select their own data center. Marketplaces with physical storefronts like automobile shops and even real estate are also exploring virtual stores and experiences to create visibility on their products online.

Innovators do not Just Weather Crises, They See Opportunity Amidst the Storm

Takeaways on crisis management:

(1) *Maintaining a healthy cashflow requires a holistic approach,* from looking at line items on the balance sheet to considering new ways to do business.

(2) *The best way to work through a crisis is to prepare for recovery or the upturn.* Develop capabilities and culture, repair inefficiencies in operations, and strengthen partnerships. Ultimately, founders that thrive coming out of a crisis are those that display *resilience and independence amid the adversity.*

(3) Digitalization is being driven by the COVID19 crisis in particular, but it will not just be about bringing business online. *There will be new expectations for the internet experience. Data will also have a larger role to play in sustaining information flows as businesses move more of their operations online.*

Chapter Nine

Exit Ahoy!

Innovators do not exit companies; they build enduring ones.

"Exploration is in our nature. We began as wanderers, and we are wanderers still. We have lingered long enough on the shores of the cosmic ocean. We are ready at last to set sail for the stars."
— Carl Sagan, *Astronomer*

In 1977, two spacecraft, Voyager 1 and 2, were sent out into the solar system. In 1990, they surpassed the orbit of Pluto and are now in empty space, with around 40,000 years before they reach the next planetary system.

Before the spacecrafts took off, NASA placed twin copper records on both. Each record is enclosed in an aluminum jacket, with a cartridge, needle, and symbols to explain the origin of the spacecraft and instructions on how to play the record.

This "Golden Record," as it is called, contains 115 images, select music, sounds from Earth, and greetings in 55 languages. The record is essentially an imprint of the Earth and humanity, meant for any extra-terrestrial life that finds it to get a glimpse of humanity.

These records are no explorers, but their exploration will endure. They will exist long after this century, and daresay long after this Earth exists. A somber thought, but such is the vastness and emptiness of space.

Tech startups are only a phenomenon of recent history, with the commercialization of the Internet, the computer, and the microchip semiconductor mid to late 20th century. And while startups seek to endure, the Internet and the markets are not as quiet as the open space.

Achieving endurance as a company has been concretized as the exit, especially from the point-of-view of investors. Exits are not only milestone that can deliver exponential returns, but they have also been portrayed as a graduation of sorts for the startup. For the wider startup ecosystem, the size, number, and valuation of companies exited is often used as an indicator of the ecosystem's health. The reason this is the case is because exits are not just events in and of themselves but culminations of several years of strategic decisions, investor relationships, and even government policy (in certain cases) that all had to fall into place.

In Southeast Asia, even as the number of exits has grown tremendously over the past decade, exits remain on the earlier side of a startup's growth, and are mostly acquisitions made by industry incumbents or tech unicorns. Then there was Sea Group's IPO in the US in 2017. As more foreign capital flows in and tech majors from other markets double down on the region, exits in the region will continue to increase, and will likely continue to be dominated by acquisitions, though channels for IPOs are emerging for local startups.

***

This chapter tackles exits from a big picture perspective — from exits as the result of strategic decisions made by the startup from day one, exits as part of a larger effort to see the upside of technology in Southeast Asia, and IPOs as the beginning to a new life for the company.

Essays in this Chapter

(44) **The decisions behind success.** Exits are already in the making long before they are discussions in the board room. How the company is built and the decisions made as it grows have a role

to play in how the startup reaches its proverbial "South Pole."
Based on "What it takes to win (in Southeast Asia)" by Paulo Joquiňo. Published on 11 June 2020.

(45) **The bigger picture.** Making an exit is not a sure win. Even then, investors are doggedly determined by the upside potential of technology (in Southeast Asia). *Based on "Making sense of the We who cried IPO" by Paulo Joquiňo. Published on 18 November 2019.*

(46) **Redefining success and exits for startups.** A look at why tech startup IPOs are almost non-existent in Southeast Asia and what it really means to IPO. *Based on "Beyond the Gong: Succeeding in the Public Markets" by Paulo Joquiňo. Published on 25 November 2019.*

(44) The Decisions Behind Success

Based on "What it takes to win (in Southeast Asia)" by Paulo Joquiňo. Published on 11 June 2020.

The path to building a great technology company is like a pioneering expedition. In a rapidly emerging region like Southeast Asia, this is especially the case. Founders in the region are faced with competition racing to lead the digitalization rush, the unfavorable odds of expanding across countries in the region, and the uncertainty in today's global economy.

Much of what prepares a company for a successful exit happens long before an exit is even in sight — from the early days of the company. A successful exit is built on the accumulation of strategic decisions over the course of the company's growth that make it suitable for an IPO or an M&A. Then the rest comes down to market conditions, as exits are ultimately judged by the buyers, whether they be stock market investors or companies.

***

On December 14, 1911, Roald Amundsen's expedition reached the South Pole. They had beaten Robert Falcon Scott by five weeks to become the first at the coveted destination, but what makes this story even more interesting is the return. Amundsen's entire team returned safely to Norway, while Scott and those with him at the Pole all perished.

Just as these explorers and many before them sought to reach the Pole and survive to tell the victorious tale, so are many startup founders in Southeast Asia seeking to create an indelible impact in the region.

I selected three aspects of their journey where Amundsen's and Scott's decisions on each spelled the difference between life and death, and between becoming first and second. Each aspect bears insight relevant for startup founders, who, like these explorers, face extreme conditions as they seek to become market leaders.

(1) Where they set up their base camp: Winners do not underestimate the impact of a compelling market entry.
(2) How they traversed Antarctica: Winners find the most suitable and simplest vehicles to scale.
(3) How they rationed food and fuel: It is not about size, but about spend. Winners do not always start with the largest war chests, but they always have the most efficient capital spend.
(4) How they set up their supply depots: Winners are able to maximize each fundraising round for the journey ahead.

Where is Your Business's Base Camp Located?

Nailing down an impactful entry into the market can spell the difference between winning and losing. "A good beginning is half the journey," the Chinese proverb says. For venture-backed startups, this means addressing a compelling market need.

For Amundsen, that meant setting up basecamp as close to the South Pole as possible. He camped 96 kilometers closer to the South Pole than Scott, at a location that would lessen the time spent at the high altitude of the Antarctic plateau. The Norwegian explorer had his eyes set on reaching the pole first, after previously failing to reach the North Pole first — the expedition's original objective.[1]

____

[1] When Amundsen's expedition failed to reach the North Pole first, he switched the expedition objective unbeknownst to his backers. Not exactly the best example to follow in this regard.

	Amundsen	Scott	Insight
Base camp	96 km closer to Pole than Scott Less time spent on high altitudes	Set-up close to area suited for geographical exploration and scientific study; longer route	Market entry should be substantial and aligned with end goals
Transport	Dog-skis	Mix of ponies and man-hauling	Vehicles to scale should be simple and suitable to the market
Rationing	More than enough for 19 men Sealed fuel cans	Just enough for 65 men Leaked fuel cans	Efficient capital spend
Depots	7:2 vs Scott Lined with bamboo flags for visibility	2:7 vs Amundsen Single flag	Maximize fundraising rounds for what the journey requires

Figure 10. Amundsen–Scott South Pole race as analogy for startup growth

Meanwhile, reaching the South Pole was only one of the multiple objectives of Scott's Terra Nova Expedition. While Scott's base was located in an area better suited for geographical exploration and scientific study, he knew that it was a poor route to the pole. That decision would lose him and his men several days and valuable resources.

In the same way, we have seen how in Southeast Asia, the likes of Grab and Gojek grew massively on top of high-frequency needs for a large market: ride-hailing for the former, and the ojek for the latter. Even then, their choice of basecamp was just the first of many more decisions optimized for scale. How the mission translates to business goals changes over time, as it did for Amundsen, who was initially set for the Arctic. But North Pole or South Pole, he made sure his starting point was optimized to achieve his mission.

Is Your Business Riding Ponies or Dogs?

These expeditions' choice of transport to reach the Pole is analogous to the various vehicles businesses use to scale. This can range from customer acquisition funnels (to scale users) to country managers and local teams (to scale the organization) and even tech stack and data storage (to scale digital capacity).

Amundsen went with dog-skis, which he was familiar with as a Norwegian and also from living with Eskimos. He also hired experienced dog drivers to make the use of the dogs as efficient as possible. Scott employed a mixture of pony and human hauling, a decision influenced by experiences in prior expeditions.

A key question to ask is, "Are these vehicles actually effective, or are they costing the business?" Effective vehicles for scale are suited to the environment and simple.

(1) *Suited to the environment:* Dogs are naturally better suited to Antarctica. When it comes to expanding the business, it is key to match local operations and talent with what will be more sustainable in the specific market or vertical.

(2) *Simple:* Scott's mix of ponies, walking, and sleds became dependent on the weakest link. Amundsen relied solely on their dogs because he had seen it work. While there was an argument to be made for not putting all of one's eggs in one basket, having a clear understanding of what works best in the market should make things simpler. For businesses, simplicity can be achieved through rapid iteration and experimentation.

In Southeast Asia, choosing ponies over dogs to trek over ice can be costly. Such is the case for businesses that have tried to penetrate and digitalize the region's rural economies. At the same time, we have seen how companies like Super and Payfazz, whose founders have roots and experiences in Indonesia's second-tier and third-tier cities, are able to leverage on deeper local understanding to pick the right "dogs" to drive digital adoption, whether it is agents for social commerce or warungs for financial services. We have also seen how companies like AwanTunai and LOGIVAN underwent rapid iteration early on to zero-in on a simple solution to tackle complex long-standing problems like SME lending in Indonesia and trucking market inefficiencies in Vietnam.

How are you Rationing?

Scholars of these expeditions found that the rations for Scott's team of 65 were inadequate, had half the required calories for man hauling at high altitudes (as part of their transportation mix) and were deficient in vitamins B and C. Tin cans of cooking fuel necessary for food and hydration (as it melts the ice for water) were found to have leaks, allowing the fuel to be vaporized by the sun. All these led to a weak, undernourished, and dehydrated team.

Meanwhile, Amundsen's 19 men — less than a third of Scott's team — gained weight from the expedition. They had packed more than enough rations and fuel. Amundsen learned from previous expeditions to solder their cooking fuel cans shut. Fifty years later, a fuel depot was found to have these fuel cans still preserved.

Interestingly, the lesson for founders here is not to have the larger war chest (though that is certainly an advantage), but the more efficient capital spend. Even if Scott and Amundsen received the same amount of dollar backing, it is highly likely that with the same resource planning decisions the results would have been the same. An efficient capital spend takes into account three things as we learn from Amundsen: quality, allocation, and control.

(1) *Quality.* Even though Scott had enough food for his 65 men, it was nutrient-deficient and not enough to support the energy required for the kind of transportation he wanted to employ. The quality of capital spend needs to match the operations of the team and demands of the market. Every dollar should be focused on what is needed to grow the business.

(2) *Allocation.* Amundsen allotted way more resources than his team of 19 needed, as he created margins for the unpredictability of the Antarctic environment. It is also important to note here that Amundsen's team of 19 was specifically formed to reach a Pole and return safely, composed of expert navigators and dog drivers. So, not only was his spending more efficient, but it was also more productive.

(3) *Control.* Amundsen made sure not to let valuable fuel leak or vaporize in his depots. The way the startup is structured should prevent unnecessary spending. Having a disciplined CFO and finance team is important in this regard.

Southeast Asia demands efficient capital spend, as a diverse startup ecosystem emerging on the heels of a market focusing on sustainability and profitability. The differences across industries and markets call for a nuanced approach to COGS and operational expenses, especially for the cross-border company. The competitive talent market, especially for engineers, also incentivizes startups to run productive, tight ships for productive hiring spend. Add the ongoing crisis into the mix, and the pressure runs high for founders to keep their operations lean and fit while having the margins to protect the business against further market shocks.

Where are your Depots?

A year after the expeditions, Scott and his men were found in their tent 11 miles away from the nearest depot. Had they reached that depot or had the depot been placed closer to the pole, they might not have perished on their return. For every seven depots Amundsen laid on the route to the Pole, Scott only had two. While Amundsen set up lines of bamboo flags for returning parties to locate the depots, Scott only used single flags.

Startups also need their depots to boost growth. The takeaway from the Amundsen–Scott comparison is not to increase the quantity of "depots", but to maximize the value of each round for the journey ahead. Just as laying out the depots strategically was critical for these explorer's survival; timing is key for startups to close in the best possible rounds. Core to maximizing each round is staying on top of company growth and having the ability to tell this story to investors.

Especially in this fundraising winter, it is all the more important to maximize each "depot". For startups that are seeing a remarkable uptake in traction, perhaps it would be a good opportunity to make the case to investors for more funding to secure this significant growth down the road.

Winning the Battle before it Happens

What I covered are just three aspects of Amundsen's and Scott's where differences in their approach spelled winning for one and perishing for the other. There are many more decisions and factors that came into play. However, what I believe truly made a difference was Amundsen's focused decision-making.

And this focus was present long before the actual expedition. The South Pole expeditions of 1911–1912 winter are a classic case of overcoming crises before they happen — or in Sun Tzu's words, "Every battle is won or lost before it is ever fought." Amundsen did not underestimate his odds, and more than adequately prepared for the harsh tundra of the South Pole. Scott had left much to chance, and ironically enough, experiences of past expeditions (which had all failed to reach the Pole).

Amundsen's every decision (or risk), from selecting a basecamp to riding dogs, was optimized for the goal of reaching the South Pole first. For startups, it boils down to what the founders want to achieve. There is a lot of space for long-term growth in Southeast Asia, even with the current crisis. The challenge for founders in Southeast Asia is not a shortage of opportunity (or arguably even capital), but having the clarity to seek out the right opportunities and focus to turn these opportunities into victories.

(45) The Bigger Picture

Based on "Making sense of the We who cried IPO" by Paulo Joquiño. Published on 18 November 2019.

Part of the decision making that will spell success or failure for a startup's exit are the fundraising deals it makes along the way and the nature of the relationship between founders and investors. This essay looks at failures from the point-of-view of investors, and the bigger picture that continues to drive venture funding.

✳✳✳

Losses are Part-and-Parcel of the VC Industry

When it comes to investing in fast-growing technology companies, risk is always part of the deal. There is the uncertainty that comes with scaling a presumably innovative business model or product, the volatility of disrupting often entrenched markets or industries, and the unpredictability of human behavior that comes with managing a fast-growing company.

For all the due diligence, analysis, and even intuition that goes into deal making, losses remain part-and-parcel of the VC industry, be it as a result of a missed opportunity or a misplaced bet. From that perspective, WeWork's fiasco and the subsequent entrenchment of Softbank does not deviate from the spectrum of possible investment scenarios.

The scale and anticipation have certainly drawn in an equivalent amount of attention and commentary, but similar cases have come up prior to WeWork in varying degrees.

More than what can be learned from the fiasco (nothing new), it is the implications for ecosystems that are much more compelling. For Southeast Asia in particular, it is a signpost for VCs in the region to re-evaluate capital flows in the region as more money will continue to flow in, especially from China. What is the bigger picture for these investments?

The Southeast Asia thesis

The recent influx of investments into Southeast Asia are largely motivated by the potential value of capitalizing on technological niches. It is not just about finding the next billion-dollar company that disrupts an industry, but the next billion-dollar industry or ecosystem that caters to the diversity of localities and needs across the region. It is not just about producing exits, but exits that can support these industries long-term. This means a good balance of growth and profitability, which is becoming more attainable with smarter money in the region.

Smarter money means investing is not just about making individual bets, but testing different theses in the market over time. Aside from capital, VCs help founders to achieve the shared vision of the company by investing time with the company. Much of the effort placed by investors into the region has gone into supporting founders post-money, providing access 24/7 to networks, services, and experience. VC is no longer simply an industry that bridges capital but also a whole variety of resources, from tech services to hiring for senior positions and PR support.

This paradigm is reflected by the region's unicorns as well. While notably loss-making, they are also taking the lead on carving a path towards sustainable growth, focusing on growing ecosystems of value rather than solely betting on market share domination. This incentivizes earlier-stage players to build their ventures not just on valuations but on value; and WeWork's story only reaffirms this.

This Southeast Asia perspective does not take away the risk that comes with investing, nor does it take away the potential losses to be had. Even with these theses, not all are proven right in the end. Ultimately, the difference lies in the process. Bets are in the momentary roll of the dice, while testing theses are in the day-in and day-out support of startup growth. Achieving unicorn status should be less the miracle that everyone marvels at but no one understands, and more catalysts of long-term value across the region.

(46) Redefining Success and Exits for Startups

Based on "Beyond the Gong: Succeeding in the Public Markets" by Paulo Joquiño. Published on 25 November 2019.

Information and quotes are adapted from a closed-door panel on "Going Public for Technology Companies" held with Aaron Tan, co-founder and CEO of Carro, and Mohamed Ismail, Global Head of Equity Markets at the Singapore Exchange in October 2018.

Startups are first and foremost businesses that drive innovation. It is easy to get lost in all the expectations of fundraising, but exiting is only a means to achieve the true goal of a startup: to drive positive, scalable impact for their industry or market.

***

The exit landscape in Southeast Asia remains driven largely by M&A deals. The pool of buyers has expanded from industry incumbents and old money conglomerates to include even the unicorn platforms like Gojek, which acquired more than seven startups in the last three years. The takeover value of tech companies in Southeast Asia has steadily increased over the last three years from \$1.7 billion in the first half of 2017 to \$4.9 billion over the same period this year, and shows no signs of slowing down moving into 2025.

Even then, the numbers still pale in comparison to more mature markets, and late stage funds are still waiting for the big-ticket M&A deals and IPOs to reach a critical mass before doubling down on the region. Liquidity events at this scale will be the ground-breaking proof for global investors that the region's technology space is ripe for heavy picking.

Opportunities and Cautionary Tales

However, when it comes to IPOs, they are less of a holy grail for tech startups in the region than they are in the West or China. The differences across markets make the whole affair much less straightforward. And this intimidating image of IPOs has only been buffed up by the failure of recent, high-profile IPOs in more mature markets to meet the prophesied expectations of investors.

Even then, as more capital flows into the region, there are more accessible pathways and opportunities for tech startups to transition into the public markets. Institutional platforms in the public market like the Singapore Exchange (SGX) emphasize the benefits of going public, and that goes beyond the reliable access to capital.

> "You would be recognized as achieving the gold standard in regulation and governance, and that gives you a lot of credibility as you go out to expand across the region. That is invaluable. It can give you opportunities and visibility that you may not have had before."
> — *Mohamed Nasser Ismail, Senior Vice President and Global Head of Equity Capital Markets at SGX*

However, if there is anything for founders to take away from the recent IPO shocks, it is that the public markets are not for everyone and it takes more than just shouting "unicorn," billion-dollar valuations, or an investment story to win over public market investors. While this approach has worked for a handful of companies, it often results in a "Boy Who Cried IPO" scenario for many, breaking the trust of public investors — a key ingredient to a successful IPO.

And these misconceptions are fed by the dominant portrayal of IPOs as an exit or end, which fails to truly capture its role in the growth of a business. For investors, IPOs are a liquidity event to realize returns, but for entrepreneurs, going public is more a beginning than an end, more a milestone than a goal on a journey into a completely different landscape.

Graduation Versus Start of a Career

There needs to be a retelling of the IPO narrative in Southeast Asia, all the more now that tech startups are becoming more exposed to these options for growth and the pressure mounts to deliver on investor expectations in the region.

If funding rounds are the different year levels in primary, secondary, and undergraduate education, the IPO is not the graduation ceremony but the first day at work and a career in the public markets. The demands of work are much more complex and high-stakes than school.

"When you are in the public markets, the demands on the company are very clear: that you should be growing the business and delivering outcomes and returns for shareholders. The demands are unrelenting and continuous. It is also about managing the complexities of the interaction with the public market, you have the different stakeholders, greater transparency, greater demands on you, so it [requires] a mindset shift," notes Ismail.

Becoming IPO-Ready

As such, it must be clear early on to founders what the motivation will be for going public and how it will play into the growth trajectory of the business. This motivation must also sync up with timing for preparations. The business should be at a fairly mature stage of growth, generally revenue-generating and able to demonstrate the path to profitability.

With this clarity and timing, the next step is to lay the foundations for the transition, which can take anywhere from six to 18 months, and involves fundamental changes in the company. The preparation generally involves meeting financial reporting requirements and listing standards in three main areas — governance, risk management, and internal controls.

If these processes and frameworks are not robust enough, even the best performing companies can fall because of singular mistakes in key departments. And the greater the scale of operations, the higher the risk. This is why strengthening these fundamentals stand to benefit every company, regardless of whether they are gunning for an IPO or not.

Building Confidence

Once the transition is finally official, setting the right targets and having visibility with investors is key. The adage "under promise and overdeliver" applies in this case when laying out expectations with public investors. This does not mean selling low. It is about leadership setting targets that it is confident in achieving.

Investors look at the captain on the deck and how capable the captain is at steering the ship to the set destination long before sailing off. Hitting targets consistently builds confidence among investors in the company's ability to achieve its future plans, solidifying them as partners for the long run.

The Real Holy Grail

These changes that come with the transition to the public markets will often stand at odds with the startup mentality and approach that prizes growth and speed over stability and security. However, according to co-founder and CEO of Carro Aaron Tan, who had seen a number of IPOs in his days in San Francisco as an investor, the road to an IPO does not have to be a zero-sum game between growth and profitability.

> "At the end of the day my firm belief is that if you build a good, sustainable company, with good gross margins especially, you will be able to exit one way or another. Even if you don't exit and build a company that's profitable and that stands alone by itself, that's good, [albeit] counterintuitive to the kind of tech companies we have today. There's a balance, where you can grow and build a great company that's sustainable."
>
> – Aaron Tan *Co-founder and CEO of Carro*

While not every company will sound the gong (or ring the bell) in the public markets and celebrate their IPO with a rain of confetti, the same mindset shifts and fundamental company transitions that go into preparing for an IPO can set a company up to be more sustainable moving forward.

Innovators Do Not Exit Companies, They Build Enduring Ones

Takeaways on making a successful exit:

(1) The success of an exit (or at least the value that will be derived from it) is already being determined by the decisions made by the startup along the way. *The more optimized these decisions are for sustainability and profitability, the better the startup's trajectory towards an exit.*

(2) The success of an exit is also influenced by *the strength of founder–investor relationships.*

(3) *An IPO is not the end.* It is only the beginning for a new stage of growth in the business, whether as part of a bigger firm (by M&A) or as part of the public markets (IPO).

Conclusion

Looking through Telescopes and Satellites

"The only true voyage of discovery…would be not to visit strange lands but to possess other eyes, to behold the universe through the eyes of another, of a hundred others, to behold the hundred universes that each of them beholds, that each of them is…"

   — *Marcel Proust, from Remembrance of Things Past, Chapter 2*

(47) The Future of Southeast Asia

By Tan Yinglan and Paulo Joquiño

"Southeast Asia's political, economic and cultural differences makes it difficult for a one-size-fits-all strategy."

   — Tan Yinglan *Wall Street Journal, June 26, 2020,*

When it comes to supporting technology companies in Southeast Asia, investors often look to more developed technology markets for inspiration. Many portfolio ideas come from technology market leaders in the US and China. At the same time, they are also driven by Southeast Asia's development as an innovation ecosystem that even the rest of the world can learn from. There is much to be excited about in the region's next 20 to 30 years.

Localization will Accelerate Digitalization in the Region

Though Southeast Asia is painted as a singular ecosystem, differences across borders make plug-and-play innovation impractical. This reality has been a bane and a blessing for founders. On the one hand, having a home-court advantage sets up a considerable (though temporary) moat against foreign players. On the other hand, it also complicates expansion.

The supply chain diversification out of China speaks to this trend. Affected products like clothes, electronics, and even healthcare equipment will see more local players cashing in and demand for local or regional products driving up.

In the decades to come, localization will accelerate digitalization in the region. The ecosystem may not produce tech giants and unicorns by the dozen, but it will populate with businesses designed to tackle specific needs and founders uniquely positioned to grow these companies.

Demographic Bonus will open up New Markets and Talent Pools

The region's young demographic bonus poses opportunities for technology companies to unlock new markets and talent pools. Investors are no stranger to the line or slide in almost every pitch deck playing this "population growth" card.

With the majority of the region's population below 40, in the next two to three decades, there will be more spending around long-term services like healthcare, education, and insurance. While there is a baseline level of expectation as to what happens as we age, consumer-facing companies will benefit from staying on top of changing lifestyles.

In terms of online culture, Southeast Asia's young population has the potential to lead even global trends on what becomes viral or socially acceptable in the future of the internet. We saw this happen with most of Gangnam Style's views coming out of the Philippines in 2013. As content creators and entertainment companies cash in on this influence, Southeast Asia will continue to be a hotspot for these cultural moments.

Apart from opening up new areas of demand for digital, the demographic bonus is a potential talent pool for tech companies. The key for this talent to be unlocked is long-term education. Aside from institutions racing to be more digital in their methodology and course options, edtechs are joining the capacity and career-building effort.

Rural Economies will see New Models of Driving Digital Adoption

As Southeast Asia is mostly composed of developing countries with technology markets that have recently seen relatively tremendous growth, a divide has emerged between the digitalization in urban and rural areas. Last year's Google eConomy SEA 2019 report cited the massive opportunity in closing this divide in the region.

We already see this in portfolio companies that have been driving digitalization in second-tier and third-tier cities in their countries. For example, social commerce platforms like Super and O2O fintech platforms like Payfazz in Indonesia have emerged to meet the affordability and accessibility needs of consumers in second- and third-tier cities.

The challenge of bringing digital to the rural economy is not new. Still, we expect more companies to succeed in the next few decades and develop new and effective ways of acquiring and retaining users. Southeast Asia is poised to lead the developing world in this regard, as rural businesses are the backbone of many of these region's economies.

Cities of Connectivity and Resilience will be the Cities of the Future

As governments and institutions in Southeast Asia become more invested in technology, we can expect more of the region's cities to become smarter, more resilient, and more connected. Singapore has long been in the lead in the smart city race globally, and we can expect urban areas around the region to follow.

Smart cities will not just be about connectivity within cities but among cities as well. We are already seeing how consumer platforms like Grab are serving customers across borders, and 4PL platforms like Janio are making cross-border logistics in the region more seamless. Platforms that can close gaps between countries will be crucial value creators in the coming decades.

The cities of the future will also be cities of resilience. We are seeing how Singapore and Vietnam, as well as neighboring states like Taiwan and South Korea, have been leveraging on technology on a nationwide scale to manage the pandemic. Being a region prone to various disasters from viral outbreaks to monsoons, Southeast Asia can lead the way in crisis management and recovery.

Talent will Come Back (or Stay) Home to Build Careers and Companies

As the technology markets of Southeast Asia develop further, and more of the global workforce participates in the digital economy, there will be more talent (and even capital) returning to their home countries to build careers and companies. Many may even forego moving abroad.

The past century saw brain drains in the region, whether due to political conflicts or better economic opportunities abroad. With the region's technology ecosystem shaping up, cities investing more in liveability, and more businesses becoming distributed, more will be spent to stay in the region than to move out.

Looking Near and Far

The current crisis with the pandemic has put a cloud over the optimism over the past decade, but we cannot afford to stop preparing for opportunities long after COVID19. We often advise our founders to look through both a microscope (short-term) and a telescope (long-term) at the same time without confusing the two images. So yes, we are going through a historical crisis. At the same time, this crisis and many other factors are paving the road for Southeast Asia (and many more would say, Asia as a whole) to lead the future of innovation.

With this perspective, it is difficult not to have hope for the future. And it is all the more important we act on it.

5 July 2020

Singapore

(48) Reservoir Engineering 101

By Paulo Joquiño

In 2007, Canadian ecologist Jean Thie spotted a 850-meter long beaver dam in Wood Buffalo National Park while tracking melting permafrost in the region via Google Earth satellite imagery. Three years later, the dam's existence was confirmed by helicopter photos taken by park rangers. In comparison, the length of an average beaver dam ranges from 10 to 100 meters, while the Hoover Dam in the US is 379 meters long.

By putting together mud, stones, and tree branches, beavers are able to engineer these natural reservoirs for their survival. These beaver dams serve as food storage for the winter and a moat against predators like wolves and bears. These dams also end up shaping the environment around it because of these functions, contributing to less drought and flooding and also storing carbon dioxide.

To have achieved this record length biologists believe that the Wood Buffalo National Park beaver dam took several beaver families, thousands of trees, and many months to construct. Another remarkable aspect of this beaver dam in particular is that it has been in construction since around the 1970s, says Jean Thie, which means it was not only an effort that likely involved multiple beaver families, but also involved multiple generations.

The title essay of this book is "The Reservoir Principle," and rightly so. Most of these pages have been devoted to engineering reservoirs and ecosystems as a way to build sustainable companies. This feat of beaver engineering uniquely reflects three key takeaways that capture this approach and best summarize this book:

(1) Navigate the market to innovate the market
(2) Data propels growth
(3) Building never stops

Navigating the Market to Innovate the Market

The market, like the environment where the beavers set out to build their dam, is full of danger. There are predators all around them, and the winter threatens their food supply. And yet, they use the environment to their advantage, building protection from resources within their grasp. And this actually contributes to the health of the entire ecosystem.

One of the tensions that arises from startup-driven innovation is between the market and the product. On one hand, founders seek to reduce inefficiencies in the market, or even create an entirely new paradigm for doing things with technology. At the same time, founders need to be able to understand and work with the market (regulations, cultural nuances, etc.) in order to make this digitalization sustainable.

The first four chapters transpose this approach onto various aspects of the early-stage startup's journey, from starting up to building a team to developing an ecosystem of services for the market.

The best example for this approach are startups in Southeast Asia's rural economy (highlighted in Chapter Four). The barriers to entry are high, especially for traditional businesses, and this actually serves as an entry point for technology-enabled platforms. A social commerce platform can distribute goods cheaper and faster than traditional retail. A farm-to-table marketplace can help farmers clear out their stock while connecting consumers directly to fresh produce more efficiently than a wet market. A fintech platform can bridge communities to financial services at a scale and speed that physical banks will find hard to beat. The high costs of acquisition in the rural economy, especially for first-movers, forces startups to be creative and work with what's already in their existing environment, like mom-and-pop shops or local agents.

Data Propels Growth

As the early-stage startup scales up, its data collection and processing become more enriched as more transactions and activity happens on its platform or with its products. A single beaver family could have made a dam 10 to 100 meters long, but because many beaver families worked on the dam over a long period of time, it came to be the largest (known) in the world. When park rangers started observing the dam, they noted two smaller dams sprouting on either side, and predicted that in 10 years (around 2020) all three would have merged to be a kilometer-long reservoir.

Just as the combined effort of families over time grew the dam's reach to record lengths, data aggregated over use cases and time can be needle-moving for the startup. Data is both what drives and results from startup growth, especially platform models — hence the Reservoir Principle in Chapter Four and platform-driven growth in Chapter Five. A truck matching platform uses data from transactions to develop more linked services and personalized user experiences, which then produces more data. An automobile marketplace uses data from transactions to branch into financial services for these car buyers and sellers, and this fintech platform also becomes a trove of data.

Chapters Four through Six and even Eight emphasize the importance of data to propel platform growth, and this data ultimately comes from accumulating and measuring activity. This data is not only analyzed to retain users for the long-term, but also to determine the revenue streams to focus on for growth, as this changes the platform's makeup over time. A platform may begin with ride-hailing — which was critical to acquisition — but soon shifts more energy to higher margin streams in food delivery to focus on profitability.

Building Never Stops

The Wood Buffalo National Park beaver dam, when it was discovered in 2007, was not a finished product. Estimated to have been started three decades ago, it continued to grow, as park rangers observed. In all likelihood, it is still being built today.

Chapters Seven through Nine emphasize the continuity and spirit of building with a repeated focus on growth and simply building a great company — whether it is for fundraising, to survive a crisis, or nail down a successful exit.

This sense of continued (and even endless) progress and endurance is what reels these investors in. The sense that years down the road, the business will be exponentially bigger than it is today. And so, it is with the ecosystem as a whole. Even in times of crises, entrepreneurs, engineers, and technologists continue to innovate. Crises periods become fertile soil for new business models to emerge. And when startups are acquired or IPO, the building still continues and remains the focus, whether as part of a larger organization or a public company.

This perspective paints an optimistic picture for Southeast Asia, at the cusp of another decade that despite the ongoing crisis many believe will be another turning point for the region's startup ecosystem to grow.

***

Exploration pushes the frontiers of possibility and heroically reimagines new paradigms of thoughts and ways of action. This face of exploration has been the focus of this book. As this book draws to a close, through the Voyager spacecrafts in Chapter 9 and this beaver dam analogy, we see the other face of exploration — one that involves the quieter, unnoticed, everyday moving forward that endures beyond knowing. While the latest innovation will continue to spark headlines and draw interest, these headlines are ultimately the tip of the iceberg. Beneath it all are the endless nights and weekends spent making things happen, until finally impact is realized simply by existing — in the same way that this dam grew to such a size that it became visible from a satellite out in space.

10 June 2020

Manila, Philippines

Appendix A

Full List of Essays

Note to the reader:

All of these essays were published on *Insignia Business Review* unless otherwise stated. Some essays were curated from interviews with other publications. Podcasts and webinars are also stated as such. Some of these essays were edited to better fit the contents of the book as a whole and update certain information and examples since the originals were first published. This list is arranged in order of appearance in the book.

(1) "Startup Ecosystem in the Philippines" by Paulo Joquiño and Yinglan Tan. Published 15 April 2019.

(2) "Big Tech's Chinatowns in Southeast Asia" by Paulo Joquiño. Published 28 February 2020.

(3) "The world is flat, but Southeast Asia is a bowl" by Paulo Joquiño. Published 18 July 2019.

(4) "Beyond the Third Wave" by Paulo Joquiño, based on interviews of Yinglan Tan with 7.5 degrees and simmondsstewart.sg (written by Liz Fox, published 20 September 2019).

(5) "Dancing skyscrapers" by Paulo Joquiño. Published 14 February 2020.

(6) "Rising above the noise: What makes great founders in Southeast Asia" by Paulo Joquiño. Published 25 November 2019.

(7) "An education on entrepreneurship" by Rousyan Fikri. Published 23 March 2020.

(8) "Leading Asia's Digital Disruption" by Yinglan Tan, originally written for Stars Insights in conjunction with the Stars Singapore Symposium 2019. Published 15 March 2019.

(9) "Tapping into traditional markets" by Paulo Joquiño. Published 24 June 2019.

(10) "Markets maketh talent" by Paulo Joquiño. Published 23 March 2020.

(11) "Developing effective local teams for cross-border companies" by Paulo Joquiño. Published 23 August 2019.

(12) "How Davids Hire Goliaths" by Paulo Joquiño. Published 5 October 2019.

(13) "Unlocking agility in middle management" by Paulo Joquiño. Published 14 May 2020.

(14) The Reservoir Principle by Paulo Joquiño. Only in this book.

(15) "Southeast Asia's retail boom fuels the rise of logistics" by Yinglan Tan. Published 23 January 2019.

(16) "Distribution insurtechs' boarding call for industry" by Paulo Joquiño. Published 22 July 2019.

(17) "Finding Healthtech's Golden Ratio" by Linh Nguyen. Published 17 January 2020.

(18) "How digital disruptors serve the unbanked in Southeast Asia" by Yinglan Tan. Published 23 January 2019.

(19) "Exploring Southeast Asia's Uncharted Rural Economy" by Paulo Joquiño. Published 9 January 2020.

(20) "Growing an edtech startup by going micro" by Linh Nguyen. Published 9 September 2020.

(21) "To change the tide, go with the flows" by Paulo Joquiño. Published 21 February 2020.

(22) "Revisiting the rural economy" by Paulo Joquiño. Published 16 March 2020.

(22a) Exhibit A "Why you don't want the APPLE to fall far from the platform" by Linh Pham. Published on 19 March 2020.

(22b) Exhibit B "Planting seeds of digitalisation in Indonesia's agriculture" by Paulo Joquiño. Published on 1 April 2020.

(22c) Exhibit C "How to be the Alibaba for cars in Southeast Asia" by Joolin Chuah. Published 19 Septenber 2019.

(23) "Cross-border logistics scaling Southeast Asia's Export Potential" by Paulo Joquiño. Published 23 August 2019.

(24) "The learning reservoir" by Bill Roosman.

(25) "Southeast Asia stepping up its esports game in 2019" by Teng Jen Ang, Yinglan Tan, and Paulo Joquiño, 8 February 2019. Also published 12 March 2019 on Business Times as "Esports streams into a new chapter."

(26) "Going social: the changing landscape of ecommerce" by Joolin Chuah and Paulo Joquiño. Published 1 March 2019.

(27) "What smart access means for the urban organism" by Paulo Joquiño. Published on 1 August 2019.

(28) "Insurtech in SEA: the big pull" by Joolin Chuah and Paulo Joquiño. Published on 22 March 2019.

(29) "Platform-first: fintech's next destination" by Samir Chaïbi. Published 9 March 2020.

(30) "Super Apps in Southeast Asia," by Yinglan Tan. Published 20 May 2019. Excerpts from the article were published as part of a Straits Times piece, "Uphill battle for South-east Asia's super apps," published 20 May 2019.

(31) "Grab and Go-Jek must show flexibility to survive" by Yinglan Tan and Paulo Joquiño, as published on Nikkei Asian Review, 11 March 2020.

(32) "Through the Lens of a VC" by Paulo Joquiño based on excerpts from interviews of Yinglan Tan featured on 7.5 degrees, TFA Geeks (Published 3 June 2020), and Business Times (Published 21 March 2020).

(33) "From betting on the future to charting its course: venture building with LPs" by Yinglan Tan and Paulo Joquiño. Published on 13 December 2019. Also published on informaconnect 5 December 2019.

(34) "Corporate venture capital landscape in Singapore" by Yinglan Tan. Published 29 March 2019. Excerpts appeared on Business Times.

(35) "Demystifying Southeast Asia's tech unicorns" by Paulo Joquiño. Published 18 November 2019. Excerpts published on Nikkei Asian Review.

(36) "Prudence and Perseverance" by Paulo Joquiño. Published on 20 March 2020.

(37) Webinar on COVID19 strategies for tech startups organized by Insignia Ventures on April 2020, with Linh Thai, former head of Vingroup Ventures and DFJ VinaCapital, and Aaron Tan, CEO and co-founder of Carro as guests alongside Yinglan Tan.

(38) Webinar on COVID19 growth opportunities organized by Insignia Ventures on April 2020, with Zhang Tao, founder and CEO of

Dianping.com, and Chih Cheung, co-founder and co-chairman of global sportswear manufacturer JAMM Active Limited, as guests.

(39) "Responding to Vietnam education's wake-up call," an interview with Edmicro founders Linh Dang Bao and Que Nguyen (Published 6 May 2020)

(40) "Acing edtech in Indonesia," a podcast conversation with Pahamify CEO and co-founder Rousyan Fikri (Published 8 June 2020).

(41) "Embrace the Vujade" by Paulo Joquiño. Published on 29 April 2020.

(42) "Making the exodus to online business" by Joolin Chuah. Published on 22 April 2020.

(43) "Data in a post-COVID world: highways of the digital economy" by Paulo Joquiño. Published 16 April 2020.

(44) "What it takes to win (in Southeast Asia)" by Paulo Joquiño. Published on 11 June 2020.

(45) "Making sense of the We who cried IPO" by Paulo Joquiño. Published on 18 November 2019.

(46) "Beyond the Gong: Succeeding in the Public Markets" by Paulo Joquiño. Published on 25 November 2019.

(47) The Future of Southeast Asia by Paulo Joquiño. Only in this book.

(48) Reservoir Engineering 101 by Paulo Joquiño. Only in this book.

Appendix B

Portfolio Companies

Insignia Ventures portfolio companies that are mentioned as well as their founders or CEOs who are mentioned or quoted in the essays in each chapter.

Chapter One

(1) First Circle
(2) None
(3) Sayurbox
(4) Janio, Super, Eezee
(5) None

Chapter Two

(1) AwanTunai (Dino Setiawan, Windy Natriavi, Rama Notowidigdo), LOGIVAN (Linh Pham), Carro
(2) Pahamify (Rousyan Fikri)
(3) Flip, AwanTunai, Carro, Payfazz, LOGIVAN, Super, Janio
(4) AwanTunai (Dino Setiawan, Windy Natriavi, Rama Notowidigdo)

Chapter Three

(1) Janio (Junkai Ng), Ritase (Iman Kusnadi), Sayurbox (Amanda Susanti)

(2) Janio (Junkai Ng)
(3) None
(4) AwanTunai (Windy Natriavi), Janio, Carro (Aaron Tan)

Chapter Four

(1) None
(2) LOGIVAN
(3) Symbo (Laurens Koppelaar)
(4) None
(5) Payfazz (Hendra Kwik), Aspire (Andrea Baronchelli), First Circle (Patrick Lynch)
(6) Payfazz (Hendra Kwik), Shipper, AwanTunai

Chapter Five

(1) None
(2) Ritase (Iman Kusnadi)
(3) AwanTunai, LOGIVAN (Linh Pham), Sayurbox (Amanda Susanti), Carro (Aaron Tan)
(4) LOGIVAN (Linh Pham)
(5) Sayurbox (Amanda Susanti)
(6) Carro (Aaron Tan)

Chapter Six

(1) Janio (Junkai Ng)
(2) None
(3) None
(4) Igloohome (Anthony Chow)
(5) Aspire, Ajaib, Payfazz, TONIK
(6) Carro, Payfazz
(7) None

Chapter Seven

(1) Appier, Sayurbox (Amanda Susanti), Janio, Shipper
(2) None
(3) Igloohome
(4) Janio
(5) None

Chapter Eight

(1) Carro (Aaron Tan)
(2) Carro (Aaron Tan)
(3) None
(4) Edmicro (Linh Dang Bao, Que Nguyen), Pahamify (Rousyan Fikri)
(5) AwanTunai, LOGIVAN
(6) None
(7) Carro, AwanTunai, Sayurbox

Chapter Nine

(1) None
(2) None
(3) Carro (Aaron Tan)

Conclusion

(1) Super, Payfazz, Janio
(2) None

Appendix C

Glossary of Acronyms

3PL	Third-Party Logistics service providers
4G	Fourth Generation (mobile network)
4PL	Fourth-Party Logistics service providers
5G	Fifth Generation (mobile network)
AI	Artificial Intelligence
APAC	Asia Pacific (region)
APPLE	Auto Pricing Project for LOGIVAN: code E
API	Application Programming Interface
AUM	Assets Under Management
AWS	Amazon Web Services
B2B	Business to Business (business model)
B2C	Business to Consumer (business model)
BPO	Business Process Outsourcing
C2C	Consumer to Consumer (business model)
CAC	Customer Acquisition Cost
CEO	Chief Executive Officer
COD	Cash-on-Delivery
COGS	Cost Of Goods Sold
COO	Chief Operations Officer
COVID19	Coronavirus Disease (2019)
CPA	Cost Per Acquisition
CVCs	Corporate Venture Capital
DAU	Daily Active Users

DICT	Department of Information and Communications Technology (Philippines)
DOST	Department of Science and Technology (Philippines)
DTI	Department of Trade and Industry (Philippines)
ERP	Enterprise Resource Planning
F&B	Food & Beverage (companies)
FDIC	Federal Deposit Insurance Corporation
FMCG	Fast Moving Consumer Goods (companies)
FX	Foreign Exchange
GDP	Gross Domestic Product
GP	General Partners
HNWIs	High Net Worth Individuals
HQ	Headquarters
HR	Human Resources
IoT	Internet of Things
IPO	Initial Public Offering
ITB	Bandung Institute of Technology (Indonesia)
JV	Joint Venture
LP	Limited Partners
LTE	Long Term Evolution (standard for wireless broadband communication)
LTV	(Customer) Lifetime value
M&A	Merger and Acquisition
MAU	Monthly Active Users
ML	Machine Learning
MRO	Maintenance, Repair and Operations (supplies)
MSME	Micro, Small, and Medium Enterprises
MVP	Minimum Viable Product
NASA	National Aeronautics and Space Administration
NPL	Non-Performing Loans
NPS	Net Promoter Score (surveys)
O2O	Online to Offline
OS	Operating System
P&L	Profit and Loss (statement)

P2P	Peer-to-Peer
PE	Private Equity
PISA	Programme for International Student Assessment
PMF	Product Market Fit
POS	Point Of Sale (system)
PPP	Public Private Partnership
PR	Public Relations
QC	Quality Control
RPA	Robotic Process Automation
SaaS	Software-as-a-Service
SAM	Serviceable Addressable Market
SAP	an ERP software
SARS	Severe Acute Respiratory Syndrome
SEA	Southeast Asia
SGX	Singapore Exchange
SKU	Stock Keeping Units
SME	Small and Medium Enterprises
SOP	Standard Operating Procedure
SVCA	Singapore Venture Capital and Private Equity Association
TAM	Total Addressable Market
UI	User Interface
UK	United Kingdom
US	United States
UX	User Experience
VC	Venture Capital/Venture Capitalist
VCAP	Venture Capital Association of the Philippines
VUCA	Volatile, Uncertain, Complex, Ambiguous
WHO	World Health Organization

Appendix D

List of Figures

Chapter Five

Platform-driven growth

Platform-driven growth: Exhibit A

Chapter Six

The learning reservoir

Building ecosystems from square one
Figure 7. Unbundling of a Bank by CBInsights (2015).

Figure 8. How Southeast Asian fintechs are creating ecosystems vs Alipay model.

Figure 9. Comparing the different fintech approaches.

Chapter Nine

The decisions behind success
Figure 10. Amundsen-Scott South Pole race as analogy for startup growth.